Occasional Gunfire

ALL INCIDENTS DESCRIBED IN THIS BOOK ARE TRUE,
AND NONE OF ITS CHARACTERS IS IMAGINARY

Occasional Gunfire

(Private War Diary of a Siege Gunner)

by

A. W. PATON, M.M.

Front cover watercolour
Hamicourt
by the author

"On the western front there was occasional gunfire."
(WAR PRESS REPORT)

Bishop-Laggett Publishing
27 Kenmare Gardens
London N13 5DR
England

First published 1998

British Library Cataloguing in Publication Data
A catalogue record for this book is available from the British
Library

ISBN 0 946273 17 0

Edited by Adrian Bishop-Laggett
Designed by Brian Whitehead

Printed and bound in Great Britain by
Arlon Printers Limited, Hemel Hempstead, Hertfordshire

SYNOPSIS OF CHAPTERS

FOREWORD by General Sir Hubert Gough, G.C.B., G.C.M.G., K.C.B., K.C.V.O.
(Late Commander of the British Fifth Army in Flanders)

INTRODUCTION by Major Robert Wilson, late O.C., the "CROWN NINE"
Siege Battery, R.G.A.

EDITOR'S NOTES

The manuscript is typed double-spaced on Bulston Extra Strong paper, stitched in chapters and trimmed to a finished page size of approximately 200 x 250 mm. In the course of trimming, up to two letters have sometimes been lost from the right hand end of a line where the typist has apparently left insufficient right margin.

The chapters and pages in the typescript have been renumbered, showing that there was originally a chapter of some 2000 words at the start of the book before what is now Chapter 1. It seems likely that this contained details of the origins of the battery and probably described their training before embarking for France.

Following the loss of the introductory chapter, Chapter 27 (covering the battery's rest period at Tardinghen) appears to have been completely retyped, in the course of which it has become a page shorter in the MS, equivalent to a reduction of no more than 250 words. The new section is typed on Andrews Duplicator paper and stapled.

The whole manuscript occupies 370 pages, including Title pages, Contents, Foreword, Introduction, two Appendices and Glossary, and is contained in a Jetleys Binder, No. D.7354/407, which has been covered in black sticky-backed plastic.

EDITING

In preparing this book for publication the author's original text has been left intact, including very occasional lapses in respect of grammar and syntax. Any editorial additions, either to the MS text or as footnotes, are shown within square brackets.

I have added a list of illustrations, an index of names, place names and some subjects, plus the following appendices:
Appendix 3: A table of battery locations and dates
Appendix 4: A list of those officers and men who are
            mentioned by name in the book.

ACKNOWLEDGEMENTS

Grateful thanks are due to:
Allan Paton, son of the author, for trusting me with his father's manuscript, sketches and photographs. My wife **Ann Bishop-Laggett** for getting me started on the typing and for her endless patience. My daughter-in-law **Dawn Bishop-Laggett** for undertaking the typing of the last half of the book. My friend **George Fox** for his encouragement. My brother-in-law **John Bunch** for his informed comments on World War I. My Polish friend **Kazio Bortkiewicz** for his help and advice on Artillery matters. My son **Ian Bishop-Laggett** for his guidance and advice on the production of the book. **Brian Whitehead** for restoring the author's artwork and designing the layout. **Arlon Printers** for reproducing and printing the finished work.

Adrian Bishop-Laggett
London, January 1997

OCCASIONAL GUNFIRE – ILLUSTRATIONS
(Unless otherwise stated all illustrations are by the author)

Page	Date	Type and approx size (mm)		Subject
vii		photograph	136 x 89	Group picture – author holding the dog
2		photograph	278 x 208	Believed to be the battery before embarkation – the author is fourth from the left in the front row
12	8/1916	watercolour	88 x 144	Vlamertinghe, near Ypres
13	4/9/1916	watercolour	121 x 175	Shrapnel Corner, Vlamertinghe
14	8/1916	pen & ink & wash	111 x 126	Moat Farm, Vlamertinghe
15	12/8/1916	watercolour	97 x 128	Vlamertinghe Church interior
18	13/8/1916	pen & ink & wash	145 x 83	Vlamertinghe (looking towards Poperinghe)
22	6/11/1916	pen & ink & wash	112 x 192	Mud Alley, Longueval (Somme)
25	14/10/1916	watercolour	190 x 79	View from TOC 1 O.P. near Flers (Somme)
26	16/10/1916	ink & watercolour	309 x 87	Panoramic Sketch from TOC 1 O.P.
34	5/12/1916	pencil	89 x 132	Bonnay (Somme)
35	7/12/1916	pencil	87 x 148	Bonnay Wood and River Ancre (Somme)
38	10/2/1917	pen & ink & wash	87 x 62	My dug-out at Le Forest, near Combles
49	28/1/1917	pen & ink	340 x 77	Panoramic Sketch from "Madame O.P." (near Peronne)
55	14/2/1917	pen & ink & wash	318 x 75	Panoramic Sketch from Bethune O.P. at Bouchavesnes
57		illustration		The Only Peace in Europe (Puck, New York)
61	19/3/1917	watercolour	151 x 109	Villers Bocage, near Amiens
62	18/3/1917	pencil	83 x 92	Farmyard Billet, Villers Bocage, near Amiens
70	27/4/1917	pen & ink & wash	80 x 83	German Observation Post, Tilloy-Les-Mafflaines, near Arras
72	4/5/1917	watercolour	169 x 106	The Chateau, Tilloy-Les-Mafflaines, near Arras
77	21/4/1917	ink & watercolour	279 x 60	Panoramic Sketch in front of Guémappe (Arras Sector)
78	29/4/1917	photograph	205 x 155	Annotated aerial reconnaissance photo of Pelves (10 Km east of Arras) showing River Scarpe
82	23/5/1917	watercolour	86 x 112	Wancourt (near Arras)
88	28/5/1917	watercolour	81 x 60	Bailleul (at the Station)
94		photographs		Souvenir piece of shrapnel
95	5/1917	pen & ink	179 x 87	From O.P in Gas Trench (Ploegsteert Wood) by Hubert Leslie
100	7/7/1917	watercolour	76 x 102	Cottage at Estaires
101	8/9/1917	watercolour	118 x 154	Chateau Segard, near Ypres
106	1/1914	pencil	148 x 172	Pencil drawing by the author of his mother
111	26/8/1917	ink & watercolour	146 x 97	Zillebeke Church, near Ypres
112	8/1917	ink & watercolour	72 x 184	Alec by Hubert Leslie
148	16/2/1918	ink & watercolour	200 x 71	Panoramic Sketch of Westroosebeke Ridge from Poelcapelle (Ypres Sector)
171	3/1918	watercolour	102 x 244	Hamicourt (*also cover picture*)
172	21/4/1918	watercolour	172 x 145	Old well at Hamicourt (Picardy)
173	4/1918	pen & ink & wash	200 x 180	Wanel Church (Picardy)

THE AUTHOR

Alexander Watson (Alec) Paton was born in Edinburgh on 1st June, 1891.

He was educated at George Heriot's school in Edinburgh and worked as a colliery clerk before enlisting in the Royal Garrison Artillery (Territorial Force) at Edinburgh on 20th October 1915. He was promoted to Commissioned Rank on 7th April 1919.

The author is in the second row holding the dog

He married Agnes Spence (Nancy) Allan in October 1917 and they had two sons, John Baker Paton and Allan Alexander Watson Paton, both of whom were at George Heriot's school. John was a Sergeant Pilot in the R.A.F. in the Second World War and was killed in action. The other son served in the Royal Navy and saw service under Lord Mountbatten in the Far East.

Alec Paton was Captain of the 38th Company Boys' Brigade, which sported two football teams and held annual swimming galas. These became so popular that the 38th Company were known as the 'Water Rats'. He also produced plays for the St. Bernards South amateur dramatic society and gave lectures on the great composers.

In business, he was accountant of the Shotts Iron Co. and after nationalisation was Assistant Area Chief Accountant of the National Coal Board where, among other things, he was responsible for installing the precursor of the computer, namely the Hollerith punched card system.

Apart from his war diary he also wrote a book called The Whipping Boys which is believed to be based on his days at George Heriot's school.

He died on 2nd January 1973 at the age of 81

FOREWORD

by

General Sir Hubert Gough, G.C.B., G.C.M.G., K.C.B., K.C.V.O.
(Late Commander of the British Fifth Army in Flanders)

Though much has now been recorded of the personal experiences of young Englishmen during the last Great War, the author of this book does well to add his story. Here again we can see the straight-forward simplicity; the gallant, cheerful, and withal good-natured devotion to duty, and a practical as well as courageous good sense in dealing with the novel, difficult, and often very critical, dangerous situations. From these pages, the youth of today (who are, in this country, often seemingly unaware that there was a great struggle in 1914-18, or that it was only due to the devotion, self-sacrifice, and undaunted, steadfast courage of their fathers and mothers, that they now live in comparative safety and comfort in "this Happy England") can learn what their predecessors did for them, and realise that they themselves and their children after them can quite possibly be called on to make the same sacrifices in order to preserve their Homeland and maintain that Empire on which its prosperity is founded.

No sensible person can look around the world today and imagine that there will be "no more war", or that those that neglect the duty of defending themselves can expect to be left in peaceable possession of their riches or their country. The story of what happened in Abyssinia, and what is happening in China today, cannot fail to shatter such ill-founded, though comfortable, illusions. Moreover, war seems tending to become more cruel, ruthless, and barbarous: neither civilian nor women or children are spared today. During all the long nerve-racking four years' struggle of the last war, never was there so much ruthless, merciless cruelty shown as we have seen in Abyssinia, and are seeing in Spain and China.

Therefore, I think such simple stories as are contained in these pages should be read, as from them our youth can draw an inspiration based on love and pride of their fathers, a knowledge of what war will mean if it comes, and some guidance in the spirit with which they should meet it, if it does come.

(Signed) HUBERT GOUGH

13th February, 1937

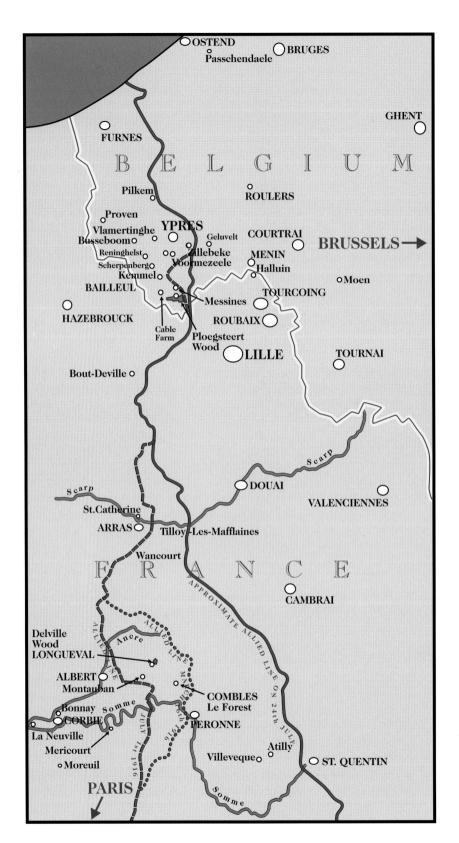

INTRODUCTION

by

Major ROBERT WILSON,

late O.C., the "CROWN NINE" Siege Battery, R.G.A.

While reading "Occasional Gunfire", one of the features which continually impressed itself on my mind was the amazing thoroughness and precision with which the author had written up his diary under conditions which were certainly not conducive to such a task. It is true that from time to time I used to observe him scribbling in his book, and I would ask him "Well, how is the diary getting on?", but I little imagined then that in later years it would be able to serve as an excellent and authoritative history of the Battery.

It may be wondered how Corporal Paton – as he was then – contrived to collect so many facts regarding incidents in the lives of not only the men, but of the officers in particular; and it should be explained that for such a purpose he was very fortunately placed. Being a Battery Commander's Assistant, he acted to a considerable extent as a liaison between officers and men for the nature of his work necessitated his presence every day in the Battery Commander's Post with the officers on duty. Under such circumstances it was only natural that he should hear much of their conversation, and accordingly his position called for great discretion, of which I am happy to say Corporal Paton was a model. The result was that he was trusted by officers and men alike.

"Occasional Gunfire", unlike some war books which I have read, does not dwell unnecessarily on the sordid aspects of war; though as the story progresses the increasing seriousness of its tone reflects the gradual transition of the writer from the stage of irrepressible youth to that of more reflective manhood. It manifests once more the characteristic which appears to be inherent in the British Tommy – that even on the most frightful occasions and at the most depressing of times, he can still see "the funny side of things".

(Signed) R. WILSON, late Major, R.A.

31st January, 1938

Chapter 1

Civilians in uniform – Vlamertinghe (Ypres)

Death is abroad and children play – Tagore

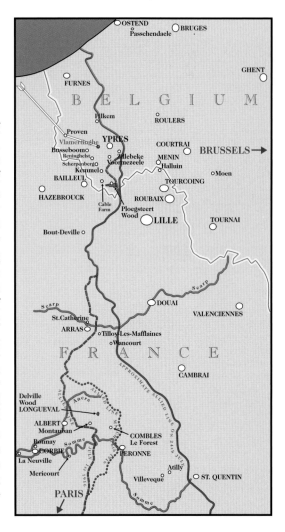

In the early summer of 1916, a battery of artillery leaving for the front was not an unusual sight; but our own battery's departure from Bristol on the night of 26th June in that year must certainly have presented some unfamiliar aspects, for our final parade then reminded me of the old Carter's Trip holiday at Leith. This was primarily due to the paragraph in morning orders stating that no one would be allowed out of the barracks that day. The news was paralysing, as we had received no hint of it in advance, and a host of engagements had been booked for that last evening with the lady friends we had made in Bristol. In the late afternoon when it was realised that there was no hope of slipping out even for an hour, the disappointed courtiers took their sorrows to the bar of the canteen and drowned them. So at parade hour, instead of a spick and span body of men, the Major beheld a collection of beings, many of whom swayed to and fro like reeds in a summer wind; some so far gone as to have forgotten the cause of their troubles, while a few had reached the stage of transferring their surplus affections to the section sergeant.

We straggled out of the "White City" into the streets of Bristol at ten o'clock that night resembling a flock of sheep rather than a military body, and it seemed as we emerged that the entire female population of Bristol had come to see us off. Soon they were drawn into the Maelstrom, and we ambled along, the ladies moving hither and thither among our ranks. Two absentees had been reported, but both joined us – one having left his whole kit behind lest the battery should be gone without him – as we neared the station. Here the battery was sorted out, the ladies being shepherded to the rear; but as we had some time to wait until our train drew into the platform, we were soon

Believed to be the battery before embarkation (author fourth from left in front row).

all mixed up again. At last the worst parade of our existence came to an end, and we left Bristol at midnight, to arrive at Paddington about four o'clock next morning. By way of contrast to the previous evening, we marched very smartly without a soul to witness us as we crossed to Victoria station, whence we immediately entrained for Folkestone, and finally embarked for France on the S.S. "Onward" early that day.

Lifebelts were issued, so that while hoping for the best, we were prepared for the worst. Most of us felt reassured by our escort of torpedo boats, but a submarine attack would doubtless have been welcomed by a select few who were seasick.

On arrival at Boulogne we were met by hawkers selling lovely peaches on the quayside, but our vigilant N.C.O.s warned us not to buy any for fear of typhoid, so we had an issue of bully beef and army biscuits. Harris, discovering a baker's shop, volunteered to get some rolls for which he tendered a shilling. He came out of the shop with two rolls and a franc piece in his hand and said, "I say, chaps, this is a grand place. I gied the wife a 'bob, and she's gien me twae rolls an' anither bob back." Later, however, on visiting the Y.M.C.A., we were informed that as the shilling was then worth one franc, forty centimes, Harris should have received two rolls, one franc, and twopence. So we came to the conclusion, to be confirmed on many occasions thereafter, that France was not such a grand place after all.

Our guns had been shipped from Avonmouth before we left Bristol, and we found them awaiting us at Boulogne, where we loaded them on special trucks. By evening we were ready for the next stage of our journey, travelling in cattle trucks to Godevaersvelde, near the Belgian border, where the guns were unloaded. The remaining part of the route was by road via Poperinghe to Vlamertinghe – the latter some two miles west of Ypres. Here we were pleased to think that the powers that be had deemed it advisable to put us straightway into the famous "Salient"; but on meeting some infantry (Shropshires and K.R.R.s), our enthusiasm received a set back. They lost no time in informing us that in the Salient the Boche 'shelled you back, front and sideways', and invited us to have a look at the mortuary adjoining the little cemetery as an appetiser. We did: and though as a result our high spirits were temporarily subdued, I confess that those Shropshires and K.R.R.s gave me the 'wind up' more than the first German shell – which is saying something. They carried at the waist a fearsome-looking weapon consisting of an entrenching tool handle, on the end of which a bundle of rusty iron bolts and nuts was strung. This they used in prehistoric fashion during night raids on the German trenches, and a cold shiver went down my spine as I thought of the effects of a whack on the head from such an implement. We were led to understand that these night raids were in the nature of picnics or side-shows, when anyone could 'have a go at the coconuts'. I felt that we could never become soldiers like these tough lads; and we never did.

As it was, we had not yet undergone our baptism of fire and did not even know how to apply the most elementary rules of warfare, as our first experience of enemy shelling (which occurred that same evening) shows. I was at the time upstairs in the schoolhouse where we had taken up our abode and from one of the windows was quietly enjoying the beauty of the closing day. The sun was just going down, and the only break in the peace was the sound of a supply waggon rattling past below the window, leaving a cloud of dust in its wake. After it had passed on towards Ypres, a hush seemed to come upon the earth so still was the air. Suddenly I head a faint whistle which almost as it was heard developed into a shriek. Instinct told me what it was, and the thought telegraphed in my mind that I ought to be lying down flat on the ground. For one crazy fragment of a second I believe I thought of jumping out of the window; then unwittingly compromising, sat down on the floor. The shell burst with a roar in the churchyard across the way; and hastily scrambling downstairs, I dashed across the yard, nearly knocking over Sergeant Bale who was standing in the doorway. "What's gone wrong with you?" he asked as I fled; but I did not stand upon the order of my going, for even at that moment I heard a second shell coming. Just then young "Sticky" Wood happened to be crossing the yard, trying to balance a mug of tea as he

3

ran. Then the shell burst with a terrific clatter among the bricks over the wall of the yard, and Wood flung himself through the doorway I was making for, at the same time casting his mug to the winds. It hit the door against which Sergeant Bale was still standing, and he received most of the contents. Judging from the language, never was anyone less thankful for a nice cup of tea.

After a few days at Vlamertinghe, however, we began to think that the war was either not so bad as it had been painted, or that the sector was particularly quiet. We inclined, of course, to the former view, though the latter was the correct one. Nevertheless we were busy each day from 4 a.m. until midnight filling sandbags, until we had converted our school billets into a veritable death-trap. For had a direct hit been obtained on the roof, the weight of material we had erected over our heads could not have withstood the shock of a shell fitted with a delayed fuze, but had [would have] come down and buried us. Being then ignorant of all this, we felt terribly safe in our billets and as no shell hit the roof, all was well. Still, we had one fortunate escape at this time. The yard was piled up with earth-filled sandbags ready for use in the school, and on these we used to sit during tea. One evening we were driven indoors by a heavy thunder-shower, and were only a few minutes under cover when a shell screamed over the wall to burst in the middle of the pile of bags. Our only casualty was the cook, John Smith, who has thus the honour of becoming the first casualty in the battery. He was not seriously wounded, and returning some weeks later, continued his Borgian experiments upon us for long enough afterwards.

When the sandbagging of our billets was at last completed, my own particular chum, Sandy Henderson, and I formed the habit of going in the evenings to a nearby estaminet for coffee, eggs and 'chips'. The husband of the proprietress[1] had a special form of entertainment for anyone willing to stand treat to a glass of beer. The entertainment consisted in the manner of consumption, for the innkeeper would raise the large tumbler to his lips and pour its entire contents over his throat in one single swallow, which performance helped to slake the artist's thirst, amuse the onlookers, and swell the profits of the business – so everybody was happy. I had never before seen a master of this doubtful accomplishment. Marie, his daughter, served the coffee, while her baby sister was usually to be seen toddling round the stove. One evening the child was absent; when Sandy Henderson, thinking to try out his French, said "Marie, où est ta soeur?" There was no reply, and Sandy remarked to me "She doesn't know her own language when I speak it." Marie turned from her cooking and said quietly in English "There is nothing wrong with it."

More amusing to the battery generally, if less accomplished in our language then Marie, was the old farmer who figured in the following incident. Our 'caterpillars', when pulling the guns into position at dusk, had made great lanes in a large field of wheat; and in order that the tracks should not be spotted by enemy planes, the Major ordered 2nd Lieut. Phipps to take charge while the gunners worked all night cutting the whole cornfield. Now the Major was held in trepidation by subalterns and gunners alike and Mr. Phipps knew that it was more than his life was worth to report the task unfinished in the morning. So he ran about all night, supervising, working, and doubtless inwardly cursing the Major; and when at 5 a.m. the work was

[1] No estaminet ever seemed to possess a proprietor; the man in the place, if any, usually sat basking in the prosperity of his wife's management.

complete, he sat down feeling he had earned a good sleep. Just then he was confronted by an irate old farmer, who excitedly demanded in French the reason for this wanton destruction of his beautiful crop. To every gesticulation, demand and entreaty Mr. Phipps had one stock answer – "No compree." At last the farmer must have thought his only remedy to consult the Major; and collecting himself in one last effort, he said in halting English, "You no compree, no compree evryting: but your *father* I bring – he compree." The picture of Mr. Phipps as a small naughty boy being chastised by the Major put all in good humour except the poor old farmer.

Three weeks after landing on Belgian soil, we washed much of it from our persons on visiting Poperinghe for a bath. Doffing our garments, we stood under the nozzles of alleged showers, which, though mere trickles, were very welcome. Afterwards we were issued with cleaned underclothing, some of which were truly 'mixed blessings'. McPheat's new shirt was body only without sign of sleeve; Brunton received a 'pair' of socks, one of which reached to his knee while the other was out of sight when he put on his boot. John Smith, as befitted our first casualty, was singled out for special honours, showing a new line in socks – one was salmon pink and the other pea green!

We felt very fresh that evening, but one of our number got too fresh, and fell into the liquid putrefaction which, in the Flemish farmyard, takes the place of our homely sweet-smelling midden. He came dripping into the billet, whose inhabitants did not wait to expostulate but vanished in the twinkling of an eye: after all we had not been asked to fight aromas! Grabbing a towel, the unfortunate one hurried off to the field behind Goldfish Chateau, where there was a small pond surrounded by pollarded willows. It had a floating surface of green vegetation, but to the contaminated one it was *aqua pura*. A brand new uniform had to be requisitioned before he dared reappear in billets.

Late on the evening of 13th July, 1916, we were ordered to pull out the guns for a new position. We worked all night, but not hard enough for our indefatigable Major; particularly when he met Mason, the battery sanitary orderly, in the middle of the night. Mason's job as scavenger was not at ordinary times an enviable one; and not being in the gun detachment, the post had its compensations when the battery moved. All he needed to do then was to collect his creosol and pails, load them on to a transport lorry, and make himself scarce until the battery was ready to move. Instead of doing this, he wandered about most of the night like a lost sheep. About 3 a.m. he was standing half asleep against the trunk of a tree, when the Major passed and, dimly seeing the human form, shone his torch upon it "Who's this loafing about here," he cried; then observing that the man had a greatcoat, he shouted "Get that blasted greatcoat off at once; before morning you'll be sweating so much, you'll want to take your trousers off." Which showed that though the Major was well acquainted with the energy required to pull out a 9.2 inch howitzer, he did not know Mason – who, like the old soldier of the song, simply 'faded A-way'.

The guns were sent on their journey before six o'clock that morning, and we were sitting in billets awaiting the arrival of our motor lorries, when we were surprised by a terrific clatter of bricks, *followed*, it seemed, by a whiz and a shower of debris. This was the herald of an hour's shelling from a 'whiz-bang' gun which we knew as "Silent Percy." The significance of the

5

adjective is apparent, but the reason for Percy I know not; unless like the tortoise possessed by my niece, they called it Percy because it was so "Shelley"! About a hundred of these whiz-bangs came over, all time-fuzed – apparently to catch traffic going to Ypres. As most of them burst in the air above our billets, we were comparatively safe, having only one casualty.

When the shelling ceased, I went out into the street to have a look at the damage. The pavé was covered with broken bricks and tiles, while Marie's diminutive sister was already on the scene, tripping merrily along the gutter picking up shrapnel bullets. I began to help her gather them, and as we laughed when I dropped the still hot metal balls, it suddenly crossed my mind that I had once heard old Dr. Whyte of St. George's, Edinburgh, say that in life we are children playing on the shores of Eternity.

Chapter 2

A burst of gunfire – Bout-Deville (Armentiers)

O people keen for change, to whom the new looks always green – Wordsworth

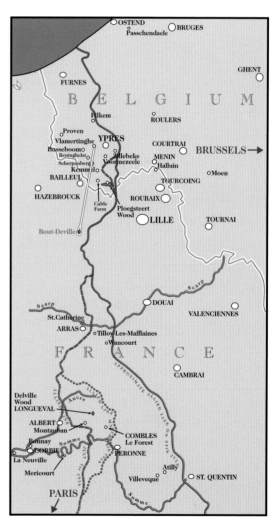

The same evening (14th July) we left Vlamertinghe for the Armentiers sector, travelling in motor lorries until 3 o'clock next morning. As the transport was required for our stores, only one lorry could be spared to carry each section's personnel of thirty-two men. So on stopping at Estaires we were stiff with cramp after sitting for six hours with our knees touching our chins; and it seemed to each of us that no one could be more uncomfortable than himself. Gunner Cox was the exception; for with a beatific smile on his countenance he sat with legs outstretched to their full extent. "I say Cox," said Sandy Henderson, "you've been long enough in that cushy position: draw up your legs and give us some room. You're sitting there like a lord in his lounge." Cox endeavoured without success to pull his feet from under a heap of other limbs. Giving up the attempt he lay back as though tired out, and still wearing that beatific smile, he said resignedly "O God, my corns are *terrible*."

It now appeared that we were to park in the square for the remainder of the night, so some of us decided to sleep on the pavement where at

7

least there would be plenty of room. I lay on the stone in my greatcoat (my blanket being among the stores) and fell asleep at once. I awoke frozen stiff at 4 a.m., to find a Field Artillery column had just halted owing to a block in the traffic. A driver, dismounting, pulled his horses to the pavement edge, and drawing the reins over their heads, lowered himself to a sitting position by hanging on to them. Then he lay on his back on the pavement, and with upstretched arm still holding the reins, fell fast asleep. Ten minutes later there was a shout that the column was again moving off; and rousing himself without undue haste, he mounted and rode on – doubtless refreshed.

We arrived at Bout-Deville, between Laventie and La Bassée, that evening, and by Sunday morning had the guns in position – two in an orchard and two in a farmyard. They were so well hidden that our observing aeroplane could not see our strip signals, and before directing our first counter-battery shoot, had to descend to ascertain our exact whereabouts.

That Sunday night we found billets in an old barn full of straw, which, though dirty-looking, promised a comfortable bed. Hardly had I lain down when a big rat *walked* across my face. Jim Brunton and I decided to retreat, and under an open shed found a two-wheeled farm cart, the wooden floor of which made an excellent bed. Though lying at an angle of thirty degrees on the sloping surface, we were in no way put out; in fact it made us fully aware of the beauty of the night, and for some time we lay awake awed by it. The countryside looked very beautiful; and looking from our cart, the poplars silhouetted against the sky seemed almost to move as the Verey lights soared slowly upward, hung poised for a moment, then sailed down and went out. Added to this, the boom of our guns somewhere far off, the bursting crackle of a occasional shell away to our left, and the distant stutter of machine guns made the night wonderful to us – for we were still new to the country and to war, and every fresh scene was an adventure, though already we thought ourselves hardy veterans.

Next morning on awaking, we were astonished to find the stone cobbles of the yard covered with slumbering forms; and later we learned that one and all had found the barn untenable, so overrun was it with rats and other vermin. Going round the place that morning, we found the graves of many Indian soldiers who had fallen at Neuve Chappelle in May, 1915, when my own brother Birnie had been killed; and I recollected he had written me just before that time saying that his billets were very verminous owing to the fact that the Indian troops previously occupying the barn would not kill any pests found on their persons, but simply threw them into the straw. And I wondered if by any chance we were in the same billet now.

Our task at Bout-Deville was a special one day bombardment of a strong point known as the Wick Salient, and on the day of the attack (19th July, 1916) we fired 397 rounds with such devastating results that the Australian infantry who took the trenches stated they had been so demolished that there was nothing for them to hold. During the shoot our numbers 1 and 2 guns each fired for two consecutive hours at the rate of 33 rounds per hour – fairly good going for our first effort of any magnitude, especially when it is borne in mind that each shell weighed 290 lb. Next evening we dropped 24 out of 30 rounds within twenty-five yards of a single German gun battery on which we were engaged. Our airman 'phoned after coming in to say the shooting was very fine, one shot being a direct hit on the gun itself, and several more within a yard or two of it. Being anything but humanitarian so far as the enemy was concerned, we inclined to plume ourselves on these successes, but pride was soon to have the fall predicted in the proverb.

We had been firing one day with good results on a German field battery close up to our trenches; and following an O.K. (the aeroplane signal for a direct hit) by number 4 gun, the order was given to cease fire. A message from the gun to the B.C. Post stated that the gun had been loaded before the 'cease fire' had been received, so the round was fired off with the same elevation as before. Instead of the expected O.K., the aeroplane sent back the signal D.9.[2] The Major, realising at once that the shell must have fallen very short of the mark, had the gun elevation checked immediately; and finding all correct, he said to Idris Williams, our wireless operator, "Are you sure of that aeroplane observation?." "Yes sir," Idris replied, "Don 9." "Then that shell dropped in our own lines", said the Major; and unfortunately this proved to be the case. The gun was left exactly as it was when the round was fired until the Brigade Colonel (whom we had immediately informed) arrived. Both he and the Infantry General who accompanied him agreed that the mishap could only be attributed to a faulty cartridge; and we then learned that the shell had dropped on the parapet of our front line. The only casualties had been two Aussies slightly wounded; but this stroke of misfortune was keenly felt by the Battery.

Our shooting generally, however, was good enough to send German planes up looking for us each evening now; but we were splendidly protected by our anti-aircraft (whose shooting was very accurate) and by our position. Despite the damage we undoubtedly did at this time, not a single enemy shell fell anywhere near the guns during the short period of our stay. Matters were less happy up the line at our Visual Observation Post. During the bombardment the signallers at the O.P. were subjected to very heavy counter fire, one direct hit being obtained on the O.P. itself, when the telephonists of another battery in our Brigade were heavily casualtied and our own senior subaltern, Lieut. Reid (one of the Territorial Officers from the Forth Defences) seriously wounded.

On Friday, 21st July, a letter was read from the Army Corps Commander thanking us for the excellence of our work, and the same evening we began to dismantle the guns. We were on the road once more shortly after midnight, and when next day we came in sight of Vlamertinghe and learnt that we should be pulling into our former position, it seemed almost like returning home. We mounted the guns in daylight as the weather was too bad for enemy planes to observe us; and we laughed and sang as we worked; for though back in the Salient, we were still journeying hand in hand with Romance.

That night in billets as we were about to sleep, Sergeant Bale entered to say that his two section corporals, Fakes and McAllister, (both of the 'regular' brigade)[3] were missing. We did not think that anything serious had happened to them, but sent out a small search party as it was possible that they might have been caught by a stray shell beyond the precincts of the battery. We hunted without success for some time and were really beginning to be alarmed, when one of the party, searching the wood behind the Chateau was startled as he parted some high bushes, to hear a voice say almost in his

[2] For any reader who may be interested, an explanatory diagram showing exactly what happened is given in Appendix 2

[3] The Battery gunners were drawn from the 'Territorials' of the Forth Defence, while the signallers and other 'Specialists' were brought from Bexhill. The N.C.O.s were regular soldiers who had served in Flanders since 1914, and were brought back to strengthen the young and untried material forming the greater part of the Battery.

ear, "Just one wee song, Mac., before we part"; and flashing his torch upon the bushes, he discovered our missing ones with their hands on each other's shoulders for mutual support. Then the night air was rent in a Sassenach imitation of Scots dialect as they sang "Just a wee *dock*-an-doris, just a wee drap that's a'." They had evidently had a few wee draps, for it took half the party to bring them in, when the whole billet was roused by the din. It was some time before things quietened down, but just as it seemed we were going to get some sleep, the voice of "Tiny" Marchant (our tallest gunner) sang out "Time to get up chaps; the cock has *crow-n*." Someone laughed and the voice of Bombardier Arnould called out "Shut up, Tiny", and for the next few minutes silence reigned. Then from the far corner of the billet a horrible muttering and swearing began. It grew in volume, died down for a bit, and then swelled up again. But no one paid any attention; it was only Chris. Grubb 'fighting bears', which he invariably did as soon as he fell asleep – the war in our sector had closed down for the night.

(See facing page)

[4] *I believe that this was contrary to King's Regulations, but can only say that we were no students of Army Law; moreover, as many found out at that time, "where drums speak, laws are dumb".*

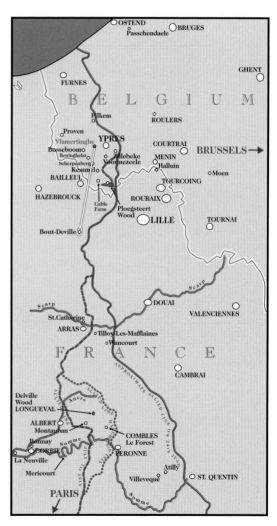

Chapter 3

Pax in Bello – Vlamertinghe (Ypres)

Vast plains with lowly cottages forlorn – Southey

When we had first come to Vlamertinghe, our impression was that it was probably the hottest part of the line; but following our return from Bout-Deville, we began to realise that the little village was something of a home from home. We still filled sandbags, but did very little gunnery, the result being that strict discipline in small matters was enforced. Dick Galliford, a signaller, was fined[4] fourteen days' pay for being unshaved; while a more drastic punishment meted out to another signaller, Tom Macfarlane, affected the battery esprit-de-corps for some time. Tom was a shy, quiet youth; and one day he was lying on his stomach on top of a pile of sandbags reading, when the Major passed behind him. Tom did not observe who it was, but catching sight of the figure with the tail of his eye, looked round. At that moment the Major also turned, and seeing Tom looking his way, put him under arrest for not having arisen and saluted. On the day following, Tom was sentenced to fourteen days' field punishment number 1, and fined fourteen days' pay. His hitherto clean record was gone; but even that would have passed without much talk had it not been that the first part of the sentence involved the practice of lashing the unfortunate victim to the gun wheel. For the first two days the Major himself came to see that this part of the sentence was duly carried out; after which, doubtless deeming discretion to be the better part of valour, he kept away and ignored the fact that the gunners no longer spread-eagled the culprit over the gunwheel. The harm was done, however, and the O.C. never recovered the prestige he then lost; for we were sticklers for fair play, and not only considered the punishment altogether out of proportion to the offence, but a barbarian practice contrary to the spirit of the age we lived in and the cause for which we had enlisted. As a matter of fact the case was appealed to the Colonel of Brigade, who remitted most of the sentence – which somewhat mollified the men but lessened still further their respect for the O.C. It would have been better for all concerned had we had more to think of at this time – for comparative peace reigned on our part of the front, due to an outburst of activity further south; the beginning of the Somme campaign.

Vlamertinghe, near Ypres

Nothing could dampen our spirits for very long however. On the arrival of parcels from home we held tea parties, when Harris was invariably cook, because he had a passion for making – and drinking – tea. On one occasion Si. Arnould (One of the few Territorial N.C.O.s at this time) swept up the debris at the conclusion of festivities. Having gathered up the remnants, he emptied dirt, crumbs, apple-skins, cigarette ends and papers into a sandbag kept for the purpose; but great was the hullabaloo when Baxter discovered that by mistake the whole of the rubbish had been put into the sandbag in which he kept his one clean shirt.

About this time, we were badly troubled by a small insect of the mosquito type. Usually it would alight on the back of one's neck or hand, and its presence was not felt until, a moment later, there was a sharp stab. Except in a few cases the bites did not require medical attention, but they were a continual source of annoyance. One night Harry Reid and Frank Baird, two officers' servants, were asleep together, when Harry awoke to see on the blanket a little ring of insects like glow-worms. "Mosquitoes", he said to himself instantly, and reached quietly for a boot. Grasping it firmly by the toe-cap, he raised himself gently to a sitting position. The mosquitoes showed no sign of alarm, so slowly lifting his arm and taking careful aim, he brought down the ironshod heel with all his force upon the circle. The action instantaneously produced an agonised yell from Frank Baird, the luminous dial of whose wristlet watch was smashed and his wrist nearly broken.

A few days later, Chris. Grubb, (a Fife miner in civil life), came up to me with something rolled up in his handkerchief. "Here", he exclaimed, "look at this b----y muckle wasp: did yae see the like o' it? How'd yae like tae be stung wi' that?" Opening the handkerchief, he revealed the deceased form of a dragonfly. Another of our Fife miners, young Sammy Nowell, on the occasion of a kit inspection at this period, informed the Major in an aggrieved tone that his "sark wis ower wee an' had nae airms intilt, his spare buits had nae laces, an' no a meenit syne somebidy had ta'en awa his gallises." The Major took all this in surprisingly mild fashion; then turning to 2nd. Lieut. Wilson (already our only remaining Scots officer), he said quietly, "Interpret please, Wilson."

Humour of a pawky type found a place too when things were not so quiet. One day after dinner we were sitting in the yard, when the Boche began to shell the meadow behind our billets. Corporal Cartwright happened to be in the field at the time and had a fair distance to run for safety. He came lumbering into the billets and sat down gasping.

Shrapnel Corner, Vlamertinghe

A moment or two later, having somewhat recovered breath and equanimity, he mopped his forehead and remarked "I like to shout 'Fire' and hear our shell sailing away to the Jerry lines, but I'm hanged if I like running for cover thinking to myself all the time 'Lord, here's another one coming.' Then a chuckle emanated from Frank Strachan, as giving Cartwright a slap on the back, he said "Cheer up, man; as Mr. Stevenson says 'It is better to travel hopefully than to arrive.'"

At this time cloud gas was still being used by the Boche, and next evening we were warned that as the wind was favourable to the enemy, a gas attack was expected. This actually took place, but the wind, veering somewhat, carried the gas north of our position. I was sent on the following morning to Brigade

13

Headquarters at Hospital Farm, and found that the farm stock had suffered considerably; the pigs in particular seemed to be still feeling the effects, as they were running about squealing, though the attack had taken place hours previously. Such occurrences were infrequent; and generally speaking, the sector was like a scene from an English countryside but for the deserted cottages in the eastern part of the village. To me, life was full of interest: in spare time I made some sketches of the village, while Albert Betts and I (both Battery Commander's Assistants) made panoramic sketches of German strong points from observation posts in the trenches.

Moat Farm, Vlamertinghe

On one occasion, when making a panoramic sketch of High Command Redoubt (an enemy fortified post opposite our front line), a piper in a trench some way to our left played for over an hour, apparently causing annoyance to the musical critics on the other side, who shelled the vicinity for some time. Any Scotsman could have told them it takes a lot to stop a piper when thoroughly under way, and the Germans gave up first. For my part, never has the pibroch sounded so fine as on that day.

A few days later, I was detailed to observe from Wilson's Farm O.P. with Mr. Phipps. We started off with two telephonists (Loveland and Sandy Macfarlane, the latter a brother of him who had been lashed to the gunwheel) at 4 a.m., and were fortunate enough to get a lift on a motor lorry to Shrapnel Corner (that on the Messines Road). From the latter point we walked to Ypres, about a mile on the other side of which lay our destination. For the last three or four hundred yards we had to crawl on hands and knees, being in full view of the Boche; and this did not meet with the approval of Loveland. "Come on, Sandy", he said, "let's up and run for it: I'm fed up crawlin' in this mud like a blinkin' beetle." "Noo, noo," replied Sandy from behind, "just keep on as yae'r daein'; when we're gaun this wey we're no' weerin' oot the soles o' our buits." We reached the O.P. safely, but as visibility was not good and became worse as the day wore on, no shoot was carried out. Our only excitement was when Phipps called to me "Look at that rabbit!" We ran round the trench bay after it, to find it was a huge rat.

14

By evening rain was coming down in torrents; and at 10 p.m. we left the O.P., walking back to Frascati (an O.P. and telephone exchange some hundreds of yards in rear of Wilson's Farm), where we had a long struggle in the rain and darkness to find our own line to the battery. At last we got through, when the Major said he would send a lorry up to meet us at the Cloth Hall in Ypres: then as an afterthought had asked whom we had left at the O.P. We replied that no one had been left, whereupon orders were given that Loveland and Macfarlane would have to go back and wait until they were relieved in the morning. This they did while Mr. Phipps and I made our way into Ypres, where the promised lorry awaited us. When we got home, I was too wet and tired even to think of something to eat, but turned in with muddy boots and wet clothes, to sleep soundly all night. In the morning on going out to wash, I met two woebegone figures dragging their weary way into our billets. They were Loveland and Macfarlane, who had sat in the cramped O.P. until 5 o'clock that morning; and not having been lucky enough to obtain a lift, had walked all the way from Wilson's Farm. And had the Major then heard what Sandy Macfarlane had to say about him, the field punishment awarded to his brother would not have been adequate for Sandy, who undoubtedly would have been shot at dawn!

Vlamertinghe Church interior

My last record during this lull is of climbing the ruined stairway to the top of the Vlamertinghe Church tower, from which point of vantage a splendid view of the entire vast plain below could be obtained. It was one of those gloriously warm, drowsy days of that summer, when one wanted to forget there was a war on. Away in the distance, some small white puffs showed that the Boche was sprinkling the Yser Canal dug-outs with shrapnel; but from my perch no sound could be heard. Nor could any movement be discerned round any of the ruined farmhouses dotted over the plain below

15

me. I thought how peaceful it looked, and how good it was to be alive – then a whimsical thought crossed my mind: 'For how long?'. As I descended the stairway, I felt half amused at my own fancy, then put the thought aside for another: St. Matthew's gospel might have been written long ago, but it stood good still, even for that fatalist element, which as the war went on tended to become more pronounced in each of us:

> *So do not be troubled about tomorrow;*
> *tomorrow will take care of itself.*
> *The day's own trouble is quite enough for the day.*

Chapter 4

Warming up – Montauban (Somme)

The earth's high places who attain to fill,
By most indomitably sitting still – Sir William Watson

On Sunday, 10th September, 1916, we received orders to pull out of our position at Vlamertinghe once more, and began the work that evening at 9 o'clock. By noon the next day we were off on foot for Poperinghe to an accompaniment of German shells, which were falling in the field where our guns had been; the latter being by that time well on the way to the railhead. Our own lorries took us from Poperinghe to Provan, where we loaded the guns on trucks to begin our journey to the Somme. The train crept along at a snail's pace; and hearing that Harris had made tea, I ran along the line, easily overtaking his truck, and was rewarded with a cup of steaming hot tea and some biscuits. Shortly afterwards most of us were asleep, and when next I awoke, we were at Armentiers. Our halt there was only for a few minutes, and when again I became conscious, it was to find that we had arrived at Longeau railhead – 7 a.m. Here we had breakfast of a kind and unloaded the guns: then began a trek by road for Montauban, some twenty-five miles distant. Our transport column had been detailed for other

Vlamertinghe (looking towards Poperinghe)

work, and we walked along beside the guns or perched ourselves on parts of the gun carriage. As each of our guns was hauled in three sections by 'caterpillars', progress was painfully slow, and the noise of the tractors drowned all else. The weather was warm and sunny, however; and all along the route the population turned out en masse to see the big guns go up. One Frenchman, finding his excited remarks falling upon deaf ears, ran alongside, stood as we passed, and shaping his mouth into a round 'O', gave a pop; then throwing up his arms, he fell back into the arms of a compatriot with whom the performance had apparently been rehearsed.

The countryside was simply glorious, and we passed through many pretty villages, the most picturesque being Blangy-Trouville, where the orchards were laden with fruit. But our progress was already too slow to permit of a stop, and it was nearly 9 p.m. when we reached Corbie. There we remained for an hour; then crawling out in the darkness, we travelled along the heights above Bonnay. Away in the distance we could see the star-shells slowly rising and falling, but our interest in these was diverted when we found that our sub-section had taken the wrong road. Each of the three sections[5] of the gun (which were mounted on separate sets of wheels) had to be uncoupled and manhandled round, and before this was successfully accomplished on the narrow road, we nearly pitched the gun carriage into the valley below. Then off again, crawling along slowly in the dark; and by this time most of us were endeavouring to lie down on any available part of the bedplate. It was impossible, however, to snatch a sleep on such a precarious perch, and at intervals I got off and walked alongside to keep awake. About 1 a.m. we passed through a long village (possibly Meault), seemingly deserted, for every window was heavily shuttered; and shortly afterwards halted on what appeared to be moorland. Here we lay down on our waterproof sheets

[5] These were (a) The gun (i.e. the muzzle [or rather the barrel and breech]); (b) The carriage (on which the gun was mounted when in position); and (c) The bedplate (on which the gun and carriage rested).

18

for the remainder of the night. I awoke at dawn with rain pattering on my face, and before long a welcome breakfast of bully beef and tea was served up. We made Montauban that afternoon (Wednesday, 13th September 1916), and there were informed that each sub-section would be temporarily attached to another battery. This we did not like, but of course, simply had to put up with. My own sub-section was attached to 42 Siege Battery, and here for the first and last time, I was a member of a gun detachment. For most of us that week at Montauban was memorable. The rain poured steadily for days, and we had neither time nor materials to make dug-outs. Our only shelter by day or night was a tarpaulin spread over the gunwheels; and as we crept under to sleep, water flowed in rivulets everywhere. We had arrived in the thick of the Somme 'Push', and the confusion was not lessened by the weather. We waded knee-deep up the sunken road for ammunition several times during each day and night, and at the cross-roads would sit awaiting the arrival of the shells, which often as not came by air from the German lines. Now and again (usually after dark) a motor lorry would turn up at the cross-roads, dump its load in the mud and scurry away; when we would rescue the shells from their muddy bed and roll them on to rafts, which we then dragged over the slime down the sunken road to the battery position. After which, caked in mud and soaked through, we crept under our tarpaulin to sleep and cared not if it snowed ink, so long as we were left undisturbed for the remainder of the night. Several times during the week we were shelled in the night by 11.1 inch armour-piercing shells; but as these went deep into the ground, there was no danger from flying splinters. The only troubles were that we might either get one 'all to ourselves', or be dropped upon by a clod of earth the size of a wardrobe; and these, of course, we had to risk, remaining under our tarpaulin throughout the shelling on each occasion.

When we had been a week at Montauban, weather and other conditions improved; and taking advantage of a lull in the battle (the infantry had now advanced beyond Flers), dug-outs were made. After ridding ourselves of as much mud as possible, we began – as was the custom in spare moments – to scrounge around. Our own gun was in the open behind the village along with others of 42 Siege excepting one, whose emplacement was dug in the bank of the sunken road. In the wall of this emplacement a pair of German legs encased in short half-knee boots protruded when I first visited the position; but a few days later I noticed that the legs were minus the boots. One of our signallers had scrounged and was now wearing them.

It was looking for trouble to wander about too much in Montauban. This was not only due to hostile shellfire, but to the fact that an 8 inch battery of our own in the vicinity was a danger to our troops, for their guns were reported to be worn out, and as a result the copper driving bands of their shells repeatedly came off as soon as the shell was fired. Coming up the street one day, I heard a tremendous whirring in the air, and the next moment a large driving band buried itself within a few yards of where I stood. The protruding end was too hot for me to pull out, and it bent quite easily. Five minutes later, when we did pull it out, it was rigid. One of the Canadian battery to which our "C" sub-section was attached had both legs taken off by one of these driving bands and died almost immediately after.

The Canadian battery's position was practically in the main street of the village, and here one night Sandy Henderson sat down behind a wall to write a letter home. Before doing so, he explained that the idea was that if, while he wrote, a shell should come over, it would hit the wall and not him. Truly a great notion which worked out entirely to plan; for as he wrote, a six inch shell blew the wall down on top of him. The letter was lost, but Sandy was dug out and sent home, being thus enabled to deliver his message in person. In losing him, I felt that the one remaining link with my schooldays was gone. Not only had Sandy and I been in the same class at school, but we had kept up a companionship since by sketching together over the Pentland hills and elsewhere, so I missed his cheerful personality.

Two more notes before leaving Montauban. One day I was called out by Harris shouting "Come on up to the crossroads and see the submarines." I went, and there we looked upon the first tanks with wondering admiration as they slowly and ponderously made their way along the road for Flers. The other incident worthy of record happened when we were engaged on a shoot. We had been fuzing shells ready for the gun, when one fuzed shell slowly rolled away along the plank on which it had been lying. To my horror, its nose scraped along the base of another shell, and I swear I heard a hiss. I threw myself flat, expecting the next moment to be my last; but as I did so, Sandy Macfarlane flung himself on top of the shell and pulled it back to safety in the nick of time. It was a mystery to me how it did not explode, and though the incident passed without recognition – and almost without comment – I have always remembered it as a very fine thing. I said so at the time to Sandy himself; but he just smiled as he sat astride the shell, and said "Ay, I was nearly awa' wi' it."

Chapter 5

The war –
Longueval (Somme)

Blow out, you bugles, over the rich Dead! – Brooke

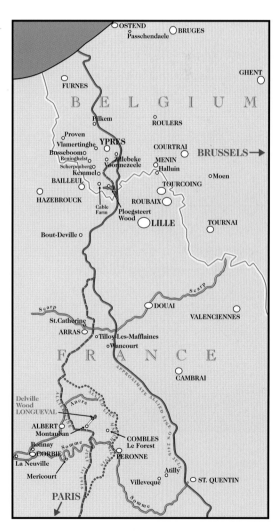

Near the end of September 1916, we resumed our identity as a battery unit, and shortly afterwards moved forward from Montauban into Longueval. Our gun position was in a switch road opposite Delville Wood, and here the dead of both sides lay in hundreds still unburied. We put in the gun transoms and bedplates on the night of 30th September and at midnight lay down in the emplacements we had made. Hardly had we done so, when a shell dropped almost on "C" sub-section's gun pit, wounding five of the gun team lying there. Then while getting "D" gun into position, Stanway had his ribs crushed. He was taken with the others to the dressing-station, and we saw no more of them in the battery.

Our position had been occupied previously by a 4.2 inch Field battery, which had moved forward earlier that evening to High Wood. I had lain down in an old tent full of their stores, the only space I could find being obtained by curling myself round the base of a square box. At 2 a.m. I was roused by the field gunners who had returned, having been unable to pull into their new position owing to the heavy enemy shelling. They were off again before dawn, and apparently made their position secure, for they did not come back.

Claude Betts, Albert Betts and I (the Battery Commander's Assistants) spent our first nights at Longueval in taking turns of sentry on the embankment above the road to watch for any S.O.S. by our infantry. What with so many dead lying and tree stumps standing, it was an eerie business; and many times during that first night of observation duty I could have sworn that those tree stumps moved.

Our dug-outs were in a sunken road which we named "Mud Alley", but as our O.C. commandeered that first made by the Betts and myself, we built another on top of the embankment to a running fire of derisive remarks from passing gunners and subaltern officers, all of whom declared we were asking for trouble up there when we could have the comparative safety of the sunken road. Time and chance vindicated our choice; for while the dug-outs in Mud Alley were flooded periodically and several were hit by German shells, our 'Au Trou aux Rats' was undamaged either by fire or water during the whole period of our stay in Longueval. When building this dug-out, we had much trouble with tree roots, and Albert Betts 'scrounged' the big axe from stores.

Now Albert was originally one of our specialists from Bexhill training school, and of course, an Englishman. While he was engaged on our dug-out, Jock Isaacs (Mr. Wilson's servant) was struggling at a similar task up the gully. Jock was a Fife miner, and on encountering a particularly obstinate tree root, he came down the gully for the axe. "Hi, Albert, hae ye gotten the aixe up there?" Albert's head appeared round the back of the dug-out, and he said "I've had enough of your Scotch jokes about our dug-out – of course I've got the aches; but if you don't clear out of here, I'll split your head open with

Mud Alley, Longueval (Somme)

22

this"; whereupon he lifted the axe from where it had been lying behind the dug-out. "Ay; that's it", said Jock: then thinking it time for someone to step into the breach, I interpreted.

Some days later, the Major took it into his head to have a special sleeping dug-out behind, but communicating with, the B.C. Post; so Albert Betts and I (the two worst selections he could have made for the task) were told to dig it. We excavated a mighty hole in the ground, made a communicating tunnel to the B.C. Post, and finally put a lid of corrugated iron sheets over the new sleeping apartment. When all was complete the Major was delighted with it, and proudly invited Mr. Wilson (who had just been promoted from 2nd Lieutenant to Battery Captain) to make an inspection. Albert and I looked on dubiously, hoping that if it collapsed on anyone there and then, it would not be the Captain. The latter got through the tunnel without mishap, and whatever he *thought* declared it to be a fine place. "Yes, isn't it topping", exclaimed the Major, and with a beaming smile disappeared into the tunnel for a further look.

Now it so happened that from the roof of the tunnel, a nasty, big, thick rooty stump projected slantwise downward. We had been afraid to remove it lest we bring the whole tunnel roof down. The Major was bareheaded, and as he went through the tunnel for the second time, the sharp projecting end of the stump jabbed him fairly on the crown of the head. Oblivious now of the Captain's and his own previous eulogies, he held both hands to his head, and emerging from the tunnel, glared at us two inefficients who stood not daring to laugh. "My godfathers," he exclaimed bitterly, "this is a hell of a place." And it was too; for although the offending stump had been removed, two mornings later the wall of the chamber caved in on the Major's bed, which fortunately he had left some minutes before.

The sleeping room was then given up, but the Officers' Mess dug-out furnished a new source of merriment to our young subalterns at the expense of the Major, whose seat in the Mess was at the end nearest the B.C. Post. Each night after dinner, he would sit back contentedly in his chair (scrounged at Vlamertinghe and added to the 'stores'), and rest the back of his bare head against the soft edge of a cloth-covered sandbag on the wall. But the cloth did not cover a sandbag: it was part of the tunic of a dead German buried there! It should be said, however, that though we thoroughly enjoyed a joke at the expense of our dapper Major, we recognised in him an O.C. who kept the strictest of discipline in his battery, and a keen 'professional' soldier. We knew that he only told the truth when, as he often did, he called us B----y Civilian Soldiers"; yet I often heard him say to officers from other units that his Scots territorials were his most dependable men, and that he would not exchange them for anybody. At this time the only total abstainer in the Mess was our one Scots officer, Captain Wilson.

The Englishmen in the battery were now taking great pride in their mastery of Scots phrases, and never tired of telling us "Yer dug-oot lum's reekin'," or less successfully "It's a fin, brikt, minlickt nickt the nickt; hook-ay." The Betts were among the foremost of the pseudo-Scots, and well I remember the evening when, after great persuasion, I was induced to ask the Major for the Officers' Mess gramophone. The request being readily granted, I returned to our dug-out with the instrument and a large bundle of records,

23

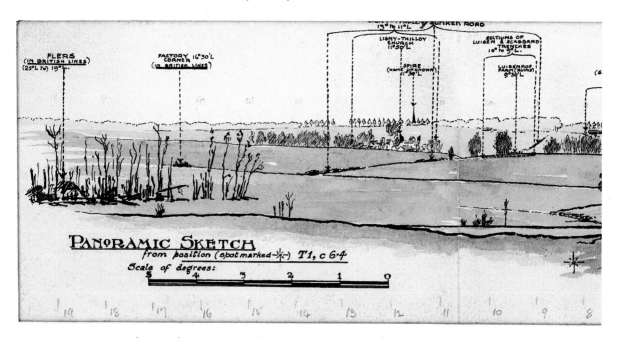

*View from
TOC 1 O.P.
near Flers
(Somme)*

and eagerly anticipated a great evening of good music – for some very good records were in the pile. Thanks to two cousins from Nottingham, all I heard that night was Harry Lauder. They insisted on hearing all his renderings again and again, and finally they thought they could sing "A Wee House 'mang the Heather" off by heart.

We spent many evenings at Longueval singing trios. Claude took the air, I the tenor and Albert the bass. After some practice, we must have become quite passable (Albert was really a first class baritone); for even Jimmy Edwards – the O.C. of our sanitary orderlies and the most argumentative Scotsman of all – would sit in absolute silence for hours in our dug-out listening to the strains of "O Who will o'er the Downs"; "Widdicome Fair"; "Sweet and Low"; "My old Kentucky Home"; "There's a long, long Trail"; "Loch Lomond" and other Scots songs, which later came to take a predominant place in the evening's entertainment. Sometimes on going outside when we had finished, the gully would contain a group of listeners, who would melt away into the darkness; Scotsmen being unable to resist the temptation of having something for nothing.

From the embankment outside our dug-out, we could see the valley in front of Delville Wood stretching to our right below us, while High Wood lay straight in front. One day the Boche got a direct hit on the ammunition dump of some field batteries on the plain about a mile in front of us. There was a terrific explosion and a huge column of black smoke, from which what looked like hundreds of human beings emerged running for their lives. From where I stood, they resembled nothing so much as a horde of black beetles scuttling from a common danger point. Pieces of shell began to drop all around us where we stood, so I too joined the horde and scuttled for cover.

At this time I often used to gather wood near Delville Wood for our dug-out fire; and while hunting in the debris one day, I came upon some boards half buried in the soil. They were somewhat firmly embedded, and I was tugging with might and main, when a head and shoulders appeared from the

24

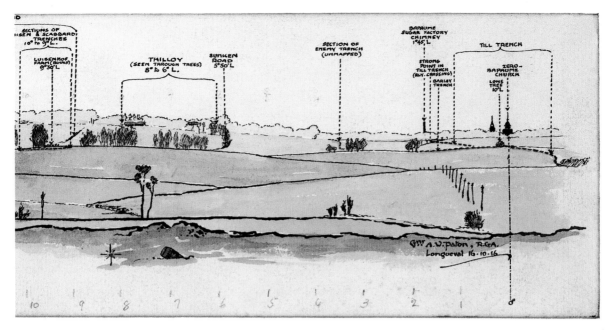

bowels of the earth, and the owner (an Australian) said, "I say, sonny, if I get any more of you pop-gunners taking the roof off my dug-out, there'll be the devil to pay." I was so surprised that I almost thought the voice was that of His Infernal Lordship himself.

I have special reason to remember a visit to "Toc 1" Observation Post on 12th October 1916, where I was making a panoramic sketch of the German lines in front of Bapaume. I stopped sketching in the early forenoon as the 'Jocks' in the front line were 'going over the top' at 1 p.m. When zero hour came and our barrage lifted from the German front line, from my position in a communication trench some hundred yards in the rear there was a strange absence of excitement. Out of the ground in front rose a long wavy line of kilted figures who appeared to walk towards the enemy lines. As a shell-burst broke the line, it seemed only a moment until the gap was closed once more. Though I knew these were my own countrymen, it was not until later that I learned that they were Seaforths, and that in that very attack I had witnessed, my brother John was killed.

My interest in our infantry had made me forget that we too were not exactly immune from danger; for I was looking through the field glasses at where our men were now swallowed up by the smoke of the barrage, when I heard what sounded like a soft "plop". I could not have said what it was, for when I next remembered anything, I was sitting on the floor of the trench. Human figures gradually formed out of the mist, and I heard the voice of Mr. Gibbs asking me where I was hit. It proved that I had only been stunned by the concussion of a 'whiz-bang' which had burst a yard in front of my field glasses; but as the Boche barrage had now lifted to our line, we had to lie low until things returned to normal later that afternoon. Coming home that evening we overtook many wounded of both sides. One West Yorks sergeant was going down with a very young German boy; they depended on each other for support, each having an arm around the other's waist. Later we overtook a Newfoundlander in charge of a party of German prisoners carrying some of

Panoramic Sketch from TOC 1 O.P.

[6] *It was considered unlucky to light a third cigarette with one match. [Behind the superstition lay the belief that an enemy sniper could spot you as you lit the first cigarette, get you in his sights as you lit the second, and shoot you as you lit the third.]*

their wounded on stretchers. When we came upon them, their guard had his rifle slung over his shoulder and was issuing cigarettes to the party. Then producing a match, he lit his own 'fag' and one prisoner's; after which he carefully blew out the match[6] and lit the others from the end of his own cigarette. We joined this party and gave the wounded the remaining contents of our water-bottles. We took a rest at 21 Siege Battery's position on the edge of Delville Wood and were standing there when one of their guns fired. Without hesitation all the unwounded Germans flung themselves on the ground, their nerves being all to pieces. We looked at them surprisedly and even laughed; but later I understood that we did not know shellfire then as these poor fellows did. Nevertheless the common bond of suffering made us sympathetic towards them; particularly towards the wounded, who lay on the stretchers mute, but with fear staring from their eyes. And although a few hours ago their main object had been to wipe us out, I felt we had more in common with these men than some of our own countrymen who, in safety at home were at this time threatening to strike for still higher wages, or profiteering without thought of anyone but themselves.

Already we had several of our gunners killed at Longueval (their number including Tom Macfarlane, who featured earlier in this story), but it was only now that we were to have the experience of getting away wounded under shellfire. An order had been issued from Brigade that if carrying out a shoot by aeroplane, we must fire whether or not German planes were over us. One forenoon (Wednesday, 15th October, 1916), we were carrying out such a shoot when a German plane came over and swooped so low above the battery that we could plainly see the observer leaning over the fuselage. We continued firing; and despite the attention of our anti-aircraft guns, the 'Allemande' got safely back to his own lines. The same thing happened on the following forenoon, and at dinner-time the Boche began to shell us in earnest, when the hunter now became the hunted. A six inch shell burst in the doorway of "A" sub-section's dug-out, four men being severely wounded. Young David Smith (a boy of 17), had his leg badly shattered, and four of us managed to get him bandaged and lifted on a stretcher. Shelling was still as heavy, but we got the stretcher lifted on our shoulders and began the journey to the dressing station, some two miles distant. We had only gone twenty yards when a shell burst very close to us. Brunton, Arnould, Baxter and I, carrying the stretcher, marvellously escaped scot-free, but Davie Smith was again hit; and after reaching the clearer zone of the main road, we had to lay down our burden and once more bandage him. I confess that when that shell burst so close to us, I was in a blue funk; and if any of the three had dropped the stretcher and run, I should have joined them. It was fortunate for me that none of them did; but our effort, such as it had been, was unavailing, Davie dying from his wounds at the dressing-station. Hostile shelling that day ceased about 4.30 p.m., and after clearing up, we had a comparatively peaceful night.

Next morning, however, the Boche again started, and the third shell which came over just cleared the roof of our dug-out, crashing into the gully below. Having learned from the previous day's experience that the best way to keep from 'getting wind up' was to be so busy as to drive away the thought of it as far as that was possible, I ran out to see if anyone was hit. Sergeant Thake called that somebody had been struck by the first shell and was at the foot of the gully. There I found two Australians lying. One had a gaping wound in the leg, while the other had his left arm almost severed. "Ginger" Hill (the signaller who wore the German short knee boots) bandaged the former, while I took the latter, and soon Sergeant Thake came up with a number of our boys to help. My patient was quite conscious; and although the wound was so big that the special shell dressing would not cover it, he watched the operations and even urged me not to take any care when cutting the arm of his tunic, but rather hasten lest he bleed to death. We were still being shelled when we got the stretcher up, but taking advantage of the comparative shelter of Mud Alley, we went by way of the gully. Just below my dug-out we passed the body of our Major's servant, who had been killed since I had passed the spot a few minutes previously.

We got the Australians safely to the dressing-station. One died on entering and the other shortly afterwards; both were brave fellows. On returning to the battery, I went up to my dug-out for soap, as my hands and uniform were in a sanguinary mess. I found a letter lying there for me and before washing, I opened it.

It is strange how that moment should have been chosen as the one on which to receive the news contained in the letter. It was from a member of the staff on which I had served up to the time of joining the army; and it informed me that the firm had awarded a staff bonus from the profits. The three members on active service would not participate as they had not assisted in earning the profits for that year. Looking back on the incident, it seems to contain an element of humour; but that aspect of it did not strike me as I washed my hands that morning in a shellhole. It seemed to me then that if I had run away from Duty at home, she had followed me up fairly successfully. For she had usurped the place of Romance by my side, and had brought me unpleasantly close to the things which I had sensed but dimly and put aside in the church tower at Vlamertinghe.

27

(See facing page)

[7] *With the exception of the Field Artillery, which generally had a sticky time and were invariably splendid.*

Chapter 6

Interlude –
Longueval (Somme)

Everything is as you take it – Proverb

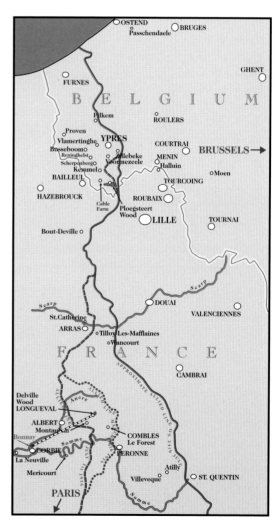

It must not be thought from the events narrated in the last chapter that we had not our good times at Longueval as elsewhere. The unpleasant experiences were remembered not because they were by any means the worst, but because it was at Longueval we first learned what war was. We saw there much of its horror and experienced some of the discomforts caused by such lesser factors as lack of drinking water and a superabundance of lice, mud, and 'iron' rations. But we realised that the full miseries of war were not experienced in the Artillery[7]: they were reserved for the infantry, which always bore the brunt of things, and had the greatest share of all the discomforts incidental to war.

For some weeks at Longueval, however, we had been living almost exclusively on army biscuits, bully beef and tea – the last made with strongly chlorinated water. The biscuits were so hard that after a week or two of nothing else, the roof of my mouth was sore enough to make eating almost as bad as not eating; while all of us were sick of the sight of bully beef tins. One forenoon, we were informed that early that morning the ration lorry had arrived with fresh meat. There were no potatoes, but green peas would be substituted. Great! There was also no bread; but the vision of stew and green peas – oh, boy! Enquiries at the cookhouse towards dinner-time elicited the information that there would be no peas: "they were as hard as shrapnel bullets" in the words of John Smith, the cook. Good: there was still stew. When the latter was served up, it was so tough that someone said it wasn't even horse – it was mule. But the last straw that broke the camel's back was when we discovered what John Smith did not now dare tell us, that there was no salt in the stew.

Such matters worried us only temporarily, but they did worry even such carefree individuals as Harris, who one day came to me and said, "I'm fed up here: I'm gaun hame." I asked him how he proposed to manage it, and he replied he would find a way all right. Some days later, I remembered what he had said, and asked him why he was still with us. He replied "Och, it's nae guid; I may as weel stey where I am. I've tried everything: when we've been shelled, I ran for wherever they were fa'in', but Jerry stopped shellin' when he saw me comin'. So I drank water oot o' a shellhole wi' a deid mule in it; an' I've never felt sae healthy in my life."

Claude Betts and I were affected differently – we went slightly 'goofy' (if Albert's opinion was worth anything) – for one night Claude challenged me to write a poem on the place we were in. The title was to be "On The Somme"; and in order that there would be some chance of reading the other's effort, it was to be in not more than twenty lines. Despite some pithy remarks of a discouraging nature from Albert, we set to; and an hour or so later I handed over the following doggerel (which is included here as it certainly will never appear elsewhere):-

ON THE SOMME

Leprous War has laid his hand
On all around:
Naught can be found
In what was once a pastured land
But stumps of trees.
The passing breeze
No longer bends the bough
And where the ploughman turned the soil,
Or weary, rested after toil,
Are shellholes now.
No more the bees
Ply honey-laden from the groves,
Nor cattle pass along in droves
With shambling ease.

Yet corn's ripe ears
Will wave where lie th'unburied slain
And here will stretch the fields of grain
In after years.

At this point, my muse gave up the ghost, and Claude soon afterwards declared his hand, which was as follows:-

ON THE SOMME

Where desolation grim and vast
Its sombre shadow late has cast
O'er leafy woods, where fragrant breeze
Has wander'd sportive midst the trees:
O'er smiling hamlet, slumb'ring still,
Sequestered 'neath the verdant hill,
The pasturage of lowing kine,
Beauteous home of luscious vine.
O'er golden fields of waving corn
In azure sky at early morn,
Sweet-throated songsters voiced their lays
In happy songs of peaceful days.

Like to some foul, contagious blast
The scorching breath of War has passed.

Unfortunately for Claude, the 'scorching breath' at this point burnt out his 'inspiratory' valves. I asked Albert if he was not going to read the masterpieces, remarking that Claude's style was that of the stanza used by Sir Walter Scott in "The Lady of the Lake", while my own seemed a mixture of all the English poets I could remember from my schooldays. Albert snorted, but adopting an air of resignation, read over both efforts. We waited patiently for the words of praise that we hoped would come. "Huh," he said at last, "you ask me to read this stuff after sitting in dead silence all night: it's been an amusing evening." We gently pointed out (1) That it had been more 'musing' than amusing: (2) That Albert had no soul: and (3) That we should write no more lines. Clause 3 is still extant.

One incident of importance to the battery and to this story must still be recorded, for it happened at this time. Owing to casualties in the battery, reinforcements were arriving from week to week: sometimes five or six at a time, sometimes two or three and occasionally a single individual. One night a single reinforcement arrived who was destined to remain a solitary in the battery, yet one of its most prominent figures, for many months to come. We had been firing at slow intervals on our night lines; and some time after one of our four-minute rounds, this reinforcement came along the sunken road behind the guns. In the darkness he blundered into the section sergeant, who was standing with his eyes glued to the luminous dial of his wristlet watch – for it was nearly time for the next round to be fired. On bumping into the sergeant, the new arrival retained his kit-bag on his shoulder with an effort, then said nasally, "I say, mate, d'ye know if there's a b----y siege battery around here?" The sergeant looked up from his watch and shouted "Fire!" If you have ever been close to a 9.2 inch howitzer firing in pitch darkness, you will know that there is one blinding flash; then for some seconds nothing can be seen but stars dancing all over the place. It is a nerve-racking first experience, and the newcomer did not wait for an answer to his question: he

31

simply flung away his kit-bag and ran – fortunately into some of the gun team who were fuzing shells, and by whom he was seized. His kit-bag was retrieved, and its owner escorted to the gully where our dug-outs were situated. I think that we must have been using lyddite shells that night, for next morning when our reinforcement came up for his breakfast, someone said "Here's Lyddite." And Lyddite he remained for the duration.

It was common practice at that time for one man to get breakfast for his dug-out companion as well as for himself; and a day or two later Lyddite held out two mugs and plates to the cook and said "Me and my mate." Food was once more back to normal, and Lyddite received two rashers of bacon, two chunks of bread and two mugs of tea. The same procedure was gone through next day; but on the third morning just as Lyddite was making off, John Smith called "Hi, Lyddite, wha's yer mate?" Lyddite hadn't thought that one out, strangely enough; so it was discovered that he had been 'doing the double shuffle' since the morning he came. After that, every man had to come for his own breakfast.

On 1st December, 1916, we were ordered to leave Longueval. Pulling out was made difficult by mud, and one of our motor lorries laden with planks and the gun transoms (the latter each weighing over a ton) went bumping up the road into Longueval dropping planks all the way. The driver never noticed the loss until the two transoms were bumped out also. Then he came back to the battery, and the gun team had to trek up the road after dark to search for the material. The transoms were eventually found about fifty yards apart, embedded in the mud. They were eventually hoisted on to the lorry and securely lashed there; but owing to the depth of the mud and the darkness, it was impossible to find more than a few of the planks. The guns were away by next morning, and we followed in motor lorries. We sometimes had to get out and push, but as it was in the right direction, no one had any complaint. We walked or waded at intervals until we reached Montauban, where we rested after having pushed the lorries up the long incline. We made Albert about 3 p.m. that day, passing under the statue of the Virgin Mary 'hanging by a tack' it seemed, from the dome of the church. After leaving Albert, the country was undulating and beautiful; and having spent the last three months in a shell-swept area, two sights especially caught my eye. One was the long avenue of trees – undamaged – and the other a team of horses ploughing.

We reached our destination, the village of Bonnay, at 4 p.m., and were informed that after nearly six months in the firing zone, we should remain here for three weeks at least in order to recuperate and have a quiet rest, with perhaps an occasional jaunt into Corbie.

The thought of it did us good; for as Harris remarked a few days later "There's nae hairm in gie'in' a body's eemagination a treat."

Chapter 7

Rest billets – Bonnay (Somme)

Short retirement urges sweet return – Milton

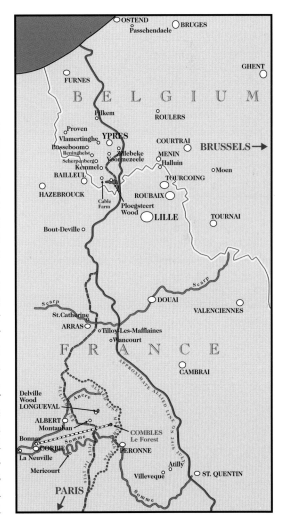

On arrival in Bonnay we found our kits (which had been taken in advance with the ration lorry) scattered along the village street. Getting out our mess-tins, dinner was served on the spot; after which our billets were shown us. My sub-section was in a barn, the side of which ran along the main street. Two long wooden platforms, one above the other, served as communal beds. Choosing between the upper and lower platform for one's sleeping place, the latter had the drawback of receiving all the dirt of the former (through chinks in the wood) while the upper platform received the rain (though holes in the roof). I elected to sleep with Si. Arnould and Jim Brunton on the upper platform near the wall, deeming fresh rain preferable to dried mud or clay. There was a large hole in the wall just beside where my head would be when I lay down; and as it was already becoming dark, I made my bed down before going out to explore. While I was doing so, Harris in the street outside, poked his head through the hole in the wall; but hardly had he done so when his hat was snatched off from behind, and he disappeared, shouting as he went "Come on out: half o' them are lost and the rest are either singin' or fightin'." On going out it seemed that the battery had run wild; but very soon the street was quiet, the gunners having disappeared into one or other of the several estaminets in the place.

Bonnay (Somme)

The two Betts and I went to look for an estaminet where we might obtain coffee, and if possible, fried eggs. We knocked at many doors, every place being in darkness from the outside, and on two occasions were nearly successful – once when the woman said she usually had coffee but had no sugar; and again when we actually found one of the estaminets. This we hurriedly evacuated when we discovered through a thick pall of tobacco smoke that a drunken Frenchman was trying to play on a trumpet to a room full of soldiers. Eventually we found one packed to suffocation by our own men, who were making the welkin ring with the favourites we had sung when marching through the streets of Horsham in the previous Spring – "O ye mind o' guid Auld Reekie", "Loch Lomand", and such war favourites as "Hold your hand out, Naughty boy", and

"Kitty, Kitty, isn't it a Pity
In the City you work so hard."

The three proprietrices, all old women, were active enough in serving out; but reminded me of nothing so much as the witches in "Macbeth". We were just in time to get the last of the coffee; then Andrew Williamson (a big good-natured Glasgow policeman in civil life, and a great favourite in the battery) came in and joined us. On asking one of the ancients for coffee, she shrugged her shoulders and said "Napu: fini." He then asked for citron, but that was also "Napu: fini." he finally had to take Vin Rouge, and tendered a five-franc note in payment. The old lady regretfully indicated that their change too was "Napu: fini." Somebody paid, and as Andrew pocketed the note, he said solemnly, "Well, there's ae thing yae seem tae have plenty o', anyway; an' that's 'Napoo: fini'."

The battery seemed all out for a grand celebration that night, and eventually the liquid resources of the estaminets were reduced to champagne. Its effects were awful, and next morning wasn't I glad I had chosen an upper-storey bed! Many sad and sober men paraded that morning for kit inspection.

34

And what a parade! Every uniform was caked in Longueval mud; so the Major simply cancelled the inspection until the whole battery, with the aid of jack-knives got rid of the mud. Such was our respect for the Major's orders that we spent most of the day 'scarting and scraping' with our jack-knives until at last our uniforms were recognisable as such.

The bells of Bonnay church tolled the whole day long, only stopping for a few minutes each hour (apparently to allow the chiming of the clock to be heard!); and though it was Sunday, we could hardly understand the incessant clanging. Jim Brunton got to a stage of exasperation when he could stand it no longer. "Here," he said, "if you won't go and see what those *bonny* bells are for, I'll go myself: if I can't speak a word of French, I'll find out before I come back." When he returned, it was to inform us wrathfully that all the 'racket' was going on because somebody in the village had died. Perhaps it was to be expected that he should add, as he did, that he could have carried out the burial himself without all that fuss and waste of time.

That day, too, I saw a flock of sheep being led to pasture. 'Led' is the word; for shepherd and dog walked about twenty yards in front of the sheep, which obediently followed the shepherd's peculiar cry of "Errr: Errr." It had not struck me before that in our country sheep are driven, not led: and the words of the bible recurred to my mind with fresh significance:

"When he has brought out his own sheep – all of them – *he walks at the head of them; and the sheep follow him, because they know his voice.*"

And again (strange how this war should bring the Bible back):

Bonnay Wood and River Ancre (Somme)

"The Lord is my Shepherd ... he *leadeth* me beside the still waters." Still waters. The same afternoon, I made a sketch of the river Ancre gently flowing through Bonnay woods – a very pretty subject, to which, unfortunately, I could do even less justice than usual; for it had to be done in pencil, as my little basket containing paints, sketching pad, and some books had been loaded up on some other battery's transport and had not since turned up. (It turned up many weeks later, however, at Le Forest.)

Next morning at 7.30, we set out for the baths at Corbie, which was about two miles away. We marched through the little town and out the other side into the country again. After some time we began to suspect that we had lost the road; and this surmise proving correct, we had to retrace our steps. It was fortunate that we had left Bonnay so early, as when we found the baths, we had just got in when other units began to arrive, and soon the place was packed to suffocation. In the congestion, several of our fellows lost their puttees; and while drying myself, my towel was pulled out of my hand. I turned round to see who had it, when a passing infantryman wiped a pair of muddy boots across my bare back. When I faced that way he was gone, and so was my towel when I again turned. One of our gunners, unable to find his boots in the crush, calmly picked up the first pair that looked big enough for him to get into.

We spent the next afternoon and evening in Corbie, where Si. Arnould and I attended the picture house run by the Infantry Division. Ushers, doorkeepers and orchestra (the latter, King's Own, being very good), were all of course soldiers; but the items of the evening were the 'ladies' in the variety turns. We had enjoyed our first day of leisure so well that on reaching Bonnay about 9.30 that night, tired but happy, we felt this was too good to last. If the remainder of our three weeks should prove anything like the day which had just closed, we felt we should indeed be fortunate.

Alas! next day we were informed that we should require to move into position in the French lines somewhere in the region of Peronne, and on Thursday, 7th December, 1916, we arrived at Le Forest (between Combles and Peronne) to find French soldiers already preparing our gun emplacements in the bank of a steep slope. I walked to "A" section's gun-pit, where the Frenchmen were digging graves for two of their number. Shortly before our arrival, a shell had burst in the emplacement, killing two and wounding seven of the working party: not a very propitious start, it seemed to me as I stood watching them.

By the following evening all our guns were in position ready for action, and we slept the night in the strongly built French dug-outs, being undisturbed until morning. While we had been sleeping, the Major's car, standing in the roadway below our dug-outs on the side of the hill, was riddled with shrapnel, and was towed off that morning to the mortuary for such equipment. Yet that was the last casualty we had from hostile shellfire for the ensuing three months, which we spent in this the most 'cushy' of all the positions we occupied during the war: winter quarters in which we hibernated throughout the severe winter until the next year's spring awakening.

Chapter 8

Winter quarters – Le Forest (Combles)

Other people are more ill-used than we,
But that is the consolation of the damned – Voltaire

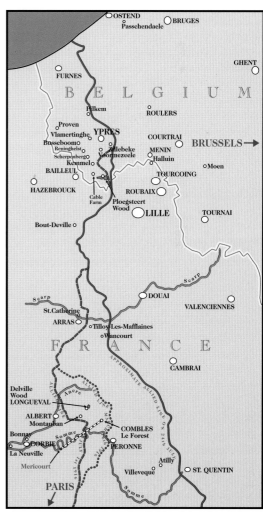

After getting the guns into position at Le Forest, we had a stroke of exceptionally good fortune; for we appeared to be the first British unit in this part of the sector, which the French were handing over to us. Consequently we fell heirs to all their dug-outs, which were excellently made, each containing wire beds and a stove.

We came to the conclusion that as our dug-outs were strong, comfortable, and situated on the steep slope of the hill farthest from the German lines, we were safe from shellfire and had found a most happy home from home. Nevertheless I had a very narrow escape a day or two later. Albert Betts and I were gathering branches for our dug-out fire along the side of the hill (which had once been tree-covered), when we heard a shell coming. Albert was some twenty yards behind me, and gave a warning shout. I had already sensed that the shell was going to drop very close, but my arms were full of branches, and to throw them and myself on the ground would have meant re-gathering them. 'He who hesitates' was saved on that occasion, for I positively felt the wind of the shell as it hit the ground a foot in front of me. My luck must surely have been in that day, for the shell was a 'dud', and ricochetted off the hillside into the valley below. But though it failed to explode, had I thrown myself to the ground, the probabilities are that it would have caught me as I lay. So on that occasion, by disregarding the accepted principles of safety, I saved both sticks and life.

My dug-out at Le Forest, near Combles

It was not long until we had to cut down tree-stumps to secure firewood, but as we were doing little heavy firing, we had time for this and for many other things. One day while sawing down trees in a wood to the north of our position, some of our gunners found a dump of German hand grenades. They speedily became expert at releasing these, and for nearly a week had daily warfare on their own with real explosive to add excitement; but one afternoon a 'brass hat', attracted by the explosions, came upon the scene and the practice was summarily ended.

We made a dump of sawn trees for general use at the battery, and while this was very handy, it had its own penalties. Si. Arnould's dug-out, for example, was a trap for the unwary. One descended two steps on entering; and as it was somewhat dark inside, a long brass rail seemed handily placed for steadying purposes. Visitors who knew no better invariably laid a hand upon the brass rail; but not for long, as it consisted of a series of 75 mm. cartridge cases (minus bases) knocked together to form the dug-out stove pipe, which was usually red hot at night – the time when visitors generally called. The heat of the dug-outs seemed beneficial to the lice, for they flourished exceedingly. From personal experience, I had considered them almost stationary pests, but one day going into "D" sub-section dug-out, I saw a garment hanging up to dry in front of the fire. The lice were racing all over it, and from its proximity to the blaze, I guessed the beasties were finding the heat oppressive.

Most of the men kept themselves fairly clean, however, and this was not difficult to do if all the occupants of the dug-out combined in the effort to keep clean. But even those who were not particular drew the line at sleeping with Lyddite, who lived alone in a small dug-out. He was constantly wriggling inside his clothes, and it wouldn't have surprised us to have seen his clothes wriggling about on their own. Eventually official notice was taken of the matter, and four gunners were detailed to bath Lyddite and periodically cut his hair. They and sundry spectators got plenty of fun out of the business, as a result of which Lyddite's person would be clean for some days; but his clothing was always in such a state of dirt as to ensure that by the next week he would be as bad as ever. Lyddite, of course, did not see the funny side of the business and submitted to it with bad grace. By this time we had built a drying-room for the battery's washing, and Lyddite was ordered to wash his underclothing and hang it with the others in the drying-room. For the next few weeks he presented quite a clean appearance, but this was followed by the *dis*-appearance of underclothing from the drying-room.

At first we thought some passing infantry or other battery gunners had been on the 'scrounge', but eventually suspicion fell upon Lyddite. A search in his dug-out revealed the missing articles – dirty of course; he had found it far less trouble to take clean garments of someone else's from the drying-room than to wash his own. For this he was awarded field punishment, consisting of marching up and down the road in the frozen snow for two hours each morning attired in full field kit. The N.C.O. on duty was instructed not to allow him to lay down his rifle or rest during the period, and for the next few mornings we heard nothing but the N.C.O. shouting "About Turn" every few minutes. Lyddite, asked one day how he liked it, said to the N.C.O., "Oh this don't worry me. I can walk about as long as you b----y well like: it'll break your heart before it breaks mine." Which seemed feasible enough, for the guard stood still during most of the period and was generally frozen stiff when the two hours were up. Lyddite's attitude on the matter came to the ears of the O.C., who thereupon changed the 'diet'. In future the O.P. party (consisting of one officer, one B.C.A. and two signallers) would go up to the Observation Post at Bouchavesnes without rations, which would henceforth be brought up by Lyddite.

This, we thought, was likely to recoil on us if Lyddite failed to turn up – and the road up to the O.P. was a long weary stretch along miles of revetted trenches, the duckboards of which only too often leapt up when a foot was placed upon them. But to his credit be it said that, from that time until the end of his sentence, Lyddite never once failed us; though he was temporarily humbled by enemy shells which he hated more than was at any rate openly shown by the majority of us. As a reward for his safe arrival, he was encouraged to give full expression to his feelings when he handed over the rations; and this he did without stint. We often felt sorry for him; but he was such a hopeless character that it was impossible to make anything of him. It was said that he had been a tramp in civil life (which would certainly account for his statement that walking about would not break his heart), and this may have been the case. He was never known to have received a letter from home; and his life in the battery was to some extent a lonely one until many months afterwards, when you will hear in its due place, another similar character joined us.

My own work at the O.P.'s here was partly visual observation and partly panoramic sketching. It beat me to know how the French had taken some of the ground on the way to the Bethune O.P. (the Observation Post at Bouchavesnes): the country was all nooks and crannies and steep wooded hills – almost ideal ground to defend, I thought. On one hillock, a German field battery had been caught trying to pull out; for its horses, guns, and ammunition waggons were scattered in pieces all over the hillside.

The trenches in this sector now became in a deplorable state, a thaw having set in and rain pouring down steadily for days. The roads, too, were terrible, and very often rations failed to come up. But we were in luxury compared with the infantry, whose case was appalling. Finding that we were a Scots battery, some Argyll and Sutherland Highlanders visited our dug-outs. They were mud-covered, haggard and hungry, accepting even a tin of bully or an army biscuit with eagerness; while a mug of tea was sipped very slowly that it might be fully appreciated. One of them told us that a mail containing parcels from home had arrived one night as they were about to go up the line with barbed wire. They took the parcels with them, but on the way got into such difficulties owing to the mud, that they were compelled to drop the material or the parcels. The inevitable delay that followed was ended by an officer ordering all parcels to be dumped, and this was done with much lamenting and cursing. Again, late one night, I had been up at the B.C. Post, and was returning to my dug-out when I saw a party of infantry silhouetted against the skyline on the crest of the hill above not thirty yards away. I heard a voice say, "What's the use of wandering about in the mud for hours looking for rations?" Another replied, "Well, I'm goin' on, anyway." Then a third voice said, "Well, I'm fed up. We don't know where to look: what the hell's the use of wandering aimlessly about all night." There was a pause, then "B----- the rations: let's go back and tell them we can't find them. I'm dead with sleep." So the party turned back, disappearing over the crest.

One day the ration lorry arrived with parcels from home, but instead of the many which we knew were overdue, only a few came up. There was one for me, the contents of which speedily vanished at the hands of our own dug-out occupants. Early that evening I was sitting writing a letter home when I heard the voice of Jimmy Hutchison outside. He and Sid Hope occupied a nearby dug-out, and the voice said, "Hi, Sid: what's that?" The awe-stricken tones made me listen at once, thinking that the shell dump at Railhead Plateau had gone up again. But Sid said, "Where in the a' the warld did yae find it?" I went outside, when I found them bending over an eggshell – thrown from our dug-out after the contents of my parcel had been eaten. The rations were unexpectedly augmented, however, at the time; some of the gunners discovering a field of potatoes, of which there were enough to keep the whole battery going for some time.

It was now nearing Christmas, 1916, and the weather was still very bad. Repeatedly in going to the O.P. I had been soaked through by rain or sleet, and was suffering from continual attacks of acute diarrhoea. One morning after such a soaking, I was compelled to report sick. We had a long way to go to be examined, and could not find out the whereabouts of our own Corps doctor. Eventually we stopped at a roadside dressing-station, where the doctor, after seeing me, said I should have to go to Maricourt and be attended at the Divisional dressing-station there. It was the first time I had reported sick since joining the army, and I was not anxious to go to Maricourt lest I should be sent to the Base, and possibly be transferred to another battery on recovering. The doctor insisted that I should go, and made me wait at the dressing-post until a lorry should pass going Maricourt way.

While waiting there, two of the Essex regiment came staggering along. They seemed dazed and utterly done, but had no intention of stopping, when the doctor called out to them and asked where they were going. One could not answer, but the other said almost inaudibly that they were looking for their Divisional dressing-station. The doctor had them into the post and made each swallow half a mugful of rum. This revived the older man, who then told us that on the Monday (it was now Wednesday) they had been going up the line with the bombs, when they had been lost in the waterlogged trenches. Some of the party had gone up to the neck in water; and in an endeavour to help them out he had himself got into difficulties, remaining firmly stuck in the mud all through Monday night. They were rescued next day and sent down the line, but the older man of the two was in a shocking state from dysentery, and the other hardly knew what he was doing. So they had wandered for twenty-four hours longer, they didn't know where, looking for their Divisional dressing station; until they had gone on automatically, having almost forgotten what they were looking for. I was so interested in them that I forgot my own trifling ills, and took them both in charge when we were put into a passing lorry, which reached Maricourt late that afternoon. It may be difficult to believe that these men had been embedded to the neck in mud, and in such a plight as to be unable to extricate themselves; but what I saw later at Maricourt was to eclipse all that, and to open my eyes to the fact that, ill though I felt, I was far too well to occupy space in that hospital; in which, as you will hear, the really serious cases made light of their ills, and many a broken body still carried an undaunted spirit.

Chapter 9

In hospital –
Maricourt (Somme)

*...who passing through the valley of Baca
make it well – Psalms*

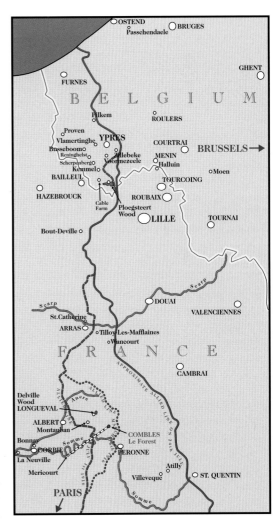

The old man (he would be about 45 years of age, which I then considered old), now somewhat revived and warmed by the rum, told me as we sat on the floor of the lorry on the way to Maricourt that he and his companion had called at a number of dressing-stations on the way down the line; but had been told at each that it was too busy to attend to anyone not in its own Division. This one could well believe; for when we reached Maricourt, the large dressing station was full to overflowing with cases of trench feet, caused by standing for long periods in the waterlogged trenches.

On our arrival, the younger of my two companions was sent away immediately in an ambulance waggon, the old man and I being left to await the attention of the medical orderlies. While waiting there, we saw some sights that eclipsed anything I had so far seen – stretchers being carried in with burdens resembling mud statues more than human forms. One man apparently had a heavy moustache, but all that could be seen of it was a mound of mud between nose and mouth. He had no helmet and the crown of his head was covered in caked mud. The doctor came forward, and after picking the mud from the unconscious man's eyelids, prised open one of his eyes, which slowly closed as he let go.

Then an orderly came and escorted us inside, where we were left on the floor of the corridor to wait for something else to transpire. Dinner, consisting of soup with bits of meat in it, came up about 3 p.m., but we were informed that there was none for the new arrivals. It was not so bad for me, as I did not feel like eating and had had breakfast at 7 o'clock that morning; but my elderly companion sat shivering in his soaked and filthy clothing. Yet no word of complaint passed his lips, though it was now Wednesday and he had eaten nothing since the Monday. One could not blame the hospital staff – they were simply overwhelmed by the number of cases coming in, and until some days later had no opportunity of getting things into some semblance of order again. After sitting in the corridor until after dark, we were taken to a large room where we were given three blankets between every two men and told to 'muck in' on the floor. The old chap was taken away and returned later, having in the interval cleansed his garments as well as he could.

Tea came up at 8 p.m. and this time we all got a share. But no system appeared to be possible in that rush of patients; for next day at 9 a.m. we were issued with a piece of bare bread; then at 9.30 tea came up; and to our great amusement, an orderly came in at 10.30 a.m. with the butter. Dinner (a bowl of soup in which meat and beans floated – it was exceedingly good too), was issued at 3 p.m.; and at 4 o'clock, when a lot of new cases were admitted, we received another piece of bread. We had to crowd closer together on the floor to make room for the newcomers; then at 4.30 p.m. we were given a piece of cheese and informed that tea would be up shortly. Between this and the time tea *did* come up, we were decidedly enlivened by the remarks of an Irishman who had just arrived.

This lad was carried in with feet like two large toy balloons and dumped on the floor, where he lay and 'shouted the odds'! Though he could not raise himself further than to a sitting position, and that with difficulty, he certainly did not mean to 'take things lying down'. No sooner did he hear that tea was coming soon than he yelled "Ord'ly; whin that tay comes up, admit him at wance and give him a bed." A minute later he called, "Ord'ly; d'ye think the man's *fell* with the dixie?" A few minutes of silence, then, "Ord'ly; if that tay don't come up shortly, I won't take it." By this time the orderly had ceased to answer the flow of remarks; but nothing daunted, the Irishman called, "Ord'ly; I could go outside and catch some of that b----y rain in me mouth." "I wish you would," replied the orderly, "it would maybe keep it shut." "'arrah, now; that's a swate one for ye," said the son of Erin; then after a moment or two, he called softly, "Ord'ly!" No answer. "*Ord'ly!*" (A shout that time). "Oh, what d'you want now," exclaimed the harassed R.A.M.C. man, "I'm sick and tired of you." "Are ye, now," said the Irishman good-humouredly; "thin just come an' lie down for a bit, an' I'll fetch the tay, me bhoy."

Tea eventually came up at 8.15 p.m., by which time our friend had plotted a scheme with another such worthy (who, however, was a walking wounded case) to get his own back for the delay; for at almost every meal for some time after, the two of them did 'the double shuffle' on the orderlies. The walking case went into the corridor whenever the first orderly arrived with bread, while the Irishman asked for his chum's ration in addition to his own. Meantime the walking case had waylaid the second orderly in the corridor, and obtained his own ration. One day there was a spot of trouble between them over the extra piece of cheese; and upon the arrival of the orderly, the story told unblushingly by each was an object-lesson on what is now termed the art of 'double-crossing'. It ended the 'double-shuffle', however, and within the next half hour the two of them were sitting, heads together, hatching some fresh plot; thick as thieves they were.

Drinking water was at a premium; and when any was available one only had to raise the communal jug to his lips, when the walls would echo to the cry of "Go gently". The weather, too, was miserably cold and wet; but though the windows of the large hut had to be open for fresh air purposes, the only method of heating was to carry a burning brazier from hut to hut. It was left standing in the middle of the floor until the hut was full of smoke; then while we choked and wiped the tears from our eyes, the brazier would be whisked off.

On Sunday, 17th December, 1916, the doctor came round to examine us with a view of sending all fit for duty back up the line, and those unfit for Bray. I was marked for Bray, but to the consternation of some of those marked for duty, I pleaded to be allowed to go back to the battery. After consultation with another doctor, and my assertion that when I got back I should be able to rest for a few days at the battery position, I was allowed to go. I had been four days in hospital, but felt very well when I looked at the cases round me. The R.A.M.C. orderly told me that they had passed 5500 cases through their hands that week – mostly trench feet – so it was little wonder that standing arrangements were hopelessly inadequate. In fact, considering that the difficulties were increased rather than decreased by some of the worthies among us, it was marvellous that meals sufficient for all came up as they did, if not with punctuality, at least with fair regularity.

I waited all that Sunday for my clearing papers; but it was considerably after dark before they were handed over, and I set out for the battery in company with old Sandy Lewis, one of our own gunners who had been sent to Maricourt before me and was now also returning to duty. We had to find our way back as best we could in the inky darkness, and for hours we plodded along in the mud. We practically waded the last two miles, the water on the roads being well over the boot-tops; while every now and again we stumbled into a flooded shellhole to go over the knees when we were lucky enough not to fall.

We arrived at the battery close on midnight, footsore (for we had been lying on the floor for the last four days), caked in mud, and soaked through. Claude and Albert Betts were as glad to see me as I was to see them; and soon I was sitting before a huge fire in our cosy dug-out, with dry garments and clean socks. As we sat there exchanging our experiences of the four days that had passed, I felt like a new man. After what I had seen at Maricourt, it seemed like heaven to be back in the battery once more, and I vowed that if ever I went sick again, I would not go down the line unless I was carried: it would not be while I had two legs to plant on the ground and stand fast.

And when in the 'wee sma' hoors' of the morning I crept into my dug-out bunk, the thought uppermost in my mind was that indeed 'there's no place like Home' – and I was there.

Chapter 10

Christmas and after – Le Forest (Combles)

Let us not burden our remembrances with
a heaviness that's gone – Shakespeare

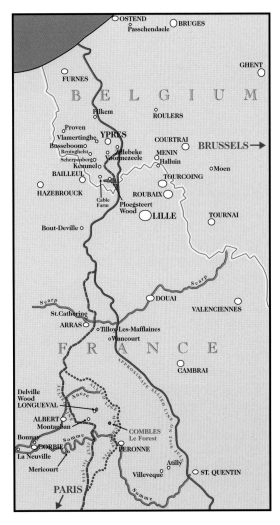

For some days following my return to the battery I was allowed to keep to my bed, the soaking I had received on the journey from Maricourt having again affected me. During these days the weather changed once more, being bitterly cold, and the snow fell to a depth of four inches.

Rations were disorganised, and for some time mails were completely held up; but on Christmas morning a motor lorry arrived with rations and no less than eighteen bags of parcels. The Officers' Mess was piled high with the latter, whose contents were also somewhat *high* by reason of having been so long on the way. Si. Arnould had any amount of green-mouldy potted-head, from which the sheen had long since departed; but the most infamous of all parcels was the one belonging to Captain Wilson. The Major came into the Mess that day, sniffed the air once or twice, then turning to his servant said, "What the devil's that smell, Reid?" "I think it's a parcel for the Captain, sir," replied Harry Reid solemnly. "Well get it removed to his own dug-out at once," ordered the Major. The offending article was

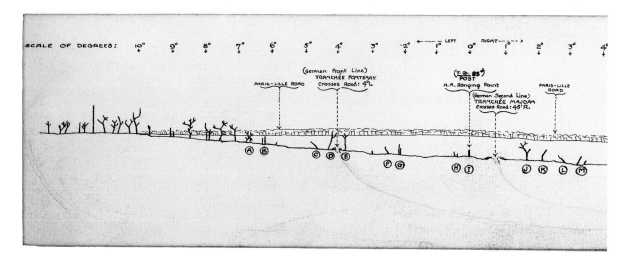

Panoramic Sketch from "Madame O.P." (near Peronne)

handed to John Isaacs, who put it in the Captain's dug-out. When the latter opened the door, he exclaimed "My ruddy ancestors"; then hastily closing it from the outside, he called "Isaacs!" His servant poked his head out of the officers' cookhouse, and without further enquiry announced, "Ah think it's yin o' they paircels sir." "Well, lay your hands on it," replied the Captain: "I expect it's one of those variety entertainment parcels with kippers in it, sent from my father. Take the kippers and let them loose on the Boche." Isaacs duly disposed of the kippers, though in answer to Captain Wilson's enquiry some minutes later, he said, "Ah dinna ken aboot the variety entertainment, sir, but they gien me a turn a' richt." "What did you do with them?" asked the Captain. "Ah went oot tae bury them, sir," said John; then with a grin he added, "bit on the way I wis passing Lyddite's dug-oot, an' flung them in." "You'd better go and see what's happened to them," said the Captain, "his dug-out is bad enough without a pair of stinking kippers in it." John went out, and on reaching Lyddite's habitation called in, "Hi, Lyddite; what did yae dae wi' they kippers?" "Ate 'em, of course," came the reply from the inner darkness, "'ave you got any more?" When the Captain was told, he was somewhat alarmed, for the state of those kippers was such that the tobacco that came in the same parcel had to be thrown away. But though the kippers would have given any normal individual ptomaine poisoning, Lyddite's interior had been trained to withstand anything, and he appeared none the worst of his fish diet.

We spent Christmas and the New Year very quietly, the only extraordinary item on the programme being that on New Year's Day everybody in the battery received a piece of plum pudding sent through the agency of 'John Bull' or 'The Daily Mail', I forget which.[8]

[8] *[It was probably John Bull since the Daily Mail can find no trace]*

One morning we saw two strange-looking figures coming down past the battery position. Both were bearded, and at first we took them for German prisoners. But as they came nearer, it was noticed that they wore no green uniform, and it transpired that they were Russians who had formerly been taken prisoner by the Germans. Finding themselves working behind the lines, they seized the opportunity to escape, and during the previous night had succeeded in getting over the German trenches into 'No Man's Land'.

48

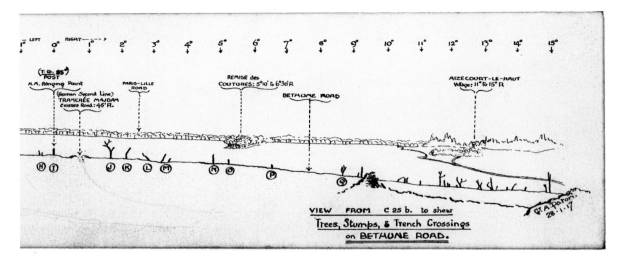

VIEW FROM C 25 b. to shew
Trees, Stumps, & Trench Crossings
on BETHUNE ROAD.

Here they had been caught in our barbed wire; and fearing that they might still be there when dawn came, they had endeavoured to attract the attention of our outposts. In this they were only too successful; for on receiving an unintelligible reply to our challenge, the wire was swept by a drum of machine-gun bullets which wounded both of the unfortunate Russians. A small party was then sent out to investigate, when the men were safely brought in. Strangely enough, the Boche had been quiet during the episode – possibly because the trenches were a considerable distance apart at that point of the line.

The Boche was very subdued, too, with his shellfire at this period, though now and again – probably as a matter of principle – he would send over a couple of 'pip-squeaks', which did little damage. These shells were fired from a high-velocity gun; and making a hole not much larger than a German helmet, were the only shells we treated with scant respect. And indeed, although a direct hit from one would have ended the career of any of us, it savoured of impudence to shell a 9.2 howitzer battery with 'pip-squeaks'.

The morning of Monday, 16th January, 1917, saw me making my way to a French 75 mm. battery position, where I had a long talk with the French officer in command regarding a new observation post (Madame O.P.) in the French lines which we had recently taken over. This officer hailed from Alsace-Lorraine, and had two cousins fighting – one in the Canadian Expeditionary Force and the other on the German side. The sergeants of the battery spoke English, having been for some time in the service of a shipping firm in Glasgow. On the following Sunday, I went up with Captain Wilson to Madame O.P. for a panoramic sketch. Snow had fallen to a depth of six inches, and the O.P. was a long distance from the battery. On the way up, we passed many dead Germans lying in shellholes unburied; though they must have been killed months before; for nothing remained of most of them but skeletons in uniform, and it was a ghastly sight to come across so many with nothing but a leg-bone in a jack-boot.

Part of our way led by a trench through a small wood south of the Bois de Marrières. As we made our way along this trench, Captain Wilson

49

remarked that a shell would have no chance of hitting it now, situated as it was on the steep side of the hill farthest from the German line. When at last we reached the vicinity of the O.P., it was being heavily strafed, and another half hour elapsed before we got into the place. The observation post was in the trench itself; a flimsy shelter of branches with a slit from which one could see right down the German front and second line trenches, which were therefore subject to enfilade fire from the O.P. The latter, consequently, was hardly a health resort; and as it was shelled at intervals every day, a deep dug-out had been made in the trench about twenty yards along from the observation post. About half an hour after our arrival shelling suddenly recommenced, and there was a scramble for the dug-out on the part of various infantrymen, artillery observers and signallers (linesmen). Unfortunately for Captain Wilson and me, we were the last to arrive. A fat officer had got wedged in the entrance, and was treated with scant courtesy – everybody pushed until he went through, then as the interior became wider, he went headlong down the stairway.

Returning home that evening, we passed back along the trench on the steep side of the hill south of Marrières Wood. A six-inch shell had just got an O.K. on it, killing an Officer and private of the Seaforths and two of the Hants regiment. The Boche had shown us without any delay that it was still possible to hit; and the soldier's superstition that it is unlucky to say that one is safe anywhere was once more vindicated.

Some days later I again visited Madame O.P.: this time in company with Lieut. Gibbs. Two little incidents worthy of mention took place on this occasion. The first was when two Staff officers came up to the O.P. and after looking round, decided that as things seemed quiet, they would take a short cut over the open to another part of the trench, which otherwise was only reached by a devious route round a hairpin bend. By taking the risk of sprinting across the open, they would save a few hundred yards if they were lucky. We asked them not to do this, as it would certainly draw shellfire on us – the risk to themselves was *their* funeral. They walked along the trench for about thirty yards from the O.P., then clambered out and bolted for the trench behind, some forty yards away. They got safely across; but the Boche, just too late, began to spray the ground with machine-gun bullets, one of which hit an inoffensive signaller in the leg. The two Staff officers never saw him, I daresay, as he lay on his stomach among the grass between the trenches. He had taken every care when crawling out to mend his line not to be observed by the Boche; and while the Brass-hats doubtless went on their way rejoicing, we had to get their victim in. This was observed just as we were getting him into the trench: then the fat was in the fire, for the Boche shelled the trench with four gun salvoes for a good fifteen minutes afterwards. The sally on the part of a couple of young irresponsibles had started a little war on its own; and that sally turned us into Aunt Sallys.

The other incident happened in the afternoon. Mr. Gibbs and I were observing, when just in front of our front line trench there was a large explosion. "Looks like a mine," I said to Mr. Gibbs, and we involuntarily crouched in the shelter as the debris began to fall all around us. "Looks like it," agreed Mr. Gibbs, who was cheery to the point of being facetious in times of crisis; "I think the old Boche is coming over on a raid. Got any weapons?"

"No," I replied seriously enough; for I was not thinking so much of defensive weapons as of my diary reposing peacefully in my pocket where the obsolete gas mask should have been, and wondering how to dispose of it should the Boche succeed in reaching our trench. "That's all right then," said Mr. Gibbs, "I've got a penknife." Just then the Boche did emerge from their front line trench, but our infantry met them with such a devastating burst of machine-gun fire that the raid withered away before it reached our front line, the survivors turning and running back to their own lines. It was all begun and ended in a few minutes, but exciting enough during that time.

I reached the battery that night feeling that I had had enough of O.P.'s to last me some time (though I knew I should be back within the next day or two). But lying down to sleep, a vague sense of security and satisfaction stole over me: something had happened which made me realise that all was well with the world. In my semi-conscious state of sleepiness I had to think for a minute or two before I knew what it was; then I remembered that my diary and sketches still lay safely in my pocket. That the cause in no manner warranted the effect did not in the least disturb the soundness of my sleep.

Chapter 11

A chapter of flights –
Le Forest (Combles)

Oh that I had wings like a dove;
For then would I fly away and be at rest – Psalms

Our Major had now temporarily left us to act as Colonel of Brigade. While he was gone a 'chit' arrived asking for the names of any officers willing to transfer to the Flying Corps (Observation Balloon Section). Lieuts. Gibbs and Phipps pressed Captain Wilson to allow their names to go forward – and indeed, since they desired it, the Captain could not refuse. Both applications were accepted; but when the Major learned that his two main observing subalterns were about to take flight, he was furious and swore that had he not been away the thing would never have happened. That may well have been the case, but now it was beyond recall, and the Major and the Captain were the only two left of the officers who had come out with the battery.

On 14th February, 1917, I was making a panoramic sketch at Bethune O.P., when I noticed that right above my head one of our older type of 'buses' (apparently directing an artillery shoot, judging from the manner in which it had been circling for some time) had been caught up by four German planes. All five planes were flying

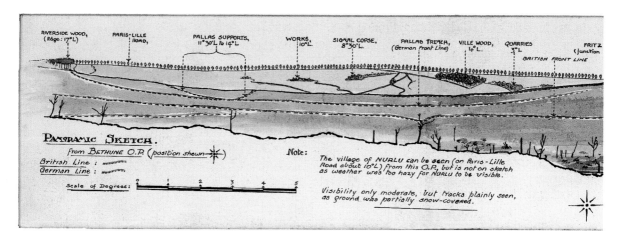

Panoramic Sketch from Bethune O.P. at Bouchavesnes

very low, and it seemed that nothing could save ours from being brought down. By twisting and turning, however, he managed to elude his pursuers, and five minutes later he was back observing. In the afternoon he was at it again, and this time was cut off by three German machines. How he escaped was a mystery to me; yet not only did he do so, but actually shot one of his assailants down. Returning to the battery that evening, I learned that it had been our own battery's observing plane that I had seen; and that after his forenoon escape, the airman had sent the message, "Sorry; hostile aircraft: repeat last round." Many weeks later, I cut the following interesting item from the "Daily Mail" of 25th March 1917:

> *"Lt. Douglas Hugh Moffatt Carberry, R.F.A. and R.F.C. (M.C.); While engaged on artillery observation he was attacked by four hostile machines, which he succeeded in driving off and continued to carry out his observations. Later he was again attacked by several hostile machines and succeeded in bringing one of them down. He has previously done fine work."*

We greatly admired the exhibition of skill and daring witnessed on this occasion, though exhibitions of daring did not always receive the same measure of commendation from our gunners, even when deserving of all praise, as the following incident shows.

One of our observation balloons had been up on several evenings somewhat closer to the line than was usual for such craft. The Boche endeavoured to shell it, but though several bursts appeared to be fairly near, the balloon remained in the air. On Thursday, 1st March, 1917, it went up for the last time. It was a beautiful evening; the balloon swaying to and fro on its anchor rope, a delicate bluish-grey against the orange sky. Suddenly I noticed that the latter was becoming flecked with anti-aircraft shell bursts, and saw a German plane making for the balloon at terrific speed. Circling round it, his tracer bullets set it ablaze in a few seconds, both our observers coming down in parachutes. From our position it seemed as though the parachutes were overtaken by the blazing mass of the envelope; but this would not probably be the case: more likely the long trailing column of smoke from the envelope

54

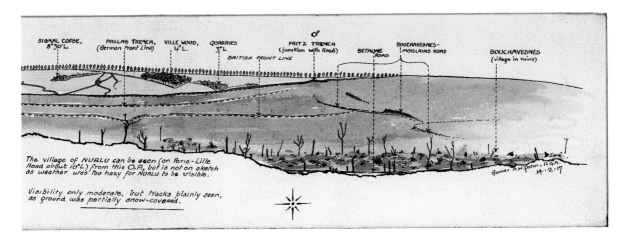

SIGNAL COPSE, 8°30'L.   PALLAS TRENCH, (German front line)   VILLE WOOD, 4°L.   QUARRIES 3°L   FRITZ TRENCH (junction with Road)   BETAUNE ROAD   BOUCHAVESNES-MOISLAINS ROAD   BOUCHAVESNES (village in ruins)

BRITISH FRONT LINE

The village of NURLU can be seen (on Paris-Lille Road about 10°L) from this O.P., but is not on sketch as weather was too hazy for NURLU to be visible.

Visibility only moderate, but tracks plainly seen, as ground was partially snow-covered.

Gunner A.W.Paton, R.G.A. 14·2·17

would hide the parachutes from view. Meantime the "Allemande" had with some difficulty reached its own lines.

That evening later, I heard a discussion on the matter by two of our gunners, when the courage of the two observers in going up so near the line was praised in these terms:- "Ay;" said one, "they've been asking for trouble, they have." "Well," replied the other, "they've got it this time." Then the first speaker rejoined, "I knew they would get it in the neck one o' these nights." Probably the observers knew that too; but it is a good thing that they went up, nevertheless; and that when they were brought down, others were ready to take their places. Yet the gunners' talk was, at bottom, less disparaging of our observers than a roundabout way of expressing their admiration of both them and the Boche airman, whose intrepidity was undoubtedly great. For as often as not, an aeroplane on such a task was shot down before it could either climb to safety or reach its own lines.

We had been at Le Forest now for almost three months without a casualty – a remarkable state of affairs, even considering that the severity of the winter had reduced shelling by both sides to a minimum. But on Saturday, 3rd March, 1917, a distressing incident took place in the battery. In order to maintain the road behind our guns in case of a move, we had been occupied for some weeks in digging chalk from a small quarry near our gun position. On the day mentioned, the gunners were having a breather, when Andrew Williamson noticed a large section of the cliff begin to topple. Shouting a warning, he dashed forward and grabbed Gunner Craig; and despite some risk to himself, endeavoured to pull him clear as the stuff fell. Unfortunately, though he retained his hold, the fallen chalk partly buried Craig and completely buried Gunner Murray. Both were dug out in a few minutes, but Murray was already dead, while Craig died the same evening. Duncan received staved or broken ribs, while Arnould, Innes and Williamson were struck by the debris and thrown clear. Had it not been for Andrew Wiliamson's warning shout, all must have been buried. But the nature of the affair, as much as its consequence, impressed itself on the battery. More than anything else, I think, we were awed by this exhibition of the frailty of the human frame; for when we pulled the two gunners out, it was difficult to believe that either could be seriously hurt: yet both were gone.

About this time, matters on the front had begun to liven up; though the weather was still very cold, it was now dry. At the beginning of March, our infantry made a determined attack on the German lines, the objective in our sector being Fritz Trench on the crest of the slope at Bouchavesnes opposite Bethune O.P. In this attack, the infantry was successful; and on going up for observation purposes next day, the whole valley beyond the crest was so plainly in view that Captain Wilson caught two enemy batteries whose gunners were in the act of taking off their camouflage preparatory to going into action – which neither did, for we engaged both at once. The mist came down that afternoon as a blessing to the Boche, who had already realised that the valley was untenable. Next morning we found it deserted by the enemy, who in the mist and darkness of the night before, had made good his own escape. On going over the ground later, we found that one of the batteries we engaged had got safely away; the guns of the other had been badly damaged and had been abandoned by the owners in their flight.

Claude Betts and Alf Gregory were ordered home for Officer's Commission the same week. These two, along with Albert Betts and me, dined in the same dug-out at Le Forest. Gregory was an amiable youth (he was the battery scout for enemy aircraft), and often after dinner he would clean up the remains of the meal from the table, on which he wanted to write a letter home. He seldom disposed of the remains, preferring to wait until Claude was about to leave the dug-out, when he would say, "Claude, if you're going-gout," (he had the habit of tacking the last letter of present participles to the next word), "you might just throw this as far as you can;" when Claude would receive a parcel of rubbish. One day he handed Claude a bully-beef tin full of remains, asking him as usual to throw it as far as he could. Claude meekly took the tin and went out, leaving the dug-out door open. A minute later a clattering can came hurtling across the table, scattering pig's meat in its wake. Gregory leapt to his feet, and looking out, saw Claude standing awaiting developments some twenty yards off. "Hi, Claude; what's the idea," he asked with a martyred air, for a letter to his best girl was somewhat badly pork-and-beaned. "Well," replied Claude with his customary twinkle, "you told me to throw it as far as I could, but you didn't specify any direction; so I threw it as far as I could in *your* direction."

The departure of Claude left a blank in the lives of Albert and me at this time; and when I next saw Claude, he was an officer in charge of as merry a band of Chinese pirates as ever ravaged the fair Flanders mud[9]. That belongs to a later period of this story. Claude's departure from the battery actually took place a day or two after the last flight to be recorded in this chapter – our own.

We were now no longer in touch with the enemy from our comfortable position in Le Forest, and early in March one half of the battery was ordered to leave for a new sector, the remaining half being due to follow a week later. I was to go with the first half, and Albert with the second: Claude, of course, was going straight to England.

The news that we were going away from Le Forest was not particularly welcome, although we had realised that it was bound to come. Albert and I were already somewhat depressed at the thought of Claude's impending departure; and when I came down from the B.C. Post with the news that the battery was going to another part of the front (usually a matter for much

[9] I have not seen either Claude or Albert Betts since 1917, but the friendship of these war years remains one of my warmest memories.

excitement and speculation), I said apathetically to Claude, "We're moving." He was studying a magazine, and didn't seem particularly interested, for he made no reply. I sat down opposite him at the table and continued my tale of woe. "There'll be a fine Spring's awakening where we're going, I expect: why couldn't they have left us in peace." Still there was no reply from Claude; and my last words setting up a new train of thought in my mind, I said more calmly, "I wonder when we'll *get* peace." It was the first time I had given expression to such a thought, and Claude looked up, roused at last. Tossing the "Tatler" across the table, he said laconically, "There's one answer."

I picked up the magazine[10], on the turned up page of which was a reproduction of a cartoon from the New York "Puck". The picture showed a shell-swept landscape, in the foreground of which lay spread-eagled just such a skeleton as I had seen on the way to Madame O.P.

[10] [Issue dated 14th February, 1917]

The cartoon was entitled "The Only Peace in Europe".

From "Puck," New York

THE <u>ONLY</u> PEACE IN EUROPE

Chapter 12

Spring's awakening — St. Catherines (Arras)

United thoughts and counsels, equal hope,
And hazard in this glorious enterprise – Milton

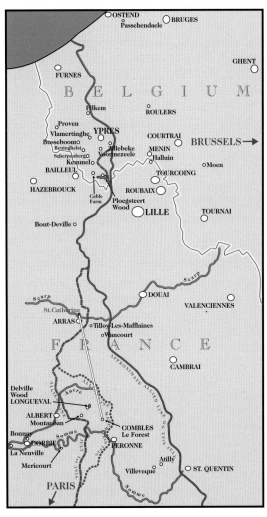

The first half of the battery left Le Forest by decauville railway on the afternoon of Friday, 16th March, 1917. When we had been about two hours on the way, the engine and one truck left the rails, and it was dusk before we got them righted. Hardly had we restarted when the Boche began shelling the valley with pip-squeaks; but following our long spell of comparative quietness, the journey was already beginning to quicken our spirit of adventure, and as each pip-squeak burst we cheered it to the echo. Then one came over that we didn't cheer – it was an eight inch! it woke up the engine driver's ideas, however, for he took us out of that valley *tout-de-suite*. Soon afterwards the engine left us with our trucks of stores, and it was reported that a motor-driven engine would come up and take us into Bray. It did not appear to be in any hurry; so after waiting until 9 p.m. we made tea and then sat around the fire. This we had kept as low as possible in case of a bomb from a Boche plane; but as the night wore on, we became bitterly cold and piled up the fire with anything we could find that would burn. Though cold, the weather was dry; and we sat singing Scots songs until after midnight, when our fuel was exhausted. Then huddling together on top of the stores, we tried to sleep; but the extreme cold made this almost impossible. The engine arrived at 2.30 a.m., the driver informing us that he had been delayed through enemy shellfire which nearly tore up the decauville railway. We reached Bray at 5 a.m., nearly frozen; and there were issued with a mug of tea, which was bad but hot, and therefore welcome. I was hungry too, and was quite ready for the bully and army biscuits given to us. But I never ate the meal; for on sticking my jackknife into the tin of bully beef, there was the sizzle of escaping gas, and I was almost asphyxiated by the smell (only on one occasion since can I remember anything comparable with that smell – months later, when three Irish infantrymen travelling down the line in the same carriage as I, took off their boots and socks). After that, I was unable to eat for some hours.

Early that morning we left Bray for Corbie, once more travelling in motor lorries along the heights above Bonnay. The road ran along the crest of a ridge, on the one side of which the village of Bonnay could be seen nestling among the trees. But though the view on that side was pretty, that on the other was truly magnificent, stretching for miles in a series of ridges and valleys. In the foreground the Somme twined its way far below us like a silver thread among azure trees indefinitely outlined in the morning haze. It was a Corot landscape in reality, and we were so impressed by its beauty that our lorry-driver stopped beside a monument at the roadside for a few minutes to admire it. Little did I dream then that fully a year later I should be observing the enemy from this very spot.

We reached Corbie about midday, and at 4.30 p.m. halted at Rivery-aux-Camons, a hamlet just outside Amiens. I visited the city that evening: it was crowded with soldiers and civilians, and it was strange to see electric cars running. We resumed our journey on the following day, and that night we spent at the village of Villers-Bocage, where there was nothing more interesting to do than make a sketch of the "Grande Mare", a sheet of water surrounded by pollarded willows. This brought us in touch with a band of children, curious to see what I was doing. When I had finished, we made the children run blindfold races, which was more exciting than it might seem; for the youngsters ran at top speed (the prizes being pennies), and several of them in their headlong flight were nearly in the pond.

Next day (Monday, 19th March), we passed through some very pretty country in the course of our journey, to arrive that evening at the filthiest village I was ever in – Gezaincourt, near Doullens. Perhaps my recollections of it do it no justice, for the weather had broken down and the barn in which we slept that night leaked like a sieve. But even so, it was as dirty as the weather; and though next morning we set off in a tornado of wind and sleet, I was glad to go. We had now reached the final stage of our journey, for on Wednesday, 21st March, we arrived at our new position in the faubourg of St. Catherines, Arras. We had spent five days on the road.

Next morning the fun began. We placed two guns in position, settled on a fighting Post, and put our stores into various cellars and houses. In the afternoon we were having a look round when a German plane flew over our heads very low. I stood in the shelter of a doorway and saw an infantryman on the other side of the narrow street standing looking up. A splinter from an anti-aircraft shell came down and hit him in the eye, so we dressed him and packed him off to the hospital. Then the Boche began to shell the neighbourhood. I had got our maps and B.C. instruments nicely spread out

Villers-Bocage, near Amiens

on a table in a house which was light and airy; and the Major was thinking of registering the two guns on some enemy point that afternoon, when the shelling started. Our shoot was postponed until next day; for one of the enemy shellbursts brought down a huge chunk of the plaster ceiling on top of the map table. This would not have mattered, but it also brought from the roof a wasp "bike"; and the next moment the Major and I were fleeing for our lives! Next morning we rescued our maps and instruments, finding a new B.C. Post in a cellar made of stone. Other cellars were made into sleeping dug-outs for the men; "D" sub-section's having at first two feet of water in it. When this was baled out, it was found that no more was coming in, so the place was used by the sub-section during the whole period of our stay in Arras. I erected a small dug-out in a garden for Albert Betts and myself; and though only splinter-proof, it was dry and comparatively light.

We decided to register our two guns that afternoon. "D" gun had the honour of firing first; and as the shell went speeding on its way, we heard a tremendous crash and a long rumble of falling debris. On going into the main street, we found that the concussion of our shell had brought down a whole four-storey tenement, the street being completely blocked for traffic. Fortunately no one happened to be passing at the time; but as we did not then know that (and a horse and cart could easily have been hidden in the debris), the shoot was once more postponed while all available hands cleared the wreckage. "Ginger" Hill was in charge of one small party after the search had proved that no one was apparently buried. A very heavy beam of wood necessitated the use of a drag rope to remove it, and while this was being done, a young lad came up and began to gather pieces of wood, presumably for his dug-out fire. Ginger stopped his working party, and walking across to the youth, said "What do you think *you're* doing?" "Collecting firewood same as you," replied the boy unabashed. But Ginger was not to be outdone so simply. "And do you think for one minute," he said, "that we took all this trouble to pull down that house for you? We want all the wood for our cookhouse: if you want some, go and pull down a house for yourself." The lad moved off, remarking that he did not know we had deliberately pulled the building down. It is to be hoped that he did not start a demolition scheme on his own!

Farmyard Billet, Villers-Bocage, near Amiens

A week later the other half of the battery arrived; and for some days we were busy bombarding targets for the big attack which we knew to be impending. The area opposite our front was very carefully allocated by zones among the various batteries, being in the strong and complicated trench system known as "The Harp" – so called because its shape on the map strongly resembled that instrument.

One dull day the Major and some of the junior officers went up to the O.P. to have a look round the enemy country. Knowing that there was little likelihood of any shoot, the gun sergeants set their teams to work cleaning up the battery position. At dinner-time, before going off to their Mess, they left instructions for the gunners to continue the good work in the afternoon. After dinner the sergeants did not reappear, nor did the sergeant-major. The latter had not been long with us, but was quite a decent sort. He had two failings in the eyes of the gunners: one was a passion for counting tubes and fuzes (in consequence of which he was known to all as "Old Toobs and Foozes"); the other was a weakness for the rum jar. He and the sergeants had apparently decided to have a blow-out that afternoon, for after 3 p.m. old Toobs and Foozes was seen making his way cautiously but uncertainly to the battery office, into which he disappeared. Shortly afterwards, the Major unexpectedly returned, having been ordered by Brigade to return and carry out a counter-battery shoot. Corporal Woods, the Battery clerk, was despatched to inform the sergeant-major, while I was given the location of the enemy battery to work our the lines of fire for the guns. Some minutes later the Major came into the B.C. Post. Bring those lines with you out to the guns," he said. "I don't know what the devil's gone wrong; the men are all at the guns, but the sergeant-major and the sergeants are not there yet. Bring out the map-board and we'll conduct the shoot from the guns."

But when we reached the battery, there was still no sign of Old Toobs and Foozes. The Major began to get ruffled. "Run and see what's happened to Corporal Woods, and come back quickly: someone's going to be sharply rapped over the fingers for this," he barked. At the battery office I found Woods bending over the recumbent form of the sergeant-major. "I don't know what to do," he said agitatedly: "I can't get him wakened." We both shook him violently, and yelled in his ear, when one eye slowly opened to give us as glassy stare like a dead cod. "Come on," I cried, "the Major's been shouting for you for ages: it's 'battery action'." The mention of the Major seemed to revive the S.M., for he staggered to his feet and waddled out of the office, buttoning his tunic as he went. When he reached the archway which led from the street into the garden in which the guns were placed, he managed to extricate his whistle. The signal for 'battery action' was a blast on this; and it was ludicrous to see the attempts old Toobs and Foozes made to blow it. He was so short of breath that he could only produce a feeble 'wheep' (for which in any case there was no necessity, since the gunners were already at their posts), and it was very obvious what was the matter. I glanced at the Major: he was speechless with fury. At last he found voice. "Sergeant-Major," he cried, "go to your dug-out, you b----y fool; you're dead drunk." Then he called for the senior sergeant, but the latter when he appeared was as bad as the S.M. For a moment the Major ignored his state and said, "The sergeant-major's under arrest; take charge." "Yessir," replied the sergeant making a feeble effort to salute. This was too much for the Major, who looked at him in utter disgust, then said, "Oh go to your dug-out too; I'll see you in the morning." The end of it all was that Sergeant Spencer (who was able to 'hold' more than any of the others) took over the sergeant-major's duties. The only gun-captain actually leading his gun team on that occasion was Sergeant Jack – the one territorial sergeant in the battery who had originally come from the Forth Defences. If the Major had any lingering doubts about the discipline of his "B----y civilian soldiers", they were dispelled that day; for the shoot was completed with every satisfaction – the gunners could discipline themselves.

For some days rumours of courts-martial were rife, but possibly owing to the facts that the big attack was imminent and that the culprit had received a lesson (for such an occurrence never again took place), the affair blew over and was not revived after the general excitement over the battle of Arras.

On the day following that incident I happened to go into the battery office. Only Toobs and Foozes and Lyddite were present when I arrived. Lyddite had just been severely 'ticked off' for something; but on my entrance, the sergeant-major wound up his admonitory remarks, and dismissed Lyddite with a caution. The latter slouched to the door, then turning round, he hurled a parting shot at the sergeant-major. "I don't wish you any 'arm, but I 'opes a b----y big eight inch shell gets you right in the back of the neck." From anyone else, such a statement before a witness would have meant immediate arrest; but Lyddite was a privileged person in the battery. As the door closed, old Toobs and Foozes just looked at me, and slowly closed the eye I had seen him so slowly open on the previous afternoon.

We were now all ready for the great attack. I still think that its preparation (along with that for Vimy Ridge – part of the same battle), planned by General Allenby, was by far the best conceived up to that time, and must have failed to attain complete success by a very narrow margin – possible only because of the breakdown of the weather again on the very day of the attack.

The infantry going up the line on the eve of the battle were in the highest spirits, calling to us just to keep on as we had been doing, and theirs would be an easy task. A sergeant of the Argyll and Sutherland Highlanders, the past winter's miseries at Combles forgotten, fell out of the ranks for a few minutes on hearing our Scots tongue. He said our practice barrages had been perfect, and departed saying "If I dinna hurry up, the boys'll be ower the tap 'ithoot me."

The hazard of the business was forgotten in confident hope as battalion after battalion marched past to take their places in the line that would be launched on the Boche in the morning. It was an inspiring sight; as still in the gathering darkness the endless streams of smiling faces and marching forms emerged from obscurity for a few minutes, then faded into the gloom. Only when the last of them had gone did I wonder what the morrow would bring – triumph or tragedy? To a great extent, both: for while confident that the attack would be a complete success, the tragedy of it lay in the certainty that so many of those laughing eyes would not see the dawn.

Chapter 13

La guerre finie? –
St. Catherines (Arras)

What he hit is history,
What he missed is mystery – Hood

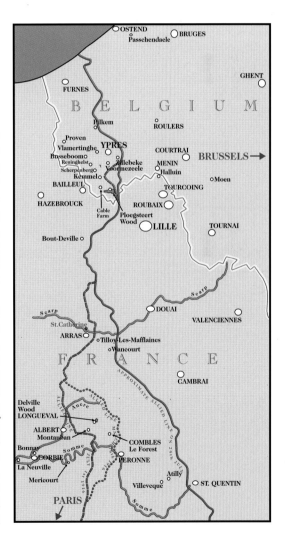

I was awake before 5 a.m. the next day (Monday, 9th April, 1917) to work out any corrections on our lines of fire necessitated by change of wind or weather. Unfortunately the latter was very unfavourable for aeroplane observation, a steady rain falling. At 5.30 a.m., the guns (which had been bombarding slowly all night) opened out on the barrage. The noise was deafening, and thousands of Golden Rain (S.O.S.) rockets went up from the German trenches.

At 8.30 a.m. we received orders to cease fire, as the infantry had already progressed to the limit of our range. By the time I had breakfasted, German prisoners were streaming in. One of our wounded told me our artillery barrage was perfectly timed and laid down: so far as he could say, our casualties were not heavy up to the time he had been hit. Later I met a Lance-Corporal of Argylls escorting a batch of over a hundred prisoners. He said his battalion had required to return from the German third system of defence, as they had been too anxious, and in their haste had run into our own barrage. The unwounded prisoners seemed glad to be out of it; and though

65

torn and tattered, most of them were quite cheerful. As they passed, good-humoured banter was exchanged between them and some of our lads; and the commonest cry was called to us, strangely enough I thought, in French: "La geurre finie; la guerre finie."

As usual, however, the wounded walking cases, mostly German, presented a pitiable sight. Nearly all looked utterly weary and dejected. Shattered arms were very common among them, and one poor fellow had his mouth half torn away by a shell splinter. Later in the forenoon, six German field kitchens went by, and also a great number of artillerymen and some batteries of guns. One infantry prisoner told me they had "stood to" for three nights in succession expecting us to attack before dawn, and on that morning – when the attack *did* take place – they were worn out. By midday it was difficult to obtain news, and prisoners were coming in very slowly. At 1.30 p.m. it was reported that we had reached the German fourth line of defence. This was the well-known double-line trench system called the Drocourt-Queant line, and it was now reported to be strongly held and fortified. We had previously conjectured that if this trench system fell into our hands, the cavalry would be able to go through; in which case the whole German defence would crumble and the end of the war be in sight. At 2 p.m. our Brigade Colonel came in to tell us that the Canadians had captured Vimy Ridge, and rumours of the surrender of whole Boche brigades were rife. The Colonel added that there was no further news of our own sector, as the infantry were now a long way from their original front line.

The afternoon wore on without further news, but in the evening the cavalry began to pour up the line. It was a great sight – dragoons, hussars, horse artillery and mounted machine-gun corps. Unfortunately the morning rain changed first to sleet and then to snow; and when the cavalry passed through St. Catherines, big snowflakes were wreathing everything in a mantle of white. I was watching from the shelter of a doorway when I was joined by a young cavalrymen who dismounted for a moment or two during a block in the traffic. To my surprise, we knew each other: when last I had seen him we were toddlers of six or seven years old in the same street of Edinburgh. But we had no time for reminiscences, for the traffic had again begun to move. Remounting, he turned to wave a hand and rode out of my life.

The next two days brought occasional handfuls of cavalry back down the line with wounded, and horses thick with mud. The only news we had was to be prepared to advance at a moment's notice to Tilloy-les-Mafflaines; so we pulled out our guns and parked our column at the roadside ready to advance. The infantry coming down did not seem to know where the Boche was by this time; but it was reported that the delay caused by the rain and snow had given him time to complete his defences in front of the Drocourt-Queant line, and that our cavalry had been held up by the barbed wire.

In our sector alone, however, we had taken two thousand six hundred prisoners, besides machine guns, trench mortars and field guns; and this we looked on as a great victory, as indeed it was. But we magnified it out of all true proportion; though our enthusiasm abated somewhat when we received orders to take up position in the village of Tilloy-les-Mafflaines, which a week earlier we had been bombarding with our own guns.

Thinking of how far Tilloy was from St. Catherines; then calculating that if, at Tilloy, we should again be within howitzer range of the enemy, it seemed to me that surely we could not, after all, have captured the Drocourt-Queant system. And as I remembered the German prisoners' cry of "La geurre finie;" la guerre finie," it looked that, while still true for them, it was not true in the sense I had imagined on the morning of the attack.

But if, as seemed the case, we had not broken through, where was the cavalry that had gone up? They had not returned in great numbers as far as we had seen, and I could not think what had happened to them. I was to see with my own eyes before many days had passed.

Chapter 14

"The harpists" –
Tilloy-Les-Mafflaines (Arras)

It is'na play where one 'greets' and anither laughs –
Scots Proverb

Early in the afternoon of Saturday, 14th April, 1917, we left Arras for Tilloy-les-Mafflaines. The road was packed with upgoing traffic, and we were held up time and again before passing Arras railway station. At that point, however, the road was fairly clear and we arrived at Tilloy about 5 o'clock. We worked all night pulling in the guns, and by six o'clock next morning were again ready for action.

We were now like rabbits standing on their hind legs gazing with curiosity at their surroundings and scenting danger in the air. And like rabbits, when the danger became real, we scurried underground. We were still optimistic that we should be in Germany before long, and none more than our Major, who revived my optimism by declaring on our arrival in Tilloy that I need not find a dug-out for *him* – it was field warfare now. He erected his map table inside a motor lorry in which he also slept that first night; but alas! overnight several big shells fell close enough to convince him that even if it was field warfare, an interim dug-out might be advisable. Thus it was that the B.C. Post came to be in a forty-foot deep German dug-out instead of a map-table in the open. The gunners too found plenty of deep dug-outs in the "Harp" trench system previously mentioned. We were warned to be careful on entering these deep dug-outs for the first time, as the Boche had laid traps in many of them.

German Observation Post, Tilloy-Les-Mafflaines, near Arras

"Comic Cuts", as Corps Intelligence Summary was nicknamed, told of places where to tread on a certain step blew the dug-out up. In others the chimney was choked with packets of explosives. We saw two casualties of this nature on the morning after our arrival, both being caused by trip wires. These lay across the ground like telephone cable, but when the foot of the highlander caught on it, the wire was found to have been attached to a bomb, which exploded, wounding the "Jock" and his companion.

There was a beautiful observation post in a ruined barn at Tilloy. Only the walls and rafters appeared to be standing; but inside the shell of the building a concrete column had been raised. From fifty yards off, the barn looked just like a ruin; but when one entered, ladders led up the inside of the concrete column to the top, from which a very fine view of our old lines and also of Arras could be obtained. Embedded in the concrete pillar was a plaster of Paris model of an Iron Cross, and this I managed to prise out to keep as a souvenir.

Not much was left of either chateau or church. On the one wall that remained of the latter were two tablets marking the burial-place of French villagers who had died a hundred years before. The inscription asked the passer-by to put up a prayer for their souls.

Our own sleeping-place was in a dug-out in the wood behind the chateau, and was a considerable distance away from the B.C. Post, to reach which I had to go through the wood for a hundred yards, cross the village street, and over part of the "Harp" for another hundred yards to the trench in which the entrance to our B.C. Post lay. One day I had just started from our dug-out for the B.C. Post when the Boche commenced shelling the wood. The first shell burst about twenty yards to my right; and when the debris stopped falling, I rose and began to run, when another came over which burst still nearer me. I had again thrown myself flat on the ground, and on picking myself up, fairly flew for the road. Just as I reached it I heard a third shell coming, and seeing a fragment of wall standing, I dashed for what shelter it might afford. A few yards from the remains of this wall a horse and cart was standing, and I flung myself down on the far side of the wall just as the shell burst. It was fortunate that I threw myself behind it on the side furthest from the cart; for I heard a voice shout "My God, look at my horse." I rose amid a cloud of black and pink dust to find the wall almost gone and the horse's entrails strewn beside it. I did not wait on getting up, but dashed on, and just before reaching the trench I was making for, a fourth shell was heard on the way. I felt sure this one would get me, but as I threw myself down the entrance to the O.P. Post, the shell screamed overhead to burst over the parapet of the trench. It seemed queer that those four shells followed my course all the way from my dug-out; and hardly was I recovering my breath when Lieut. Leslie came rushing down the steps. He stopped short on seeing me, his eyes almost starting out of his head. Then he said, "How did you manage to get in here? I thought you had been killed. I saw you run across the road and drop behind that wall where the horse was standing; and when the dust cleared away, the horse was dead and the wall almost gone, and you nowhere to be seen. I thought you had got the whole shell." Thorough 'wind up', however, had lent wings to my feet on that occasion, but I never think of the incident without remembering that as I went clattering down those dug-out steps hearing that fourth shell roaring in my ears, I was quite certain it was coming down the entrance too (being a German dug-out, the entrance now faced German lines). But I was apparently more fitted to be an underground "Harpist" than a celestial one. That night the Boche put 200 shells into the wood, without further casualties than three candles extinguished, the canvas screen over our "window" torn down, and Idris Williams (our wireless operator) flung on top of the stove by the concussion of a near one.

Though most of the dug-outs used by the battery were made by the Germans and "safe as houses", there was one man in the battery who did not take advantage of their safety. This was Gunner Brebner, (known to all and sundry as 'Auld Dougal'), the oldest man in the battery, and one of the former Forth Defence gunners. He was over the age for going abroad when the battery was formed, but was so keen to go that the Major had agreed to take him as battery storeman. Auld Dougal was the most privileged old rascal in the battery, and was an expert at hedging when anyone went to him for an issue of clothing. If you asked for a new pair of boots, he would look sympathetically at the worn out pair, and then say, "Eh, man; I'm awfu' sorry: had yae come juist twa days ago, I could've daen somethin' for yae; but noo I've nae buits, nae tunics, nae puttees, nae shrapnel helmets, nae rum – nae anythin' hardly." Then leaning forward, he would say confidentially, "Dae yae happen tae be needin' a new pair of gallisses? We've got some fine gallisses in the noo." But there is a limit to substitutes, even in war-time, and this was reached one day when Jim Brunton went to draw an issue of bread for an O.P. party. "I've nae bried;" said Dougal solemnly, then cheering up, added, "Take a set o' bats and wickets."

Dougal's store at Tilloy was a ramshackle square shelter, whose walls consisted mainly of tea and biscuit boxes, the roof being composed of corrugated iron sheets laid flat across and supported in the centre by a long wooden deal. One day the Boche put a shell right through the roof. The quarter-master sergeant, Auld Dougal and two other gunners were inside at the time; and of the quartette, one gunner was killed outright, while the other and the quarter-master sergeant were severely wounded. Dougal had been sitting on top of a pile of biscuit boxes smoking his pipe; and when the smoke and debris cleared away, an amazing sight was revealed. Everything except the pile of biscuit boxes on which Dougal had been sitting was razed to the

71

A.W.Paton
4th May 1917

*The Chateau,
Tilloy-Les-
Mafflaines,
near Arras*

ground; the roof was gone, and nothing remained except the tall column of
boxes, on top of which Dougal sat dazed, pipe in hand, wondering what could
have happened. He was quite unhurt; but if the incident had its funny aspect,
it held tragedy also, and more than a touch of grim humour. For the man who
was killed was thrown high in the air, and his body dropped on the shoulders
of another of our gunners at "A" section's gun, fifty yards off. The gunner was
injured and somewhat unnerved by the shock; and it was Si. Arnould who
first grasped what had happened. With his usual presence of mind, he
grabbed the gun cover and threw it over the body, then set about putting
things in order again and cleaning up. When this had been done and the
corpse laid on a stretcher, he went to report to the sergeant-major. Old Toobs
and Foozes asked if the body was entire, when Si. replied that a leg was
missing. "Well," exclaimed the S.M. irritably, "go and search for it until you
find it: you're not going off without it." It was eventually found, when it was
placed beside the other remains and taken to the mortuary.

But a repetition of the experiences incidental to war breeds, if not
contempt, a cloak of indifference – for by that evening Auld Dougal, with the
help of some of the gun detachments, had rebuilt his store; when one of the
gunners referring 'sympathetically' to the incident in general and Dougal in
particular said, "Ay, Dougal; the de'il aye looks after his ain."

All and sundry lived in the "Harp" at this time. There was a Field
Ambulance Station (of which more will be heard in the next chapter); while
in the trenches which led to our dug-outs were little bays or cubby-holes in
which odd infantrymen – goodness knows how they came and went – would
sleep for a night or two. One morning I was in the B.C. Post when the carbide

72

lamp began to splutter and 'fizz'. I turned off the water, thinking too much must be getting into the tank, and called for Harry Reid (the Major's servant) who attended the lamp. He asked what was wrong, then opened the tank and looked inside. I held the lighted burner closer to enable us to see; but as the tank was full of carbide gas, the latter exploded and burnt off our eyebrows. I put the light out by pressing the rubber tube, and Harry seized the tank. Rushing up the wooden steps into the trench, he emptied out the water and carbide together, The stuff ran along the trench into a little bay, over which hung a blanket. "I say, Harry," I said, "if anyone is in there, they'll be soaked with that stuff." We ran along the trench, and lifting the blanket, found the carbide and water floating and hissing among the blankets of two of the London regiment. They had been asleep; but by the time we lifted the blanket covering the bay, both were sitting up feverishly endeavouring to don their gas masks!

At this time we were firing mostly on enemy batteries as these were located; for maps were not yet available to show the exact position of our new front line. But if we did not know exactly where our infantry were located, I wondered still more about that cavalry which had gone up through Arras.

Chapter 15

Stalemate – Tilloy‑Les‑Mafflaines (Arras)

But things like that, you know, must be
After a famous victory – Southey

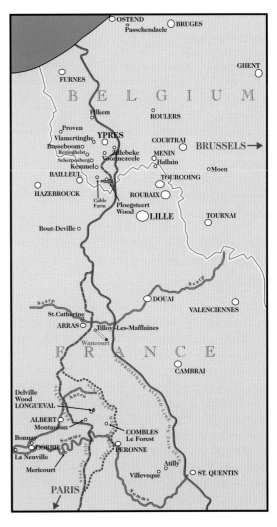

On 21st April, 1917, I went up to the O.P. near Guemappe to make a panoramic sketch of the Boche country, and to prepare for visual observation of our fresh attack which was due to take place two days later. On the way up, I passed over two hundred dead horses, some in the open, others in trenches: horrible sights, and beginning to smell badly. Then I learned that the cavalry had been completely held up in front of the Drocourt‑Queant line. What I saw must have been a mere fragment of the whole; but bodies of horses and men lying across each other everywhere on the road up testified to the desperate nature of the heroic but unavailing efforts of the cavalry to break through. Now I understood what had happened to the cavalry, and later I learned that their casualties included their General. They had arrived too late (probably no fault of theirs), and it looked as if they had simply determined to do or die. The snow had proved a saviour to the Boche, and a disaster to these poor fellows.

On reaching the O.P., I found visibility excellent; and shortly after beginning my

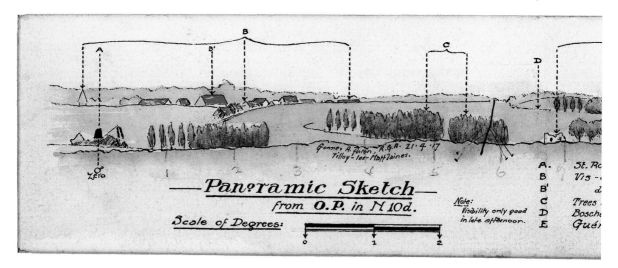

Panoramic Sketch from O.P. in N 10d.

Scale of Degrees:

Gonnel, R. Paton, R.G.A. 21.4.17
Tilloy-les-Mafflaines.

Note: Visibility only good in late afternoon.

A.	St. Ro...
B	Vis – ...
B'	d...
C	Trees ...
D	Bosch...
E	Gué...

Panoramic Sketch in front of Guémappe (Arras Sector)

panoramic sketch, I discovered a German gun, apparently of large calibre, in action. It was very far off; but calling Mr. Phipps (who had not yet actually left the battery for the Air Force) we watched for the next flash. Then crawling over the parapet, we each wormed our way in an opposite direction to prearranged points, and by means of measuring the angle between these points and that from which the gun flashes emanated, we roughly plotted the position of the gun[11]. We also spotted a German working party of about fifty men emerge from a wood and begin working on the road. Phoning the battery, we fired a shell which fell short of the road, but which had the effect of scattering the working party, which did not resume work there that day. Then after showing an officer of the Black Watch his final objective for the attack which was to take place on the 23rd, I was looking through the field glasses at a particular spot, when one of our shells burst in the field of vision of my glasses. I had been looking intently at the spot for several minutes, and had seen no sign of life whatever; but the moment that shell burst, a Boche rose from the grass and bolted. Perhaps an observer too.

Our own target for the 23rd – the village of Guemappe – was badly damaged; as were also Monchy-le-Preux and Wancourt. The villages of Pelves and Vis-en-Artois, however, looked completely intact; but all were to present a different appearance two days later after the attack had taken place. I was again at the observation post on that day. The infantry went over at 4.45 a.m., and this time the Boche was ready for us. Immediately our barrage opened, up went his S.O.S. rockets, and within two minutes his barrage was down all along the line. We took Guemappe and most of our first objective, but so heavy was the German artillery retaliation that it was impossible to hold the village, and our infantry retired, forming a semi-circle round it. Meanwhile our artillery was informed that the village had been evacuated, so we barraged it. Both German and British artillery simultaneously were shelling the place all that forenoon, and nothing could be seen but a mass of pink brick dust and black smoke. A very similar state of affairs seemed to be existing in Monchy, Wancourt, Pelves and Vis-en-Artois. Our own guns were red hot, having been firing 'rapid' from 6 a.m. to 4 p.m. The battery fired altogether fully 3000 rounds that day, at the end of which we did not appear

[11] Some days later, "Comic Cuts" contained the news that on information received from artillery visual observers, an aeroplane had located a 9.3 inch German naval gun. Its position was officially given two hundred yards from the point we had estimated.

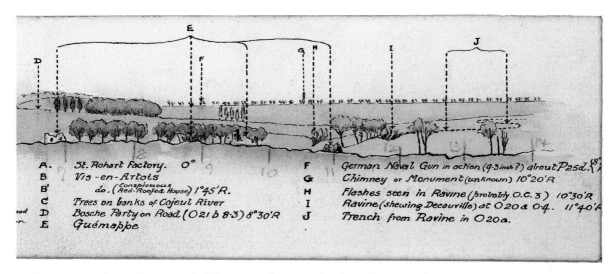

A.	St. Rohart Factory. 0°	F	German Naval Gun in action (9.3 inch?) about P25d.
B	Vis-en-Artois	G	Chimney or Monument (unknown) 10°20'R
B'	do. (Conspicuous Red-Roofed House) 1°45'R.	H	Flashes seen in Ravine (probably O.C. 3) 10°30'R
C	Trees on banks of Cojeul River	I	Ravine (shewing Decauville) at O 20 a O 4. 11°40'R
D	Bosche Party on Road (O 21 b 8·3) 8°30'R	J	Trench from Ravine in O 20 a.
E	Guémappe		

to have gained much ground. The casualties on both sides were heavy, every inch of ground being bitterly contested by the Bavarian division opposite us. These Bavarians were "bonny fechters": they had held us up in Loos in 1915, and again at High Wood on the Somme in 1916; and in my opinion were the best troops in the German army at that time.

On the way back to the battery that evening, I spoke to a Bavarian prisoner. He told me that two days before the attack, his Company's ration party set out for the ration, but could not get back owing to our bombardment; consequently he and the remainder of his company in the front line had had no food for two days. He had been fighting for nearly three years; the first of which had been in Russia, which he declared to be worse than France, being a perfect morass; but shellfire was nothing like so intense. Despite his hunger and the fact that he was wounded, he was very confident – not that Germany would win the war, but that we could not drive the Germans further than they themselves wanted to go. Thus, he said, a few months previously they had evacuated the shell-swept Somme valley; not because we had driven them out, but because by retiring voluntarily they had good roads over which to bring their supplies, while ours had to be transported long distances from our base over barren and shell-pocked country. My reply was that they did not go until we had captured such points of vantage as made it impossible for then to hold the ground they occupied; and he had apparently overlooked our genius for road-making and moving our supply railheads quickly over them to forward zones. His confidence, however, remained unshaken. We reached the Field Ambulance Station at Tilloy early that evening, when I left the Bavarian drinking a cup of tea. And here I should like to pay tribute to the work of the 3rd London Field Ambulance, which was stationed here, Perhaps they had opportunities which other groups did not have; but the fact remains that the station itself was kept spotlessly clean, and though wounded of both sides poured in from Guemappe in hundreds, this company never seemed to get flurried. Every man who was able to take it, friend or foe, received a cup of hot tea the moment he arrived, and his wounds were immediately attended to. We often watched this R.A.M.C. unit at its work, and it was the unanimous opinion of

Annotated aerial reconnaissance photo of Pelves (10 Km east of Arras) showing the River Scarpe top left

our battery that they were the finest lot we ever saw in France.

All units in Tilloy were not so happy in their work. The six inch naval guns of the battery behind us were worn out and had twelve prematures in one day, the shells bursting about a hundred yards in front of their guns. Our own guns too were showing signs of wear, having fired approximately 33,000 rounds since we had landed in France. Our number 3 gun was shooting short so consistently that we now invariably cocked her up a degree more than the others to ensure her shots reaching the range of the target.

On Thursday, 3rd May, we had another attack on Guemappe and took our objectives; but once more we were driven out by enfilade fire. The losses on both sides were again very heavy, the Bavarians suffering terribly but holding us up nevertheless. Our infantry (Black Watch, Camerons and Seaforths) were badly cut up by machine-gun and shell fire, and all day long the wounded poured down the line. The casualties were not confined to the infantry, but our battery got off comparatively lightly; for though one shell dropped right on top of a stack of ammunition at "D" gun, scattering some and blowing up others, only one man was hit. Our other casualties were caused by gas shells, which were rained on our position during part of that day; but we were fortunate compared with our neighbour battery (116 Siege) who had forty casualties including their Major and the Vickers expert, who were both killed. A neighbouring Field Battery had one man killed and several wounded (they considered they had got off very lightly) through one of their own shells bursting prematurely and blowing up the gun. So the day ended, and it looked at the moment as though the position was stalemate. And now Albert Betts was sent home for Officer's Commission, consequently I was the only one left of the four original Battery Commander's Assistants. So for some days I felt rather depressed, and somehow the confidence of that wounded Bavarian stuck in the mind. But my mercurial spirits were somewhat raised by an order that we were to move two guns forward into Wancourt.

On 6th May, while preparing our gun pits at Wancourt, we were called up at Tilloy by Brigade for a counter-battery shoot. I informed the Brigade adjutant that all officers were at Wancourt, when he replied that the plane had already gone up – had we anyone who could carry out the shoot? I said I would do it, and was instructed to go ahead, but after twenty rounds to 'phone Brigade and give the aeroplane observation. The range of the enemy battery was 9900 yards, just about the limit of the range of our guns; but as it was a fine afternoon, I asked the sergeant-major to have all cartridge cases put out in the sun, as by doing so, the increased warmth of the cartridges would help to get distance for our shells. I conducted the shoot from behind the guns, taking cartridge temperatures and adjusting our gun elevations accordingly every few minutes. Had we been shelled in return, the cartridges lying in the open would probably all go up, but we had to risk this. Our first three rounds were given Y7, (theoretically eight yards short of our target); and at the end of the twenty rounds, on reporting to the Brigade I was instructed to carry on to fifty. The observations being satisfactory, Brigade instructed us to fire in all a hundred rounds, and of these, thirty-three were given as direct hits. When our Major returned, I reported what had occurred. He looked at the record of aeroplane observations, then shot out one word – "Rubbish!" Well, it must be admitted that our airmen were sometimes optimistic with their observations, but that evening the airman himself came up to the battery and reported to the Major that the shooting had been excellent. I think the Major told him it had been carried out by his B.C.A., but I was curious enough to want to see what he would say about it in the official diary which was at that time kept, showing the record of all shoots. So before going to bed that night, I turned up the page on which the entry was already inserted. It read: *"Fired 100 rounds by aeroplane observation on Enemy Battery O.B.2 to-day from 4.5 to 5.25 p.m. Many hits."* I carefully copied the entry into my own diary, adding what seemed the only appropriate final word of comment: *"Rubbish!"*

That was our last shoot at Tilloy-les-Mafflaines; for two of our guns went up into Wancourt on the following evening, and the other two a few days later. And as even a small advance was better than stalemate, "Up we go, and the best of luck."

Chapter 16

Near the German line – Wancourt (Arras)

Music when soft voices die,
Vibrates in the memory – Shelley

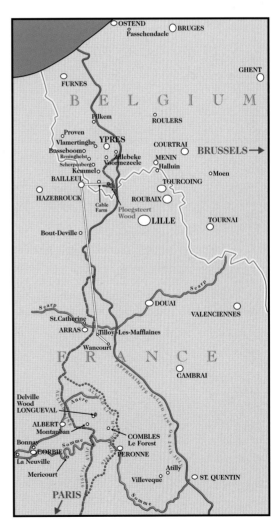

On going up to Wancourt with the last two sub-sections, I found that though "B" and "C" guns were in position, they had not fired a round, and had actually received orders to hold themselves in readiness to move to a new front. They had been having quite a lively time, however, since arriving in the village, which was shelled at regular intervals each day. At night the Boche indulged in spasms of gunfire; sometimes a few scattered rounds, at other times almost a bombardment.

"C" sub's dug-out had been roused during the previous night by someone looking in and calling for help, as his working party of infantry had been badly cut up. The night was pitch dark, and when Andrew Williamson and Arthur White (the latter a signaller in the battery) led a small party of our fellows in response to the call, the man who had given the alarm was nowhere to be seen. Noises were heard, however, apparently from the German end of the village, and the party made its way in that direction. Then the Boche took it into his head to put down a barrage on the edge of the village, but the party carried on, Andrew Williamson leading. They found the infantrymen, several of whom had been wounded; and after helping to dress the wounds, the party returned. The incident is worthy of mention here, as being typical of these two gunners to carry on through the darkness under shellfire, though there was no guide to lead them to the object of their search.

Wancourt must have been a lovely village in pre-war days; for even now, although only a thousand yards from the German front line, it still possessed remnants of pretty gardens. The village was situated on a crest south of

Wancourt (near Arras)

Monchy-le-Preux (our infantry's final objective on the first day of the battle of Arras), and commanded a good view of the valleys to the north and west – particularly the latter, where the road from Wancourt stretched like a ribbon across the long valley to Tilloy. Our "B" and "C" sub-sections now went into rear billets at the latter place for a day or two before departing to the new front; and each evening two volunteers traversed the road from Wancourt to Tilloy to bring up the rum ration for the half battery at the forward position. Wancourt was too near the line for the ration lorry to come up in day-time, while the rum was too precious to be put in the handcart which brought up the rations daily. One evening we were anxiously scanning the valley for some sign of the return of our 'rum-runners', who on that occasion were Gunners Price and Harris. At last we saw two small figures coming from Tilloy in our direction, but almost immediately the Boche began to shell the road along which they were moving. As the smoke of each burst cleared away, we saw that the two figures were still plodding along; but when they had come about half way across the valley, it appeared to us that the shells were falling dangerously near them. They seemed to halt now and again to take cover, but invariably they resumed their journey after the smoke of each shell had cleared, and mentally we gave them a cheer for their courage. The shelling became heavier, but the two figures came steadily on without making any attempt to take cover; and soon our fears for their safety became swallowed up in concern for the safety of the rum. Alas! these fears proved only too well founded; for when our two worthies reached Wancourt they were arm in arm, singing lustily and fearing "no foe in shining armour." As Harris explained it later, "Yae see, when the first shell burst near us, we stopped an' had a tot o' rum – jist tae gie us courage, like: then when the next yin burst, we thoucht we'd better hae anither wee drap; an' by the time we had had eight or nine, it wis a' the same tae us whether they fired pea-shooters or eicht inch."

If Harris was happy, however, no one else was; and the gunners used some language, when instead of a full issue of rum, only a thimbleful was available. Harris's heroism reached the peak when he came up for his rum issue, and this time he was really chased for his life. Price, unlike Harris, did not laugh. He looked upon himself as a martyr, and was ready and willing to defend himself against all comers. It looked as though there might be civil war, when the Boche created a diversion by having another go at Wancourt. We all scuttled into the deep German dug-out except Price, who was still taking on all comers, shells included. Seating himself on a big stone in the middle of the yard, impervious to flying fragments of brick and shell, he called us for all the cowards under the sun. Some of the gunners attempted to get him in by force, but it was of no avail, and we spent the next half hour crouching in the dug-out entrance listening to him declaiming and waiting for him to be hit. But the saying that a special Providence looks after drunken men and bairns proved true. When the shelling ceased, Price rose from his seat, and coming down into the dug-out, withered us with a look – and lay down to sleep in his German bunk; one of our unsung heroes!

Next evening Captain Wilson and I were sitting outside the B.C. Post watching the Tilloy road again being strafed, when on looking up, we saw coming over, high above our heads, the actual German shells. They seemed like express cricket balls, and never previously had either of us seen enemy shells actually flying through the air before bursting. Even then we could only see them by facing the road on which they fell a second or two later: that is to say we could not see them *coming*, but only after they had passed over our heads *going* for the road.

On Saturday, 19th May, we were informed that next morning we should have to evacuate Wancourt for that day, as the Corps on our right was putting down a bombardment, and a heavy retaliation was expected on Wancourt. On the Sunday morning, I rose at five o'clock and went to the cookhouse to waken the cook on duty. Then going down the hill to the German side of the village, I became so interested in some pansies in a garden, that I was still there when I noticed that the bombardment had commenced on our right. As I hurried back, shells began to fall in Wancourt, and I made for the cookhouse to find out if breakfast was ready. On the way, a shell whizzed over my head and it seemed to me that it must have burst very near the cookhouse. On reaching the latter, I found it empty and the floor littered with debris and broken brick. I ran down into the adjoining dug-out, and found Sergeants Jack and Spencer bandaging the head of Bombardier Tommy Ross, who had been in the cookhouse when the shell burst, and was seriously wounded in the head and back. His shrapnel helmet lay near the stretcher, and looking at it, I thought nothing but a miracle could save the life of the man who had worn it; for a huge piece like an equilateral triangle with sides of six or seven inches had been taken out of the helmet. We carried the stretcher across country to avoid the roads, which the Boche was shelling; but after travelling a mile and a half, we reached a by-road where a passing ambulance relieved us of our burden. On the way back we were unanimous that Tommy would not see the day out, but we were wrong. And if at Le Forest, we were

12 At the time
of writing,
Tom Ross is
Sanitary
Inspector for
the Royal Burgh
of Dysart, in
Fife. For many
years after the
war he was
troubled by an
incessant
buzzing in his
head, but that
too has now
almost gone.

impressed by the frailty of the human frame, we were on this occasion amazed at what it could withstand[12]. By the time we got back to Wancourt, the two sub-sections were ready to evacuate the village; so, waiting for our chance to get away in peace, we once more turned for Tilloy.

I received permission from the Captain (the Major had gone to the new front with "B" and "C" sub-sections) to go into Arras, as I wanted to buy a birthday present to send home. Harris and Sidebottom came with me; for though the former declared he had "sair feet", he wanted provisions so badly that he was prepared to walk into Arras for them. We got a lift part of the way in a lorry, and got off at St. Catherines. I thought, sentimentally, that it would be nice to have a look at my old dug-out there. The sentiment was driven out of me at once on going inside, for the dug-out was re-occupied – by a horde of wasps! We then had a fine swim in the Scarpe (being careful to avoid the barbed wire that remained); after which Harris got his eatables – though he moaned about the price; apparently he could not now bargain as he once had at Boulogne – and I bought a silk scarf.

We then recommenced our return journey; and what with being loaded with syrup, Quaker Oats and other provisions, all of which were telling on his "sair feet", Harris was moaning bitterly. He had no rum to "gie him courage, like", and the heat was oppressive. To make matters worse, I had suggested what looked like a short cut to Tilloy, but this landed us in the village of Beaurains (where a few days previously. Captain Fownes, our old O.C. on the Forth Defences, had been killed). Here we sat while Harris relieved himself of his provisions and opened the flood-gates of wrath against everything in general and myself in particular. However, after letting out steam, he resumed his cheerful outlook on life, and with a "san fairy ann", shouldered his bundle once more. We reached Tilloy in the early evening, footsore and fairly exhausted by the heat of the day, but happy to think we could now have a good tuck-in of porridge made with Quaker Oats and washed down with syrup instead of milk.

Suddenly in the middle of the street of Tilloy, Harris let all his provisions deliberately fall; and staring along the road said, "B----y H--l! Did ever yae see the likes o' that?" *That* was a travelling canteen which, during our absence, had taken up stance in the village, and was doing brisk business at reasonable prices in the very goods we had walked miles and paid through the nose to obtain. Harris's final comment was "It's bad enough tae hae sair feet; but when yae end the day wi' a sair hert as weel, I wad drap doon deid if it wasnae for wastin' they messages." But the provisions were not to be enjoyed just yet, for we had orders to proceed at once to Wancourt, which we did on foot. Half an hour after our arrival, the corps on our left put down a barrage on the German trenches, and from our battery position we watched the British shells bursting. The barrage was well put down, but there was an equally good retaliation, and as part of the latter was concentrated on our village, we had to bolt, with the porridge half cooked, into the dug-out.

On 25th May, we were ordered to fire 200 rounds at a German battery and then immediately pull out our guns. It seemed asking for trouble; for on the previous day we had only fired twenty rounds when we were forced to stop by heavy shelling of our position. Moreover, a Boche observation balloon was up near the line and staring us in the face. We fired off the rounds without mishap; and to this day I can only account for the comparative absence of retaliation by assuming that either the German H.Q. would not believe their balloon observer's report that a battery of such calibre was so near the line (though later many batteries, including our own, were nearer), or that the observer must have been having an afternoon nap while our shoot was being carried out. We began to pull out that night, and leaving Wancourt very early next morning, arrived at Tilloy before 6 a.m., to find our motor lorries waiting to take us to a new sector of the front, "B" and "C" sub-sections now having been gone for over a week. We had breakfast at the roadside, and were congratulating ourselves in getting away so easily from Wancourt, which we could at that moment see being heavily shelled, when – *whiz-bang!* – a shell dropped twenty yards from where I sat. Immediately following it came another, and it seemed that our transport had been spotted. Captain Wilson gave the order to start up (our kits were all ready to throw into the lorries), and in a few minutes we were on the Cambrai Road half a mile away. It was an exciting five minutes, for while we were moving along the road in Tilloy, high velocity shells were bursting very near the column, and shrapnel bullets poured into some lorries through the waterproof canvas covers. Several were rolling about the floor of the lorry I was in, and two were lodged between my tunic and gas respirator. The Captain's prompt order on this occasion showed a good sense of discretion: we had already experienced proof of his courage, and very soon were to have further proof of the latter, when (as will be told in due course) he went up with the infantry over the Messines Ridge.

The two sub-sections under his command reached Habarcq late that afternoon. During the week that the other half of the battery had spent there, one exciting incident had taken place – when the Boche had fired a large ammunition dump in the village. There had been great commotion among the villagers, for whom Andrew Williamson was the hero of the hour, having rendered yeoman service in carrying children out of the danger zone of flying shell splinters. Andrew was fated never to receive any official recognition of his good work on this and other occasions – possibly due to the fact that everything he did was carried out so unobtrusively that no one in authority ever seemed to observe that something out of the ordinary had been done. Two men in the battery stand out among all others (and many of these were good fellows) for solid worth and unassuming character: one is Andrew Williamson, the other Si. Arnould. Habarcq was peaceful enough when our half battery arrived, and that night we slept in an orchard on the grass. It was fine to awake at 6 o'clock next morning with the smell of the dewy grass pervading the whole air.

We left Habarcq on Sunday, 27th May, reaching Aubigny-en-Artois early the same afternoon. The simplest things are often the best remembered; and so it is with me on this occasion, when I attended evensong in the Church Army hut in Aubigny. It was an unaccustomed treat to hear the voices of the nurses (from the large casualty clearing station there) singing during the service; and to me the most memorable part of it was the sound of these voices, for we had not heard a woman singing for almost a year. After the service was over, a Bombardier of 90 Siege Battery (I believe he had been an organist of St. George's, Worthing) played very beautifully on the piano, and as we sat in silence listening, the war was forgotten. Probably, too, as the sweet melody of the Entr'acte from Schubert's "Rosamunde" rose softly on the air of that calm evening, none of us remembered that we and our allies in war were fighting against the countrymen of that modest little man, who though long dead, still had the power to waft our minds from a world of war's alarms to one of magic dreams!

(See facing page)

[13] *The hum of the Mercedes engine on German planes was quite distinctive.*

Chapter 17

Among the pig-styes – Cable Farm (Ploegsteert Wood)

Low in Glory's lap they lie – Montgomery

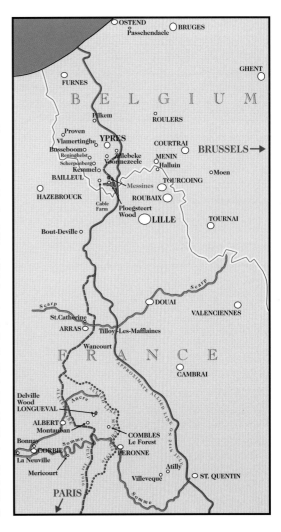

The guns were loaded on trucks at Aubigny, which we left that evening, the battery personnel sleeping in open trucks. It was a fine night, and as I lay on a stretcher in my truck looking up at the stars, I began to wonder what our next position would hold for us – for at twenty-five years of age every change of position was a fresh adventure, to be anticipated with much eagerness, and perhaps a touch of foreboding. The latter became uppermost in my mind for a moment on hearing the hum of an aeroplane in the darkness; but as it came nearer, we knew it to be one of ours[13]. It hovered over the train for some minutes. and I must then have fallen asleep, for the next thing I remembered was waking up in broad daylight at Bailleul railway station. Here we unloaded the guns and travelled by lorry to our new position at Cable Farm (west of Ploegsteert Wood), which we reached at dusk that evening. Our arrival was greeted by a few pip-squeaks and 4.2 inch shells from brother Boche, no casualties resulting. The farm people were still in possession when we arrived, but were ordered to evacuate a day or two later. On the day this happened, I heard such an inhuman screaming that it seemed someone was having his throat cut. That was what had actually happened – to the big sow. Then hay-carts were requisitioned, and furniture, bedding, farm implements, live stock (little pigs, poultry and the farmer's children) piled high as possible; until from every available corner of the carts material hung, swinging and threatening to fall off at each lurch of the carts as they departed.

The farm was comparatively small, the house being out to use as the Officers' Mess and servants' cookhouse. The barn held only one sub-section of the battery; and while a few dug-outs had been built when the farm people went out, half the gunners still had no available sleeping places, the only remaining shelters being the pig-styes. There was a considerable number of these, as the farm seemed to have been largely concerned with the rearing of pigs. The styes were brick built and strong; so our gunners got to work with creosol, pails and brushes to clean them out. It is wonderful what can be done even with a pig-sty, and the next day they became the habitation of the gunners who were not already accommodated in the barn. Indeed, a few days later it might have been difficult to believe that pigs had ever been there – though from the German point of view, it

Bailleul
(at the Station)

must be admitted that we had one or two 'English pigs'! – and the styes made much safer habitations than our splinter-proof dug-outs.

We were now preparing for the Messines Ridge battle, and the first week at Cable Farm was spent mainly in registering our guns on various targets. In the evenings, the gunners off duty went scrounging in the direction of Nieppe. One evening, Jim Brunton, returning from a foraging expedition, put his head in at the door of the barn and cried, "Ho! chaps: eggs and chips for half a franc!" A dozen recumbent figures immediately sat up with a chorus of "Where?" "Ay, where?" echoed Jim sadly, "that's what *I'd* like to know;" and he gently closed the door from the outside and returned to his pig-sty.

It was early evident that our anti-aircraft had orders to prevent enemy aeroplanes coming over; for the moment one appeared, the sky was flecked with anti-aircraft shell-bursts – very good shooting too. On the evening following our arrival, one of our observation balloons, up at a later hour than usual, was set alight by bullets from a German aeroplane which had succeeded in reaching the balloon without being hit. Immediately its work was done, the plane made off for the German line at great speed. It seemed that he was going to get safely back, when the machine seemed to wobble; then bursting into flames, it fell like a burning faggot.

By Tuesday, 5th June, 1917, it was generally known that the big attack was imminent, and on that day we were shelled at intervals while firing. On one such occasion we ceased firing for a bit, as it was suspected that a Boche plane in the distance was attempting to register a German battery on us. "C" sub-section were in a slip trench which we had dug for emergency shelter in front of the gun, when Corporal Newcombe (the gun-captain on duty) suggested that to lessen the chance of the gun being definitely spotted, it should be temporarily covered up. The whole gun team leapt out of the trench, and climbing on top of the gun, began to pull the cover over it. Then another shell came over. It dropped a couple of yards behind the gun and hit no less than nine out of the ten men on it. The nine men had over fifty wounds between them, and among those killed were the gun-captain and Andrew Williamson. Poor Andrew! He was perhaps the one most missed by the battery. Gunner Cox (whose corns had once caused a spot of bother) was hit in many places, though not mortally wounded, by shrapnel bullets; and he actually stood on his feet while we stripped him and dabbed iodine on so many parts of his body that he resembled nothing so much as a human leopard.

On the morning of 7th June, the attack on the Messines Ridge was launched. It was timed to begin at 3.10 a.m., and at 3 a.m. I gave the gun lines to Sam Dunkley, the telephonist on duty as runner to the guns. "A" and "B" guns duly reported by 'phone that they were ready; but when at 3.5 a.m. no word had come from "C" and "D" guns, I was sufficiently alarmed to emerge from the B.C. Post; and fixing my gas mask (for the air was saturated with both phosgene and tear gas), I ran for the gun position. As reported, "A" and "B" were ready; but on the way to "C" gun, I pitched into a shellhole over the form of Sam Dunkley, who was lying gassed, still grasping the remaining gun-lines. I did not wait to see how bad he was, but taking the lines out of his hand, I ran with them to the guns. Some of the gun detachment came back and brought in Dunkley, who was removed to hospital. We were all ready by 3.8 a.m., and I then stood outside the B.C. Post to await the zero hour. It was not yet daylight; but at that moment the darkness was lit up by our gunfire in one fearful sheet of flame which seemed to stretch right along the horizon, lighting up the whole countryside. In the far distance I could see through the incessant gun flashes huge columns of smoke, while the ground under my feet – even at that distance – heaved with the concussion of our exploding mines. Rockets went up in hundreds, and the indescribable din of barrage had begun. Then a dull prolonged roar reached our ears – the boom of the tremendous explosion which had levelled Hill 60 and hurled its thousands of occupants into eternity. Captain Wilson and Mr. Rees were up there with the infantry that morning when the attack took place. One servant and a signaller accompanied them. The signaller was one of the most imperturbable men in the battery – he had already been censured for being found up the line in the trenches without a shrapnel helmet – and seemed to know no fear. His words may briefly give an indication of the inferno that raged up the line that morning. Our party were standing in a trench at zero hour when the mine went up; and as the explosion rent the ground, the whole party were lifted off their feet. And when our signaller felt the ground going beneath him, he was at last impressed with the fear of death. "Suffering Christ," he cried, "the world's ended."

According to all reports (some of them from infantry and from the forward parties of neighbouring batteries) the Captain did some very fine work that day, and it was freely rumoured for long afterwards that at last our Major had recommended one of his battery for an award; but later we understood that the Captain had only been mentioned in dispatches, a reward that seemed to those who were with him quite inadequate.

For the next week the battery was kept very busy on counter-battery work; and one evening we were firing so rapidly that "A" sub-section's gun became almost red-hot. On running cold water through the bore, it came out steaming and bubbling at the other end; and almost immediately afterwards, just as the gun was being elevated, the cartridge in the bore became ignited with the heat of the metal. Our sister battery, 116 Siege, were in position a hundred yards in front of our guns; and their gunners flattened themselves to the ground, as with a mighty roar, our 9.2 inch shell screamed over their heads, to burst – fortunately – in a field in front of their position. At the same time the buffer cap flew off the gun, and several of our men were severely scalded by boiling oil. Someone jocularly suggested that the O.C.'s liver should be pickled in it; and indeed at this time his temper was so uncertain that it was vented upon the officers in presence of the gunners. Phipps and Gibbs (now gone to the balloon section of the R.A.F.) had not worried over such trifles; but the new officers, typified by more mature men like Leslie and Rees, very much objected to being "ticked off" before their own gun detachments. One day when the former (an artist by profession) had received a tremendous dressing-down, I was amazed to see him "make a thumb" as the Major walked off in a tantrum. Such a thing had not been heard of on the part of an officer in the battery, where the O.C. was a law unto himself absolutely. But a few nights later we were further enlightened in the psychology of the new officer by Lieut. Rees (who had been a member of one of the pre-war Antarctic expeditions). That night, I remember, Frank Strachan (now battery clerk) and I were preparing for bed in our dug-out, which contained two wire bunks, one above the other. Our despatch rider came in to ask if we could put him up for the night – he would sleep on the floor beneath the lower wire bed if we would not mind him doing so. We told him to go ahead, when he promptly made his bed and crawled under. Shortly afterwards the blanket covering the doorway was pulled aside, and Mr. Rees (who happened to be the night officer) entered. "I've just called round for a minute's chat before I go to bed," he said. "That b----y Major's been ticking me off all day – before the gun detachment too; and for two peas, I'd have knocked him down on one occasion." He went on relieving his feelings for some time, and we hardly cared to mention that the motor-cycle man was under the bed. Having let out steam, Mr. Rees concluded, "Well, I'm off to bed. If you get any S.O.S. during the night, let me know direct; and for the love of goodness don't waken the old man, or he'll be coming in asking why the hell I don't stand at attention on my bed while he wakens me." When he had gone, there was silence for a moment or two, and we thought that the despatch rider must be asleep; but his head peeped out from under the bunk as he exclaimed, "Gee; is that what the officers think of the Major too?"

It was bad discipline all round, but perhaps sufficiently humorous to keep it from being harmful to the work of the battery. It must be said, too, that if the Major's rule by force was not in accordance with the spirit of the new army, he kept a firm hand on everybody, and had no favourites. After all, his methods had been successful in creating and maintaining an efficient unit – which I really think we were by this time – from a motley collection of miners and clerks.

90

Besides, he always gave us something to croak about: and talking of croaking, our nights at Cable Farm were filled with the croaking of frogs. We never saw many of the creatures during the daytime, but we knew that the sound emanated from a small pond in the field behind our dug-out. This pond, like many others we had come across in the course of our wanderings, was surrounded by pollarded willows; and one warm day Frank Strachan decided to have a bathe in it. After stripping, he found it somewhat difficult to wade in; so throwing caution to the winds, he took a flying leap into the middle. He got the surprise of his life when hundreds of frogs jumped out in every direction. Frank crawled out of the pond feeling like Alice when she upset the jury-box, though he did not wait to put the frogs back!

On Sunday, 17th June, we moved forward to a new position, stated to be an hour's journey from Cable Farm. Owing to heavy enemy shelling, we had to go by a circuitous route. It was becoming dark as we travelled in motor lorries through the woods, and after some time our driver made the discovery that he had lost the remainder of the transport column. We turned, and a mile back tried a road which branched off to the left. Ten minutes later, we were informed by a sentry that we were on the wrong road; so we turned again. Where we went I have no idea; but as dawn was beginning to break, we found ourselves on a ridge with what looked like a valley lying in front. Here we stopped and got off the lorry to discuss what our position might be. Spreading out a map, we began to examine it by the aid of an electric hand torch; but our discussion was rudely shattered by the arrival of a high velocity gas shell which burst immediately in front of the lorry, and was followed by a salvo of tear gas shells and several bursts of machine gun fire – the latter sounding too near at hand to make us feel comfortable. 'Turn again, Whittington,' this time in a mighty hurry, and off once more. We found the remainder of the battery soon afterwards, when it appeared that we had been very near to Messines itself in the course of our journey. So it was little wonder that the lorry had been shelled.

Our stores had been unloaded by the roadside and were screened from view by tall trees which lined the road on both sides. A long trench ran parallel with the road and within a yard of its edge; and after seeing that the B.C. stores were safely gathered together in the trench, I opened out a stretcher for an hour's sleep. My small bundle of clean underclothing made a fine pillow; and as I sat on my stretcher and looked down the trench in which the forms of our gunners, already asleep, could be dimly discerned, it seemed to me that sleeping in an open trench was greatly preferable to damp and draughty dug-outs or even to purified pig-styes. Then lying down and pulling my greatcoat over my head, my stretcher felt like a feather bed. Pigs in clover.

Chapter 18

"Plug Street" Wood – Messines ridge (Messines)

Wee, sleekit, cow'rin, tim'rous beastie,
O what a panic's in thy breastie – Burns

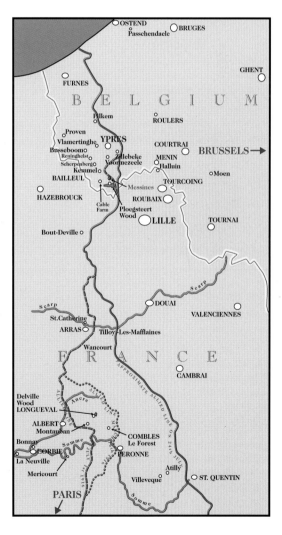

I awoke in the trench shortly after 6.30 a.m. hearing high velocity shells bursting in the neighbourhood; but though splinters were whizzing round up above, I considered it safe enough to lie where I was. As I lay on my back on the stretcher, I looked up and saw a human figure high up in a tree whose branches stretched from the roadway over the trench far above my head. It was Idris Williams, our wireless operator, taking advantage of nature's provision to erect a super aerial. "Hello, Idris," I sang out, "you'll be getting one of those splinters where you won't be able to sit if you don't come down." Idris, though he had heard my voice, did not hear what had been said, and I repeated the words. "Get off your back, you lazy blighter," he answered, "I can't hear yet what you're saying." Inwardly giving him blessings for disturbing my comfort, I raised my head from the pillow (my clean underwear) and was just about to speak, when '*pring...*' – a large piece of hot shrapnel came whack into the centre of my pillow. I kept that piece as a souvenir of Idris, who used afterwards to say that he saved my life on that occasion; my reply being that the label with

0 | 1 |

inches

my name thereon became detached from that shell in its flight.

We pulled in the guns that morning, and spent all day making our new position. That night I secured a small concrete dug-out in the trench. Si. Arnould, Frank Strachan and I literally occupied it, for when we lay down side by side, the dug-out was completely filled up. We had not gone to sleep, however, when word came that some of our gunners were missing, and a search party was organised. After some time it was learned that Gunners Millman and Sinclair had been found far down the trench. Both had been wounded and had been removed to hospital; but McGill, who was supposed to have occupied the same dug-out, was still missing. We had no idea where they had been sleeping, and after a short consultation on the part of the quartette composing our own little party, the Major and Idris Williams went off in one direction, Mr. Leslie and I going in another. We carried hand torches, and climbing over the trench parapet, we began to search among the little splinter-proof dug-outs on the bank above. Gas shells were coming over, with now and again a high explosive; and we had constantly to throw ourselves flat as they burst. I could see Mr. Leslie's torch moving about in the darkness, and we agreed to keep within hail of each other by this means. I had examined nine or ten dug-outs when I crawled into one in which lay the object of our search – dead. He looked so peaceful that at first I thought he was asleep; then I was able to see that a gas shell had come through the roof of the dug-out. It was ascertained later that Millman had died at the dressing-station, and Sinclair was thus the only one to survive[14].

Next day we carried out a counter-battery shoot by aeroplane observation, but we were heavily shelled and at last had to signal the plane to call a temporary halt. The airman knew what was happening; and though a thunderstorm was coming up rapidly, he went off on his own to locate the battery shelling us. Later he informed the Brigade adjutant that he was amazed to see us continue for so long. The incident had its humorous side, nevertheless. When the Boche first began to shell us, Jim Brunton found Lyddite standing beside him. "Hello, Lyddite," he said, "what ye doing here? You'd better clear out; the Boche's coming over." Lyddite faded away, and Jim thought no more about him. That evening, however, a Corporal of another battery came in escorting Lyddite, who was arrayed in full kit. "This man belong to you?" he asked. "Yes," was the reply, "where's he been?" "Oh," rejoined the Corporal, "he came down the line and told us the Boche was advancing; but after questioning him, we thought he was either loopy or shell-shocked." Lyddite was asked what he meant by clearing off and spreading false rumours; but the most amusing part of the incident was when Brunton was asked if he had stated that the Boche were coming over. He stood open-mouthed with astonishment; but when he was made to realise that his joke might have had serious consequences, he decided that to "play with Lyddite" was dangerous. Nevertheless, as will be

[14] The names convey nothing to the casual reader, but are inserted because, to those who shared such experiences, they bring to mind some who were once with us but who were not spared to return.

told in the next chapter, he and Lyddite were to be central figures in at least one more incident.

As on the Somme during the previous autumn, cartridge cases were the means of several temporary romances between some of the gunners and the munition girls who had packed the cartridges. Inside the cylinders we used sometimes to find the name and address of the packer, when a correspondence – usually brief – would ensue from one of the gunners to the damsel. One day a signaller came to me and said, "Here, I've gone an' done it this time. Yae mind yon lassie's name I got frae Sandy Mac. a little time ago? Wee, onyway, he gien it tae me, an' I wrote a nice letter endin' up wi' love an' kisses; but the same nicht I wrote tae the wife's sister, an' pit the letters i' the wrang envelopes. The wife's sister showed the ane she got tae the wife: I've just had a letter frae her kickin' up her heels aboot it." It is pleasing to note that the matter was amicably settled when the signaller went home on leave.

At "Plug Street" Wood, both Germans and British had many observation balloons up each day, and on Saturday, 23rd June, we had no less than thirteen balloons up in line. It was an unlucky number, for shortly after midday (when our airmen, usually very vigilant at this period, may have been having a bite of lunch!) a Boche plane came over. Our anti-aircraft shooting was very poor on this occasion, and the Boche had a merry time. Racing along the line of balloons, he set fire to three of them – and talk of flying angels! The air was full of parachutes – twenty-six of them – but the show was brought to a premature close by the arrival of two of our planes, which chased the Boche to his own lines. The Germans had a fine row of their own balloons up; so half an hour later some of our planes flew over, and the heavens discharged once more. Did we cheer? We were like schoolboys witnessing a raid on a rival establishment, and that day the war seemed ridiculously absurd rather than only senseless. But if it seemed a senseless way of settling disputes, there was apparently no other way then; and we too

From O.P in Gas Trench (Ploegsteert Wood) by Hubert Leslie

were quite capable of senseless procedure in the field of war, as the following incident will show.

Our visual observation post was in a trench on the slope facing Messines Ridge. Messines village, still in the hands of the Germans, stood on the crest of the ridge opposite, and in the valley between lay the German and our own front line. The O.P. in "Gas Trench" was therefore in full view of the enemy on the opposite slope; and on that account, Mr. Leslie, Captain Wilson and I used invariably to come over the crest and down the hillside under cover of a hedge about a mile from the O.P., then drop into the trench and walk along it to the observation post, where a large splinter-proof dug-out had been built – for many batteries used this place. The dug-out and O.P. were well camouflaged, but this was discounted by the fact that the officers and signallers of several batteries repeatedly came over the crest of the hill in the open, to skelter down the slope and drop into the O.P. itself. The Captain, Leslie and Rees had each remonstrated with these careless individuals; but they simply would not trouble to make the detour, and we knew that unless the Boche was blind – and we did not think he was – the existence of an O.P. at that point must be well known to him. So we expected trouble, and were not disappointed.

One morning I woke Mr. Leslie at 5 a.m. as we were due at the O.P. at 7 o'clock. Rain was falling in a steady drizzle, and we decided that as observation under such conditions would be unprofitable, we could wait until ten o'clock. This we did; when, the weather showing signs of clearing, we set off for Gas Trench. As usual we came down the hill by the hedge although already late, for it was nearly noon and the weather was definitely clearing up. On reaching the vicinity of the O.P., it was apparent that something had happened, and that within the last half hour; for part of the trench was almost unrecognisable through shellfire, and on crawling over the debris we found that the O.P. dug-out was blown in. Everybody at the O.P. had taken shelter in the dug-out when the shelling started, and all (three officers and eight signallers) were killed. As the telephone lines were cut and tangled, we could not report to Brigade until our signallers had repaired the breaks. Then Mr. Leslie had to report that we had not gone up earlier; but apparently the adjutant took a lenient view of the matter: better perhaps a live dog than a dead lion. The fact remained, however that eleven lives were lost unnecessarily because a few people disregarded the elementary rules of the game, if game it can be called. And though on many other occasions I saw our men adopt the same unhappy-go-lucky methods of bravado, never once do I remember the Boche carelessly betraying the whereabouts of one of his observation posts.

We left Messines at the beginning of July, 1917; and though the position was not a bad one, I left without a pang of regret. While there, we had continual thunderstorms, and often it was difficult to distinguish between claps of thunder and enemy shellbursts. And although no great reason existed for it, I seemed there to have a permanent feeling of 'wind-up', though I hoped it had not been apparent to others as it was to myself[15]. Perhaps one reason for it was the daily running of the gauntlet from the dug-outs in the trench to the cookhouse, a distance of some 500 yards, the path to which seemed particularly to attract the Boche shellfire at mealtimes. There was

[15] *Strangely enough, many months later, Captain Wilson, Mr. Leslie and Frank Strachan – all usually imperturbable souls – confessed to having had this same feeling of continuous "wind-up" at Messines, though at the time I did not suspect that any of them felt as I did. On the other hand, Si. Arnould says he was quite happy there.*

also the strain (for those of us whose duties took us almost daily to Gas Trench) of waiting for the O.P. to be demolished; for we were certain it would happen long before it did. Another somewhat unpleasant memory of Messines was our morning awakening, when we usually found at least one huge black-beetle crawling in our hair. Occasionally one of the three in our dug-out was awakened through the night by one of these monsters creeping up his back; though a liberal use of Harrison's pomade on wrists, ankles and neck before going to bed proved a fairly effective barrier. On such occasion (Frank Strachan was generally the victim) Si. Arnould and I had to get up in order to allow Frank sufficient room to grope for and eject the intruder. We used to sprinkle the dug-out floor with creosol before putting our blankets down at night; but that did not prevent these beetles making their way through chinks in the wooden floor; nor could we hit upon any satisfactory method of keeping them from nesting in our hair overnight.

So farewell, "Plug Street"! Despite the intensity of our attacks at that period, I doubt if we gained anything but experience while we sojourned in your sultry, yet 'windy' atmosphere.

Chapter 19

At the Chateau Segard – Voormezeele (Ypres)

***An ounce of vanity spoils a hundredweight
of merit – Proverb***

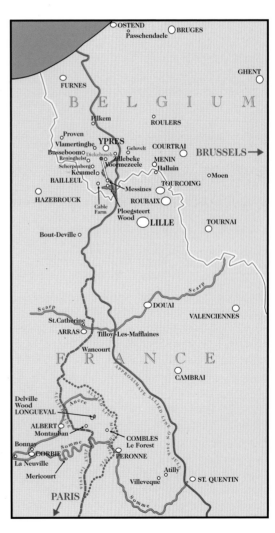

We pulled out from Messines one evening at the beginning of July, and after travelling throughout one night and the best part of the day following, found ourselves on the outskirts of Estaires. Here the lorries were parked, and it was rumoured that we should have a rest of a week or two. The battery had now been in Flanders for over a year, during which time it had only been out on rest for the few days spent at Bonnay in December, 1916. Idris Williams and I secured a bed on the floor of the kitchen in a very pretty cottage at Estaires; but after two nights the battery moved back to Poperinghe, where we slept in tents in an orchard, and remained for the next four days. During the latter period we were not idle, though in the evenings many of the gunners went to the Toc. H. hostel in Poperinghe, where one could always depend on quietness to read or write. During the day the gun detachments went up in motor lorries to prepare our position at the Chateau Segard.

The Major was away, either temporarily in command of Brigade or on a course; but after

99

three days in Poperinghe under the command of Captain Wilson, the Major returned; and considering our tent quarters too far removed from the scene of our day operations, he ordered the whole battery to move up next day. This we did; but as there was no shelter except two small cellars at Chateau

Cottage at Estaires

Segard, we halted at dusk that evening just at Dickebusch Lake, where we had espied a large number of little dug-outs empty. The field in front of the dug-outs contained numerous shellholes, apparently made that day; but these did not worry us, and we entered into occupation congratulating ourselves on such a find. We were then informed that the field had been used as horse lines by a battery of field artillery which had been shelled out that day; their loss was our gain, and we dug ourselves in. I got into a small dug-out on my own, while Jim Brunton was in another close by. We settled down for a comfortable sleep, but about ten o'clock the Boche began an hour's shelling. Most of us remained where we were until the spasm passed; but at half past one in the morning he began again, and the place grew so hot that a goodly number of our gunners cleared out; and though quite unfamiliar with their surroundings, most of them succeeded in finding safer retreats in the larger dug-outs made in the bank round the lake. Jim Brunton lay still until one shell hit the far corner of his dug-out. Then he hurriedly crawled out into a deluge of rain and fled for a new shelter. Noticing a glimmer of light percolating through a blanket doorway, he made for it. Then he heard the next shell coming. As its opening whine developed into a shriek, he know it was going to be a near one; and he floundered through the slippery mud gasping. The shell was roaring in his ears when he was still a yard from the dug-out; so taking a flying header, he sailed through the blanket and landed on his stomach on the floor inside to the accompaniment of a shower of debris and mud on the roof. Breathless and winded, he lay exhausted for a few moments; then raising himself on his elbow, he looked round to see if anyone was there – for though the candle-light had guided his footsteps to the dug-out, no one had spoken. In a corner of the dug-out he saw Lyddite, nonchalantly picking bully beef with his jackknife from a tin. Now it will be remembered that no matter what position we occupied, Lyddite slept in solitary state; for no one could be found who would share his dug-out. Seeing Jim begin to take stock of his surroundings (though still too exhausted to speak), Lyddite paused in the act of conveying a bladeful of bully to his mouth and said casually, "You cawn't come in 'ere: I'm lousy." The shelling ceased about 3 a.m., and next morning we went up to Chateau Segard, where I remained. The gun detachments took day about between the chateau and our billets at Dickebusch Lake until dug-outs were made at the gun positions.

The chateau itself was in ruins, but we built the B.C. post against the remaining part of one of its walls, while a cellar below housed a number of the gunners. The others built dug-outs in the wood behind; and the signallers, wireless operators and myself made dug-outs against the high brick wall which had at one time surrounded the chateau. This wall was broken down in many parts by enemy gunfire, and we used up much of the rubble in making foundations for the gun transoms. One day I was coming from the B.C. post at the chateau to my dug-out at the wall when I overtook Ginger carrying a large stone from the chateau. "What are you going to do with that?" I asked. "Going to knock a chunk of the brick wall down with it," he replied. "Then I'll use the bricks at the entrance of the signallers' dug-out to keep the mud from being dragged in – compree?" I said I 'compreed', and stood by to watch the results of his efforts. He was a big, strong fellow; and raising the heavy stone, he cast it as high as he could at a part of the wall which looked weak. The shock was quite sufficient to cause the immediate appearance of a large crack, which widened rapidly to a gap as a huge section of the wall toppled down. To our utter

Chateau Segard, near Ypres

astonishment, a figure rose from the debris. It wore a tunic, beneath which appeared only a shirt tail and a pair of legs: the feet were buried in bricks and rubble. The apparition glared at us, and from its mouth the unmistakably nasal accents of Lyddite were heard saying "Wot's the gime? You knew I was on the other side of that b----y wall, and I suppose you knocked it down on purpose." Poor old Lyddite. I'm afraid that in his eyes our laughter discounted all protestations of innocence and he remained unconvinced that the incident had not been deliberately planned.

Our new position was at first subject to considerable shelling, and though matters improved later, the Boche had two direct hits on our emplacements before we got the guns mounted. Our experience had taught us, however, that a bad start often heralded quite a good position; and once we settled down at Chateau Segard, we liked it – during daytime at any rate. But well do I remember our nights for the five weeks during which our guns were in position there. We could depend upon it that invariably at midnight, at 2 a.m. and at 4 a.m. the Boche would fire from eight to a dozen 11.1 inch armour-piercing shells at the chateau. These did no particular harm unless they obtained a direct hit, in which case it was 'all up'; but they made a hole the size of a bedroom, while seconds after they had burst, clods a cubic yard in volume would come hurtling down from the sky.

About twelve yards from my own dug-out in the wall, six of our signallers had made a dug-out in the ground. This was roofed with heavy 'elephant' iron, and was considered safe from anything but a direct hit. One morning during the 4 a.m. spasm, a shell just cleared the roof of my dug-out, burying itself between the latter and the signallers' dug-out referred to. No one was hit by the shell, but the signallers received the full force of the blast. The roof of elephant irons was lifted clean off the dug-out and deposited thirty yards away; while the six signallers, who one moment had been lying in the dark of the dug-out, were left gazing at the paling stars. All were shell-shocked. The worst part of this nightly shelling was undoubtedly the anticipation of it. It acted like an alarm clock; for Idris Williams would regularly wake me with "Five minutes to two, Alec. Get ready for another do." It was almost a relief when the shelling commenced – and *what* a relief when it was over: we could count upon two hours of peace, and never were we disappointed in this.

We did not altogether go scot-free during the daytime. One afternoon the Boche had a concentration on us; and it was fortunate that when it began, most of the gunners were either in the cellar beneath the chateau or in the dug-outs in the wood in rear; for so suddenly did gunfire commence that we had no chance of clearing out even if we had desired to do so. Idris Williams, some signallers and myself were sitting in our dug-out when the shelling started, and in ten minutes we could not see the hedge twenty yards away for smoke. How our dug-out was spared was a mystery; for several shells came through the wall, though fortunately for us on this occasion they were instantaneously fuzed. Shell splinters were whizzing all over the place, and one flew through the entrance of the dug-out and caught a signaller (recently arrived in the battery) behind the ear. He tried to bolt out of the dug-out, but we grabbed him and held him down until he quietened, when we got him bandaged. An infantryman in a trench nearly two hundred yards away poked his head over the parapet, and said to his mate (who was making tea in the trench) "The battery in the chateau's getting it hot." Hardly had he said so, when a piece of shell came skimming along just above the ground; and though the shell had burst at the chateau, that splinter caught him on the forehead, and killed him instantaneously.

One day later, while our transport was unloading shells, the Boche got an O.K. on the lorry, setting it on fire. Mr. Walker, our transport officer, was inside at the time; and though it was a hopeless proposition (for blazing cartridges were shooting up flames to a height of thirty or forty feet), Ginger attempted to get him out. Mr. Walker was already dead, however, and Ginger Hill was badly wounded. Then Gunner Payne was killed by a bomb from a German aeroplane which visited us daily shortly after dawn. These were among the more unusual types of casualty; but here too we finally lost our Major, who went down the line gassed, and was sent to England. But before he goes out of our story, an incident which happened just at this time must be told.

I was in the B.C. post one afternoon with Captain Wilson (the Major having gone to visit Brigade Headquarters), when Harry Reid entered and asked if I would phone across to the signallers' dug-out at the wall for one of their number to assist him and Jock Isaacs to bring some cases of aerated

102

water and a small case of whisky from the road to the Officers' Mess. It was raining heavily, and I offered to assist. Captain Wilson agreeing (for I was nominally on duty), we set off down the muddy path through the wood. On reaching the road, Harry and Jock Isaacs agreed to carry the cases of aerated water if I would take the small case of whisky. We returned with the cases on our shoulders, and I was proceeding up the path, when I felt the case slipping over the back of my shoulder. In the endeavour to recover it, my feet went from under me in the mud, and the case crashed to the ground. At that moment we were passing the dug-outs of another battery, whose gunners were on the way to their cookhouse for tea. When I picked up the case, whisky was running out of every corner, and I was pursed by gunners trying to catch the flow in tea mugs. Harry Reid was in a state of nervous prostration when on opening the case in the Officers' Mess, only four bottles were intact, while from the eight which were broken, we rescued about half a bottle. The smell of whisky, however, could have been felt yards away.

The Captain undertook to explain to the Major on his return, and must have done his job well; for late that night after working out the S.O.S. lines for the guns, I thought it my duty to go into the Mess and make my apologies to the Major. This I did expecting to receive a good round volley for my carelessness; but the Major was in excellent form. Waving my apology aside, he said "Oh, its Wilson there that's to blame: what did he want to send my B.C.A. to carry whisky for? It looks to me like a conspiracy between two teetotallers." I was relieved to hear such remarks, though I am afraid I was ungenerous enough to conclude from their tone that the O.C. had managed to secure his due share of the four bottles which had been left. Yet he never referred to the matter again, except jocularly in the Mess.

With that incident and the following note, I take leave of our first Major. Despite his overbearing and often passionate nature, he was perhaps the best man we could have had to whip us into shape – perhaps we did not realise this sufficiently. And had it not been for his temper, which was responsible for every hasty thing he did, he might have been an ideal O.C. He could be very charming in manner when he chose; was an excellent conversationalist, no mean artist and extraordinarily kind to dumb animals. The last trait may sound somewhat surprising, considering his harsh treatment of several of the men under his command. Yet if he soundly rated both officers and men on many occasions, he was both proud and jealous of his battery as a unit, and repeatedly stated to Brigade and to other battery officers that, though himself a 'regular' soldier, the most reliable gunners of his experience were his own "B----y civilian solders" – a phrase he used so often that it might well have provided the title to these pages. He had a sound knowledge of his job, and did not hesitate to give others the benefit of his experience. In addition to all these, he was invariably immaculate in personal appearance to the point of vanity; and perhaps if one characteristic stood out above his temper in our eyes, it was his vanity. But we benefited by the latter; for he thought himself and his battery of such importance that on several occasions he pushed us into comfortable quarters by sheer bluff. On one particular occasion, when the Brigade Colonel wanted his B.C. post and all the battery dug-outs for the more important uses of Brigade, our Major not only refused to give them up, but 'stuck to his guns' and eventually won the day, apparently without incurring any permanent rancour on the part of the Brigade staff.

Thus while our main impressions of him during the war years were apt to be those that were largely the effect of his hasty temper (and those to a large extent recorded in these pages), the passing of years, brushing away surface matters from the mind's eye, has revealed a figure which we 'civilian soldiers' could not then understand; perhaps because we were not what he undoubtedly was – one who loved soldiering as his profession in which he had experienced no small measure of success.

If hitherto his name has not been mentioned, it is because that only at this point, where we bid him farewell, can I feel that justice has been done to the name of Major E.H. Lovell.

Chapter 20

Blighty and back – Dickebusch (Ypres) and home leave

Ave, atque vale – Latin Quotation

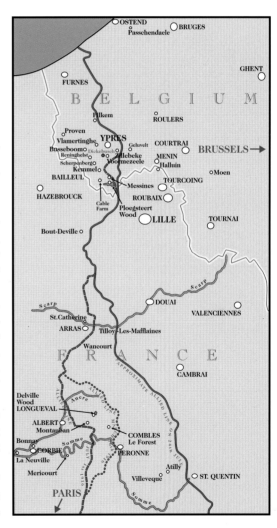

For the past month I had been continuously at Chateau Segard; but the gun detachments were still alternately there and at our rear billets beside Dickebusch Lake. Here they renewed acquaintance with Mr. Phipps, whose observation balloon floated daily above the lake. He came up to Chateau Segard one evening, and before going into the Mess for dinner, spent quite a time with me talking over O.P. experiences (for it was he who had taught me the rudiments of visual observation) and recounting such episodes as the cornfield at Vlamertinghe in 1916. On each of the two following evenings, his balloon was brought down in flames by a Boche aeroplane, and on both occasions Mr. Phipps descended in safety by parachute. On the third evening he was again up; and though we could see his balloon from the Chateau, it was from our man at rear billets that we learned the full story of what took place that evening. The balloon was again brought down, and this time Mr. Phipps, descending by parachute, dropped into Dickebusch Lake. He swam for some yards, but hampered by the harness of his parachute and accoutrements, he sank before rescue could be effected; and though his body was very quickly recovered, all attempts at resuscitation failed. Mr. Phipps was a fine type of a young officer, a first-class observer and fearless under fire. We remembered him with real affection, and his death cast a gloom over the whole battery for a time.

Pencil drawing of his mother by the author January 1914

On 5th August, 1917, I left Chateau Segard for home leave. On the way down to Poperinghe, I spent a few minutes at our rear billets at Dickebusch. It was Gunner Goldie's washing day, but he suspended operations to tell me how lucky I was to be going on leave. Then turning to the cartridge cylinder in which his underclothing was boiling he threw some N.C.T. underneath. The flames blazed up and caught some petrol which had been poured into the water with the object of killing lice. The floating petrol took fire, and Goldie stood frantically endeavouring to poke the protruding parts of his shirt beneath the surface of the water. It was all over in a few minutes; and picking his shirt out of the cylinder with the aid of a stick, he examined it. It might have been worse – three holes, each the size of a saucer, were burnt in it.

Sleeping that night in one of our motor lorries at Poperinghe, the column was bombed, the lorry next to mine being set on fire and reduced to a charred mass. I left in the morning for Boulogne, where the night was spent in St. Martin's camp: then up at 4 o'clock next morning to catch the boat. Who having experienced it, can ever recall without some feeling of emotion the first sight of the white cliffs when nearing the English coast? We had experienced disease and dirt, fear and sudden death, but none of these things had so profound an effect upon us as the sight of these cliffs. Our feelings found some kind of outlet as we bawled with all our might, "Take me back to dear old Blighty … Blighty is the place for me." When we had finished, a silence fell upon us as we gazed at the approaching land; then some sentimentalist began to sing "Loch Lomond". We must all have been sentimentalists, for in a moment the song was taken up by all aboard, and this time there was no bawling: in these few minutes the pent up feelings of our hearts found expression as the sound of the song floated over the waves. I had a feeling that it was worth while going through the horrors of a war to have such moments as this. Then all was changed to bustle and excitement as we struggled down the gangways on to the quay at Folkestone – then into the train for London. Were ever such green fields as these, I thought, as we sped on our way for Victoria. Arrived there, I stood alone on the platform watching the joyful faces of women meeting the men they loved. My own experience of that came next morning – and such an experience is too intimate to be put to paper.

I pass over the days of my leave. Happy they were in some ways, yet clouded over by the fact that my mother lay on her death-bed and could hardly bear to let me out of her sight. Little wonder perhaps, for both of us knew that after these few days of leave, we should not see each other again. Sudden death in war seemed more merciful than this. (She died a month later.)

Leaving Edinburgh again on 21st August, 1917, I arrived at Folkestone next day. Here those returning from leave remained in billets while awaiting the boat to cross the Channel. The billets were the pre-war boarding houses on the front, and the walls were covered with pencilled messages, humorous and pathetic. I noted a few:-

> Pte. ...., 1st Connaught Rangers.
> Left India 10th August 1914 – 120 degrees in the shade.
> Went into action at Messines 4th October 1914.
> Since then engagements too numerous to mention."

Beneath this another hand had written, *Drink up.*
Another message read:-

> Pte ....Regt.
> Left for France for the third time on 7th Aug. 1917.
> Finis soon, please God.

Beneath this again, someone had pencilled *God rest his soul.*

It struck me that both of these wall diarists had in a few short sentences indicated greater and more extensive experiences than I had been able to put into four notebooks!

Late that afternoon we re-embarked for Boulogne, where we arrived after dark and once more marched up to St. Martin's camp. I lay down on the floor of a Nissen hut, and soon was blissfully unconscious. A sudden scramble and I found myself on my feet, realising dimly that the time had come to parade for my train. We marched down to the station, where I got into a carriage that was minus a door. As I was in a seat nearest where the door ought to have been, and facing the engine, the draught of the moving train had me nearly frozen when at 9 o'clock next morning we arrived at Poperinghe. I meandered on my own from Poperinghe to Chateau Segard, to find that the position was now being occupied by two guns only; the remaining two having gone up to what proved to be the best-remembered position we ever occupied – that in Zillebeke, about two hundred yards from Hellfire Corner on the Menin Road. No less than five attempts were made before our two guns were got safely into position; and in the course of these operations we lost 2nd Lieut. Rees, who was very badly wounded. His sojourn in the battery had been a short, but merry one. The original battery had been gradually 'acclimatised' to the vagaries of war, but not so Rees. He had joined us at Tilloy only a few months previously; and coming straight over from England had the misfortune, on coming up the line, to run into an exploding ammunition dump. That was a nasty baptism; but on arriving the same afternoon at Tilloy, the Boche was shelling the village, and it had been a somewhat shaken and dishevelled figure that gulped down his tea in the Mess that day. Then Major Lovell had said there was nothing like getting broken in at once, and sent him straight up to Wancourt. Captain Wilson had demurred, but the Major was adamant; so the Captain had offered to accompany Mr. Rees. When they arrived at Wancourt, the Boche was pumping gas shells into it, and it was only after several narrow escapes that they had succeeded in reaching the Mess at Wancourt late that night. Mr. Rees was then so down and out that it had required half a bottle of whisky to pull him together, after which he became so wide awake as to declare that a sandbag in the corner of the Mess was a dead body. Then at Messines Ridge, he had accompanied Captain Wilson 'over the top' with the infantry when Hill 60 was blown up. Now, during one of the attempts to pull our two guns into Zillebeke, he was standing with Captain Wilson on the Verbrandenmolen Road, where the convoy had been halted owing to a heavy Boche barrage being put down between it and the village. As a matter of fact, the Verbrandenmolen Road had been chosen instead of the Menin Road as the easier way to reach our position, but it now appeared that the column was 'between the devil and the deep sea'. Suddenly the shrapnel shell burst right above them, and Mr Rees fell at the Captain's feet. The latter, with Corporal Cartwright, carried him into a ruined cottage by the roadside, where they dressed a wound in his arm. They were surprised that a usually plucky officer like Rees should be making such a fuss, for he kept repeating he had been badly hit in the stomach. The Captain examined him, but could find no wound there; so, imagining that his nerves had got the better of him, he spoke sharply and told Mr. Rees to pull himself together. To get him to the dressing-station, the party (consisting of the Captain, Corporals Cartwright and Bell, and Bombardier Bird) had to carry the stretcher through the barrage, and none of them seemed to know afterwards how they ever reached the place. When they did, it was to find the dressing-station a shambles. The Medical Officer and orderlies were working frantically to dress and attempt to evacuate the wounded, while those killed were put on one side to await burial at a later date. It was not until three months afterwards that a letter from England (where Mr. Rees was then slowly recovering) explained what had been the matter. The shrapnel had gone in a slanting downward direction clean through Mr. Rees' right arm; then penetrating his body with great force, had passed through the lungs and lodged in the lower part of his other side. Thus his departure had proved as exciting as his arrival.

Since the departure of Major Lovell, Captain Wilson had been in command of the battery[16]. He had now returned to Chateau Segard, Lieut. Leslie being in command at the forward position in Zillebeke. I was now sent up there, and for the next three months made the place my home. And what a home it was to prove: farce, light comedy, melodrama, and tragedy – all had places there; and it became the final resting-place of almost half of our battery.

[16] *The permanent command of the battery was at this time offered to the Captain by the Brigade C.O., Colonel Winter, who pressed for acceptance, urging that on several occasions already Captain Wilson had assumed command, and had both the ability and experience necessary. The Captain declined to become Major, insisting that as he was yet only 21 years of age, he desired at least some months further experience before assuming the responsibility of full command with rank of Major. Eventually the Colonel had to agree.*

Chapter 21

Falling shadows –
Zillebeke (Ypres)

***When clouds are seen, wise men put on
their cloaks – Shakespeare***

I arrived at Zillebeke to find our two guns in position on the edge of the road between Zillebeke Church and Hellfire Corner. So far, we had experienced a good deal of trouble, both guns having been put out of action by hostile shellfire, while several hundred shells meant for the battery had been dumped in the mud near Dormy House, some two hundred yards in front of our position. This was due to the fact that one of the three trucks bringing it up by decauville had been hit by a shell, and the railway torn up at that point. Thereupon the ammunition from all three trucks was unloaded on the spot and left there while the railway was repaired and the trucks got away. There was no means of getting the shells across the intervening area of flooded shell-holes except by dragging them across the mud on rafts. This we tried, but it was a hopeless task. In one day we recovered about forty; next morning the remainder had disappeared under the mud, and there they remained. Already, too we had suffered some casualties among the rank and file as well as among the officers. But though missing the cheerful personality of Mr. Rees, we had a worthy

successor (though of a different type) in Mr. Fryer, whose tubby form had first appeared among us at Habarque. He had been a regular army sergeant-major before his appointment to commissioned rank; and judging from the mixture of uniforms upon him, the appointment must have been made in the field. He was a pure-bred cockney, afraid of nothing and nobody; and made no pretentions to be anything more than he was – honest and straightforward enough to cause us to revise our ideas regarding regular army sergeant-majors in general. He, too, had a hand in putting our two guns in position at Zillebeke. When the work had at last been completed on the night of pulling in, Mr. Fryer was preparing to return to Chateau Segard with one of the gun detachments. The whole sub-section and some Jamaican gunners (the latter allotted to us for the purpose of unloading shells) had to get into one motor lorry. They were packed standing; but when a number were still left in the road, someone inside shouted that the lorry was packed to suffocation. "'Old your breath and yew'll pack closer," replied Mr. Fryer, "Come on, it's got to be done." Another five or six men were pushed in, when again a smothered voice from the interior was heard calling "We cant get another soul in, Mr. Fryer." "Yew'll 'ave to get in," bawled the latter, "even if yew b----y well get inside each other." The task was accomplished without resorting to such desperate measures, and Mr. Fryer got up beside the driver. His stock, however, underwent a severe slump as the lorry lurched over the shellholes down the Verbrandenmolen road; for the language emanating from the lorry might well have set it on fire.

The mention of Jamaican gunners reminds me that a detachment of thirty of these men had been allotted to each battery in the Brigade at this time. They were hard workers; and lifting shells, each weighing two hundred and ninety pounds, seemed easy to them. Our battery's detachment was under the command of a black sergeant, with a half-caste corporal as deputy. I escorted this lot up to Zillebeke the first night I went up, and found them sleeping-quarters in an old cottage still boasting part of its roof. Then I went to bed in a dug-out opposite the church, in which Idris Williams and his wireless assistant Fred. Newsom were already installed. Overnight the Boche rained gas shells into the village and we lay for hours with gas respirators on. About 2 a.m. the shelling practically ceased and I took off my respirator, taking care before doing so, to see that the blanket over the doorway was properly covering the latter – for the air was full of gas. I had hardly got back under the blankets when that over the doorway was pulled aside, and a voice said hoarsely, "Corporal, are you there?" "Come in, you ass," I replied, "You'll be gassed if you stand out there with your gas mask off." The intruder proved to be the Corporal of the Jamaican gunners, who said that his men refused to sleep any longer in the cottage and were now roaming about looking for some place which did not threaten to fall about their ears every time a shell burst – would I tell them where they could go? Idris told him in such unmeasured terms that the Corporal departed hurriedly – though not for the destination indicated, which he could not have reached unless the Boche had blown him there. Feeling uneasy on the matter, I shortly afterwards rose, and accompanied by Idris muttering either Welsh or swear words (probably the former, for Idris seldom swore) made my way to the ruin where the Jamaican gunners were lodged. Things were quiet by this time, and on flashing my torch inside the place, I found them all lying there. Apparently

Zillebeke Church, near Ypres

most of them had never moved from the cottage, for their blankets were covered with plaster and debris which has fallen from the roof. I did not wonder that they had wished to clear out; but assuring them that the rest of the night would be peaceful (I devoutly hoped my forecast might be correct), we went back to bed. Beyond a few desultory rounds, we were left in peace until morning. Next day, however, Mr. Leslie arranged that as no accommodation was available for them at Zillebeke, they should come up from the Chateau each morning and return at night, an arrangement which pleased them exceedingly.

Some of the Jamaican gunners were very good fellows. They were not afraid to work if the Boche gave them peace to do so; but when he didn't, they often cleared out. As they were blacks, we did not know who were our gunners and who were not; but we observed that if we were unloading shells while one of the batteries round about was being shelled, we would have twice the number of Jamaican gunners we ought to have; while if we were being shelled, all we had was a mere handful and the half-caste corporal. The last-named was an excellent fellow; never missing from his post, he shepherded his men at every turn. Unfortunately, when we had only been a week or two in Zillebeke, he was killed while unloading shells at the guns.

During the initial period at Zillebeke, I lived in a small dug-out which was used by Mr. Leslie as a B.C. Post. We could not stand upright in it, as it was simply a 'lean-to' three feet high behind a ruined wall. Here Mr. Leslie and I used to creep into bed at night and exchange reminiscences. One night

111

after putting the candle out, I heard him chuckling away to himself, and on asking what had tickled his fancy he replied, "Oh, I was just wondering if you wear kilts at home." Doubtless the picture of my lean form in kilts gave him some cause for amusement, and I replied "I'm afraid that if I wore the kilt at home, I'd be arrested for having no visible means of support." He hadn't heard that one evidently, for a day or two later he handed me a cleverly-drawn cartoon of myself without sign of leg between kilt and hose-tops.

ALEC.

The author by Hubert Leslie

We had to be up with the lark in these days, for quite often our Brigade C.O., Colonel Winter, visited us to ascertain how we were progressing. He invariably arrived about six o'clock in the morning; and while we often wished he would either come later or go somewhere else, we were really glad to welcome him. He must have been sixty years old, I should think, at that time; and we could not but admire the hardihood and self-discipline, not to mention the interest in us, shown by these daily visits. It helped us in no small measure; for as the white-haired old figure emerged from the trench at the end of Zillebeke Lake and came trudging across the duckboards, we felt that if he could come up here alone or accompanied only by his adjutant, surely we could stick the place without grousing.

After some weeks in Zillebeke, Mr. Leslie went back to Chateau Segard for a few days, being relieved by a new officer in Lieut. Cruttwell, a man of about forty years of age. He had newly joined us, but had seen service in another battery, so was quite accustomed to war conditions. He brought up with him a little fellow of about eighteen years old as servant, and spent most of his first day going over the maps while his servant made merry in the cookhouse, about fifty yards away. The little lad was a recruit to Flanders and rejoiced in the name of Baga. He was, however, a regular army soldier, having seen service as a band boy in India; and doubtless was imbued with the spirit of the "Old Contemptibles", for he ran the gauntlet with Mr. Cruttwell's dinner, when the Boche was shelling the village with six and eight inch shells. He waited in the little dug-out while Mr. Cruttwell took dinner, and during this time, several shells dropped very close to the dug-out. "That was a near one," said Cruttwell after one of these had fallen; "Just run out, Baga, and see where it fell." Baga crawled out, and was gone for nearly half a minute when Mr. Cruttwell said, "I wonder what's happened to Baga? I only wanted him to *look* outside." Then an eight inch shell came over. It cleared the roof with nothing to spare, and for a minute or so mud and filth pattered on the roof. "My God," said Cruttwell, "I hope that hasn't got Baga." We both struggled to our feet in the small dug-out, but before we could reach the entrance, Baga quietly and slowly came in. He was covered from head to foot in mud and slime, and wiped his face with a handkerchief that had once been khaki-coloured. We gazed at him speechless, and he shoved the handkerchief into his pocket as if ashamed of having used it. Then in a half bent position he saluted and said

112

"That one come over me 'ead, sir, an' 'as burst ten yard from the dug-out."
No night sentry reporting "All's Well" could have been more nonchalant; but
like the rest of us, he soon learned when and how to run.

Next day the Boche shelled the vicinity of the village for three hours.
During a lull, Gunner Stevenson looked out of the wireless dug-out (where he
had taken shelter) to ascertain if it would be safe to make for the cookhouse.
As he stood there, another shell came over, a splinter from which killed him
instantaneously. About one in the afternoon, the Boche restarted in earnest
again, and this time we all cleared out of the village and watched the
proceedings from a trench at the end of the lake. It was well for us that we
did so, for the enemy had selected our two guns for a destructive shoot. Idris
Williams warned us of this, having heard the Boche plane giving "Fire",
shortly after which an eight inch shell dropped near our position. It was after
his aerial had been smashed that we had run for the trench, from which we
could see the German plane in the distance directing the shoot.

Our cartridges at both guns went up in a blaze, and the whole position
was thoroughly strafed. When the shooting had ceased and the fires burnt out
in the early evening, we returned to examine the guns. Little more was left of
either than heaps of scrap iron, and we knew that we should either need two
new guns or bring up the remaining two from Chateau Segard. The latter
procedure was adopted next day; and leaving the two old guns to become
objects of wonder to passing infantry and transport drivers, we pulled our two
remaining guns into position in almost the same spot as before.

We had not yet had an opportunity of building some decent dug-outs
nor could they have had much chance of remaining had they been made.
Already our latrines were non-existent for the third time, while the
cookhouse also had been demolished and its position changed to a cellar. But
all these things were mere preliminaries to our existence in Zillebeke. For if
they had begun to teach little Baga the truth of the proverb "Discretion is the
better part of valour", they were to prove to us also the truth of Lochiel's
warning – "Coming events cast their shadows before."

Chapter 22

Dwellers in the tombs – Zillebeke (Ypres)

Anything for a quiet life, as the man said wen he took the sitivation at the lighthouse – Dickens

The two days that followed the destruction of our guns were like calm after storm. Hardly a shell dropped in the village on either day, though at night we had the usual dose of gas; and we were fortunate indeed to be able to pull in our two remaining guns under such peaceful conditions. A psychological sidelight was thrown on the situation by the fact that while hitherto the gunners had been in the habit of going about with gas respirators loose ready to adjust at a moment's notice, before that second morning of calm was well advanced they had not only fastened up the respirators, but were going about without shrapnel helmets.

On the third day, however, the period of quietness ended; and, as if to make up for his neglect, the Boche started a real 'hate' on the Zillebeke area. He began with 1 Siege Battery at Dormy House about 6 a.m., and gradually lengthened to our position; then he had a systematic sweep of the whole district. By 5.30 that evening, he had poured over a thousand shells into and around the village – for nearly three hours they fell at an average rate of five rounds per minute, nearly all 5.9 inch shells. Idris Williams repaired his aerial six times within two hours in the early morning, and on the last of those occasions we had both run out, Idris climbing up his mast to refasten the aerial. I was just handing him the wire when we heard another shell coming, and recognising at once that it was going to be a near one, Idris leapt from the top of his mast. We both dashed across the intervening ten yards to the dug-out, flinging ourselves through the doorway on our faces as the shell burst. When we rose up after the falling debris had subsided, Idris looked at me with a pair of startled eyes, and said "That was a near one, look you." And it was, 'indeed to goodness'; for on looking out, the shellhole was where his mast had been. We then cleared off to the hidy-hole at the lake, where we remained all day.

About 6 p.m. the shelling ceased; and on returning to the villa we found that John Smith, the cook, had both dinner and tea ready in the cellar. At 7 o'clock the shelling was resumed; and this time we remained in the wireless dug-out as the shells were falling between it and the lake. Some were going into the water, throwing up great spouts which fell in beautiful cascades; but most were dropping in the vicinity of an eighteen pounder field battery at the Zillebeke end of the lake, and about a hundred yards behind our gun position. Already the Boche had caught six or seven dumps of cartridges and ammunition, including one of our own which had just been brought up and stacked on the previous day. Now he got one of the eighteen pounder battery's cartridges, a large flare resulting. This seemed to be the signal for increased activity, as shells poured into the position and also into the lake beyond. As I 'chanced one eye' from our dug-out doorway, one shell caught the field gun itself fair and square. There was a terrific explosion, and the shower of hot metal and debris reached as far as our position. After this the shelling slackened off, and at 8.30 p.m. ceased. I was intending to go down to Chateau Segard that evening to have a clothes-washing next day; and when, soon after the shelling had stopped, Mr. Leslie returned to relieve Mr. Cruttwell, I suggested to the latter that we should go while we had the opportunity. "We'll wait for five minutes more," he said. "It would be just like the wily devil to give us a quarter of an hour and then put over a salvo to catch us by surprise." That was exactly what happened; for two minutes later four shells came over in rapid succession, to burst just short of the lake. Then the whole show started all over again, though the shells were now going further over the lake, and to the decauville railway at its far end.

We decided to stay the night at Zillebeke, as if we left we should require to cross the shelled area on the way to the chateau. Apart from gas shells, the night was fairly quiet; but at 6 o'clock next morning the Boche began to drop one eight inch shell into the village at regular five minute intervals. He was becoming a most tiresome fellow, and I was glad to be relieved by Corporal Murray (now the other B.C.A.) at 9.30 a.m., when our small party consisting of Mr. Cruttwell, two telephonists and myself, left Zillebeke. We had not gone more than a hundred yards when the rate of shelling began to increase; but as we had deviated from the trench alongside the lake, we decided to push on for the railway, judging we should be safe once we reached the shelter of its embankment. At one time we thought we should never make it: shells dropped just short of us, just over, and to right and left; while lumps were whizzing and 'phutting' all over the place. We blundered on, throwing ourselves flat every minute; and when at last we reached the shelter of the far side of the embankment, we lay utterly exhausted for ten minutes, the perspiration running down our faces.

Late that day, a message came from Mr. Leslie (who had been unable to get in touch with us earlier owing to the shelling) asking how many of our party had reached the chateau, as from where he had been watching, it seemed impossible that we had got through unscathed. At Zillebeke, the gun detachments had cleared out to the lake trench early in the forenoon, and from that point Mr. Leslie had timed the rate of shelling. At one time shells were falling at a rate of thirty to thirty-six rounds per minute, and of all calibres up to eight inch. Our cartridges were again blown up; but strangely enough, the damage done to the two guns was not more than could be repaired by our artificer staff-sergeant in a day or two. 1 Siege Battery in front of us had five out of their six guns knocked out that day. Wasn't I pleased to be quietly washing out shirt and socks at Chateau Segard!

There I learned from Captain Wilson that a new Major was expected within the next few days. That night I slept in peace in the Captain's dug-out, and when next morning I stood inside the entrance shaving (for the weather was wet and a strong wind howled outside), I felt it needed a week or two in Zillebeke to make one appreciate the safety of rear billets such as the chateau had now become. Suddenly there was a rumble, then a loud crash on the roof of the dug-out. It was fortunate that the latter was made with elephant irons, for the chateau wall that remained on that side had collapsed on it. The dug-out entrance was completely blocked by fallen masonry, but a squad of our men soon had the debris removed, when I was released from my involuntary prison. I did my washing that forenoon, and in the afternoon had a swim in one of the old 11.1 inch shellholes. It was flooded and one could swim three yards in one direction and two across in eight feet of water. It was easier to go in than to get out, for the yellow mud at the sides was slippery and a sponge-down was necessary after emerging.

Though a stormy wind was still blowing, the rain had now ceased; and as I made my way back to the chateau, I observed some of the gunners sitting in a row on a bank near an old rusty iron tank, which lay on its side and was used by Lyddite as a dug-out. I asked 'Sniper' Brown (one of our cooks) why the men were sitting there, and he replied, "If you want to see a pantomime, come and watch this." While we sat, he told me what had transpired up to then. It seemed that some weeks before, another character somewhat similar to Lyddite had arrived as a reinforcement. I could hardly believe it; but Lyddite himself had summed him up shortly after his arrival, when he had buttonholed him, saying "Look 'ere: I've been the b----y laughing stock of this battery for months now. You can come and muck in with me if you like in that tank, and take a share of wot I've 'ad coming to me." Lyddite the second (for so he had been dubbed) had been quite agreeable, and the two of them had slept, eaten (and been eaten!) in the tank since then. 'Sniper' informed me that Lyddite the second had been seen an hour previously carrying a cartridge cylinder for water. As washing clothes was outwith[17] the programme of the Lyddite clan, someone had asked where he was going with the case, and elicited the information that he (Lyddite the second) had been deputised by Lyddite to fill the cylinder with water, boil the latter, and then pour it over Lyddite's legs, thus giving him what he hoped would be a 'Blighty one.' The gunners were now awaiting the re-appearance of Lyddite the second with the boiling water. Meantime Lyddite (the original) lay inside the

[17] [SCOT: not part of]

117

tank like Diogenes in his barrel, with bare feet and legs protruding. When a shout of applause greeted the appearance of his confederate, struggling along under the combined weight and awkwardness of the hot cartridge cylinder, Lyddite sat up, and peering out, said "Now none of your b----y nonsense: pour it all over at once – not a cupful at a time." Then lying down, he awaited the onslaught. But as we knew from experience, it is nearly an impossible task to empty a long cylinder of water all at once on something on the same level as its base. Had Lyddite the second put the vessel on a box two or three feet high and then poured the water down on to Lyddite's legs he might have made a job of it. As it was, he tried his best, but only succeeded in tipping about a pint on Lyddite's leg. With a roar, the latter bounded out of the tank, and shoving his astonished ally out of the way, ran for his life while the water from the now completely upset cylinder flowed into the tank among the blankets. Whether or not Lyddite ever meant to get his 'blighty' that day I cannot say; for I should not have put it beyond him to have in this way tried to 'put one over' on the gunners. When asked the same evening if he hadn't got a blighty yet, Lyddite replied, "Nao; that b----y fool messed it all up; but you wait and see. You don't need me any longer now that you've got 'im, and I'll get a blighty all right – b----y soon too."

I returned to Zillebeke that evening to find everything quiet. But what a mess! The ruined houses were all practically razed to the ground, and the only dug-outs left were the signaller's and the wireless operators'. Our lean-to B.C. Post and its protecting wall were both demolished. Sleeping accommodation of some kind was urgently needed for the gun detachments on duty; and while some cellars had been found, these were then flooded and it was impossible to use them until they had been baled out and dried. Some of the men found sleeping quarters in a passage under the ruins of the church. This passage ended at a door leading to burial vaults; so breaking open this door, we examined the stone chamber in which we found ourselves. It consisted of a broad stone-flagged passage with recesses leading off in something after the following manner:-

In four of the recesses were coffins with remains; but the others were empty. As each recess held a man very comfortably, as many men as could in the gun detachments occupied the vacant recesses; those who could not secure one finding sleeping accommodation on the stone floor of the centre passage. Thus did the quick and the dead sleep side by side, a state of affairs that lasted during the whole three months spent in Zillebeke. We had slept in strange places before now; but dwelling in the burial vaults of a cemetery with the dead for daily companions was surely a step lower in the social scale than the pig-styes at Cable Farm. Pigs and burial vaults – a strangely familiar association of ideas, though at first I could not recollect its source.

Then I remembered the story of the madman and the Gaderene swine; and indeed, as there was a distinct prospect of the constant shellfire either cutting us to pieces or depriving us of reason, it seemed to me that we had only to remain here long enough to become modern demoniacs among the tombs.

Chapter 23

"The dogdays" – Zillebeke (Ypres)

Cry havoc! and let slip the dogs of war – Shakespeare

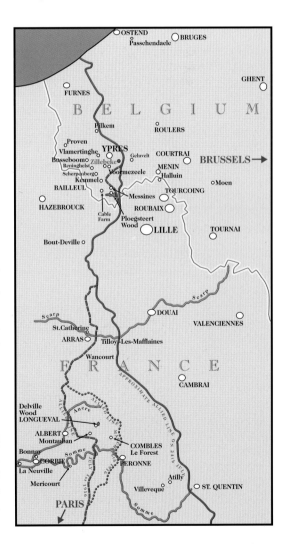

The history of the next few weeks would seem to show that if not quite demoniacal, we were well on the way towards lunacy. Our two remaining guns which had been brought up from Chateau Segard were now so old, and their shooting in consequence so erratic, that Mr. Leslie and ten men were sent to Calais to bring up six new Mark II guns. Up to this time we had been a four gun battery, and it was now reported that a half battery of gunners would be coming direct from England to man the two additional guns. Meantime the detachments spent most of their time scurrying between the cookhouse and the vaults, while the occupants of the wireless dugout continued to use their own particular funkhole in the trench at Zillebeke Lake when shelling became intense.

And now the stage was set for a series of tableaux ranging in such quick succession from comedy to tragedy that sometimes it was difficult to distinguish "t'other from which". A detachment of Royal Engineers had come up and built a new B.C. Post inside the ruins of the church.

Though built in the usual splinter-proof fashion, it was considered shell-proof, owing to the provision of a double roof of straight elephant irons and stone rubble. Between the top and bottom roofs was an airspace of about two feet or more, the theory being that if a direct hit was obtained, the shell would go through the top roof, its shock being taken up by the airspace below; and while the lower roof might also be damaged, the shell would not penetrate to the dug-out. We were not anxious to have this theory tested, though there seemed every likelihood of it; for owing to constant interruptions by the Boche, it took nearly a fortnight to build. Then on the day following its completion, we were unloading shells, when one of the hostile spasms began. Captain Wilson and I were in the new B.C. Post at the time, and noticed not only the gun detachments running past the doorway for the protection of the vaults, but also a fair number of Jamaican gunners. We were unaware that the latter were in the habit of going into the vaults; but when the shelling had ceased, we went outside to look for them. At first not a sign of life was to be seen; then Captain Wilson's eye was attracted by a slight movement on the roof of the B.C. Post. "Good Lord!" he said, "Look at that." The first thing I saw was two eyes and a row of white teeth; then one by one our Jamaican gunners wriggled from the airspace between the two roofs. They had decided that in the event of a shelling, this would be the most secure place in the village! Warnings had therefore to be given that the airspace was meant to receive German shells and not Jamaican gunners. I wonder what the Engineers who built the B.C. Post would have thought had they seen their scientific theories turned into farce through the all-important airspace having been filled up with living bodies.

Then we had a touch of melodrama that afternoon; for later while standing outside the B.C. Post with Harry Reid watching Hellfire Corner being shelled, a horse and rider emerged from the black cloud of smoke and came galloping furiously down the road towards us. "Ho," chuckled Harry, "here comes Tam o' Shanter wi' the de'il at his back." Then as the horseman rapidly approached at the same breakneck pace, he remarked "I'll bet that chap's got the wind up all right." Well, either he had, or his horse was out of control, for with flying hoofs it sped past the spot where we stood. As it was passing, Harry dashed out into the road after it shouting "Jim! Jim!", for all he was worth. But hard though he ran, horse and rider disappeared in a few minutes over the ridge in a cloud of dust. Harry returned to where I stood wondering what had taken him, and said "Isn't that the blooming limit? Here have I been looking for my brother for the past fourteen months, and that's him."

Since the destruction of the old lean-to B.C. Post, the officer on duty slept in the wireless dug-out where I too had now made my sleeping quarters. That night Mr. Cruttwell was sleeping in the upper bunk, the lower one being occupied by a young officer named Hansen[18], just out from England and up in Zillebeke that evening for the first time. Cruttwell remarked from above, You'll get some prime Zillebeke down there tonight Hansen." Idris and I laughed; but Mr. Hansen, not realising the significance of the remark while feeling that some rejoinder was expected, answered "I don't think I'm very safe sleeping under you, Cruttwell." "You're a long way safer sleeping under me than that blanket," Cruttwell replied. "Prime Zillebeke is a particularly large brand of lice, my lad; you can tell me what you think of them in the

[18] [This officer's name is later spelt Hanson p. 130]

120

morning." Then he began to tell Hansen what else he would experience in the morning, suggesting that I might take him round to choose the particular recess in the vaults in which he would like to be buried, and after that introduce him to our Jamaican gunners. I replied that it could not be done, as I had obtained permission to go to Reninghelst next morning to visit Claude Betts, who was officer in charge of a company of Chinese labour Corps. Hansen said thoughtfully, "I think it would be a good idea to use the Chinese as infantry, there are so many of them: I wonder what the Germans would do if they saw ten thousand Chinamen coming over the top?" "Run and bring their washing, I should think," replied Cruttwell.

Next morning I went to Chateau Segard, and thence by side-car to Reninghelst. I had a long chat with Claude Betts, who had already learned many Chinese phrases; for his labourers spoke no English at all and were cunning enough to pretend not to understand any signs if the latter indicated work. I left him shortly after tea, and on the way through Reninghelst noticed that Headquarters had put up a large notice for the benefit of our troops. It read:

DO NOT SPEAK TO THE CHINESE

Beneath this, in equally large letters, some wag had chalked:

WHO THE HELL CAN?

Next morning (17th September, 1917) I went up again to Zillebeke along with the two gun detachments about to go on duty. We reached the railway embankment about 6 a.m., and thereafter continued in small parties, as the Boche balloon was up. About half a mile from Zillebeke we tailed into a working party of infantry, resulting in a long string of men in single file. I ran to the head of the column (where a youthful 2nd Lieutenant was leading the infantry) and suggested that as the Boche balloon was staring us in the face – and with the morning sun behind him must be able to see us quite clearly – it would be wise to split up into small parties, as our men had done. The officer was quite nice about it, but thought the precaution unnecessary; so I returned to the rear of the column and instructed our men to make a detour in order to gain the shelter of the trench which ran the whole length of Zillebeke Lake, and this was reached a few minutes later. Meantime the working party of infantry was travelling parallel to us over the open. Then the Boche opened a cross fire upon them from two batteries, when they turned back, apparently with the intention of making for the railway embankment. I called to the officer that there was plenty of shelter in the trench; and after some little delay and confusion they reached it with the loss of one man. We reached Zillebeke without further incident, except that I had palpitation once when a time-fuzed high explosive shell burst right above my head with a terrific crackle. I stood rigidly to attention while chunks went 'phut' into the ground about me, and I had visions of sharing the fate of Mr. Rees.

At six o'clock that evening the enemy had a short but merry strafe; and though the new B.C. Post and the wireless dug-out were only twenty yards apart, no less than six shells fell between them without one direct hit on either, though all our beautiful sandbags were burst by splinters. Late that night we were sitting in the wireless dug-out. The Boche was sending over occasional gas shells, with now and again a high explosive. Suddenly we

121

heard a voice some distance away singing – apparently in the open. From the tones, we adjudged the gentleman to be slightly merry; but as it was raining heavily, no one immediately offered to investigate. As the singing continued, Frank Strachan said "That sounds like MacPheat's voice; I'll go out and see what's up." Guided by the sounds, Frank slithered across the mud, and in the darkness blundered into Arthur White, who was standing on the edge of a shellhole part full of water. Half way down its muddy side sat MacPheat, his legs trailing in the water as he sang:

There's an ol' mill by th' stre...em, Nellie Dean,
W'ere we used to sit an' dre...em, Nellie Dean,
An' th' waters as they flo...,
seem to murmur sweet an' lo...,
You're my heart's desire – I luv you, Nellie Dean.

"He won't come out," said Arthur, "and if we go down to get him, we'll be pulled in and get as wet as he is. He must have got some extra rum somewhere; he's drunk as a lord." "Come on, Mac.," called out Frank, "what about it?" "Tha' you Frankie?" asked Mac. "Yae've juist cam' tae th' rescue when I wis gie'in' up hope o' getting Arthur oot o' that shellhole; an' noo you're intae. Gie's a grup o' yer paws an' I'll sine hae ye baith oot." And with that, he reached up his hands. Arthur grasped one and Frank the other, when Mac. was dragged out and eventually dumped in the signallers' dug-out for the night. Next morning I asked him what all the trouble had been the previous night. He swore even then that he had pulled both Frank Strachan and Arthur White out of a shellhole. Truly our world was a topsy-turvy one!

But if our men's behaviour savoured of lunacy, no less so was that of our guns, which had now become permanently 'deranged'. The rifling of the gun muzzles was so worn out that accurate shooting was impossible, and we could not fire on the German trenches lest our shells fell on our own lines. Neither could we fire on back areas, as we no longer had the necessary range. Our shooting was therefore confined to enemy batteries, and terrible stuff it was. One day, for example, during an aeroplane shoot, we fired three rounds in succession at the same gun elevation. Theoretically, of course, these shells ought to have fallen on about the same spot: actually, the first was nearly 300 yards over the target, the second was 40 yards over, while the third was nearly 600 yards short. One day we were supposed to be firing on a Boche battery, but could not reach within 250 yards of it. To the surprise of our airman, the enemy put up a smoke screen in front of the area in which most of our shells were falling; and so was discovered a new enemy battery to add to the sector maps. The limit of the Boche's endurance was apparently reached on the day following the last episode; when one of the shells, falling 300 yards short of our target, dropped in a wood and set fire to a very large German ammunition dump, the existence of which had not been suspected hitherto.

The proverb says 'Mad dogs do not live long', and doubtless the Boche thought it time to destroy this particular specimen; which if not entirely mad, appeared to be in the throes of 'dogdays'. At any rate he sent across two aeroplanes, and an hour afterwards began another destructive shoot on our position. We cleared off to a safe distance and watched the end of our original guns. By evening, both had been rendered useless beyond all repair by direct

122

hits, and scorched all over by flaming cartridges, 870 of which were blown up that afternoon. So ended this crazy period of comedy and tragedy. That it contained he latter we had reason to know; for up to now, of the battery personnel of a hundred-odd men who had first come to Zillebeke, over seventy had been lost by casualties.

As I stood that night looking at the charred and mangled remains of the four guns we had brought from England, it seemed almost fitting that their end should come as it had, rather than that they should have been taken intact but useless to the base, there to be laid aside neglected and forgotten. Perhaps too, these iron ruins, shortly to become the main object of interest to all who passed through the village, were fitting monuments, not only to those who had gone from us, but to the passing of the original battery. For already many reinforcements had come – and gone – while within the next few days we should have six new guns and two sub-sections of gunners fresh from England to man them. A new Major was on the way to take over command; and it seemed that all that remained of the old battery was one officer and some fifty other ranks and the 'Crown-Nine' mark[19].

Yet there was something else. For though the fires that had destroyed personnel and material were now cold and dead, the spirit of the old battery still burned in a small, but steady flame.

[19] *Each unit had its own distinctive mark, which was painted or branded on all stores and equipment. Our mark was a Crown (for King and Country) with the figure Nine (considered by our first Major to be a lucky number) beneath.*

123

Chapter 24

Calm before the storm –
Zillebeke (Ypres)

A lull like the lull of a treacherous sea – Hood

A s we could not again go into action until the arrival of Mr. Leslie with our new guns, the next week was occupied attending to urgent matters which we had hitherto been too busy to think about. Our main task was to make the position as secure as possible against further battery casualties; and with this end in view, the flooded cellars were baled out and made habitable, while the cookhouse was removed from the cellar and a new one built in the open – the cellar being required for the additional men. A telephone dugout was built near the B.C. Post, and the vicinity cleared of such encumbrances as dead mules, no less than three of which lay in the few yards of roadway between the wireless dug-out and the B.C. Post, and stank abominably.

Then up to now we had no permanent observation post. I had gone up one day to find one and had got no further than Sanctuary Wood, which that day shockingly belied its name. Captain Wilson found an O.P. in our front line of trenches, though not before having had several narrow escapes – not all from shellfire. The day on which he discovered the O.P. was very misty, and after passing Sanctuary Wood, he had gone on for some considerable time, when it was borne upon him that in the sea of shellholes he was metaphorically as well as literally befogged. He crossed over a sap, but after proceeding for some minutes among barbed wire entanglements, decided to retrace his steps. Re-entering the trench, he proceeded along it until he reached a dug-out which proved to be the Bedford's Headquarters. The Captain enquired of their Adjutant the whereabouts of the map point he wished to reach, adding that he had been over the open beyond the sap, but could see nothing but barbed wire. "Good Lord, man," exclaimed the Adjutant, "it's mighty lucky for you it's so misty. You've been wandering about in no man's land."

The Captain had been in temporary command of the battery once more for about a month when our new O.C. arrived in the person of Major Hall. He was giant in physique and brusque in manner; but in the short time during which he was to remain our commanding officer, we found that he was a capable officer and a fine man. On learning that a half battery of recruits from England was expected to join us as reinforcements and bringing their own N.C.O.s, he swore that he would have all the latter reduced and the remaining gunners of the original battery promoted before a month had passed. The morning after his arrival, learning from Captain Wilson that the gunners had the cellars ready for our expected reinforcements, and that they were now engaged in preparing emplacements for the new guns, Major Hall went out and spent the whole day along with the Captain superintending the work. That evening he came into the B.C. Post mud-covered to the knees, dumped his colossal weight into the one chair we possessed and in a stentorian voice that reverberated through the dug-out, called "Bennet!"

Bennet (Major Hall's servant, who had come with him to the battery), had been installed with us in the wireless dug-out; and hearing the call, came running in. Major Hall's legs were stuck straight out in front of him; and without any further instructions, Bennet proceeded to take off the O.C.'s boots. This became a nightly performance which afforded us not a little quiet amusement, though Bennet performed it as a rite. And the boots! They were not only big, but seemed correspondingly high. Often I stood looking at them in wonder as they stood side by side on the dug-out floor, and never did I do so but I thought of the seven-league boots in "Hop-o'-my-Thumb". Everything about Major Hall was big. As he moved about among the men, his words – whether of encouragement or censure – came booming out in tones like Big Ben; while his appreciation of acts of gallantry showed that his heart too was something of an outsize.

Bennet, his servant, was a big chap too. It took us what we could do to find a corner of a dug-out large enough to dispose of his person at night. His first night in Zillebeke was none too happy. The Boche had some long spasms of gas shelling, and we spent a great part of the night with our gas masks on. The next night was worse, and we were awake until nearly 4 a.m. About three o'clock Bennet remarked for about the tenth time "That was a near one", and was told to shut up. Then there *was* a near one! It fairly shook the dug-out, and Bennet declared it to be a direct hit. We were inclined to think that being new to the village he was somewhat windy, and told him not to mind the shelling but to lie quiet. Shortly after this the shelling ceased, and we took off our box respirators; which, of course, meant that we could now sleep as well as rest. "There's an awful smell of gas across here," said Bennet. We felt it too, but as that was not unusual, we thought little about it and settled down for the rest of the night. I was just dozing off, when Bennet's voice came, it seemed from a long distance away, saying "There's an awful draught here, Corporal." Astonishment at such a complaint brought my sleepy senses to a state of wakefulness at once. "Did you say there was a *draught*?" I asked. "Yes," said Bennet, "I'm about blown away in this corner." Idris chuckled from his bunk, and said "If you wait until morning, I'll send your mother a postcard to come and tuck you in." "All right," replied Bennet pacifically, "I was only telling you." But when I awoke in broad daylight, on sitting up I chanced to look over to the corner where Bennet was now snoring peacefully. Within a yard of his head gaped a hole two feet wide at the bottom corner of the dug-out. Bennet had been right in both his statements – it *had* been a direct hit, and there *was* a draught! When Bennet was wakened, he openly remarked quietly "I knew it had hit the dug-out near me when I felt the gas so strong afterwards; but you fellows thought I had the 'wind up', so I thought I'd better say no more."

Our new guns arrived during the latter part of September, 1917. Four of them were pulled into position close to the remains of our old guns in Zillebeke, the remaining two being put at Westhoek Ridge, on the north side of the Menin Road near Bellewarde Lake. The half battery of reinforcements arrived with its own N.C.O.s; and for the next two days we were hard at it pulling in and unloading ammunition for a projected attack on Passchendaele Ridge. It was fortunate – particularly with so many men just out of England – that the weather was bad during these two days; for the Boche seemed to think it time for a lull in his Zillebeke activity, and we got the guns into position without undue trouble, and completely free from casualties; and for these blessings we had to thank the elements.

But if the stormy wind and scudding rain seemed to indicate that the Boche might cease his activity for the winter, this was far from proving the case; for within the next few days, a storm such as we had not yet experienced broke upon us with full blast.

Chapter 25

Passchendaele ridge – Zillebeke (Ypres)

And hearts that once beat high for praise
Now feel that pulse no more – Moore

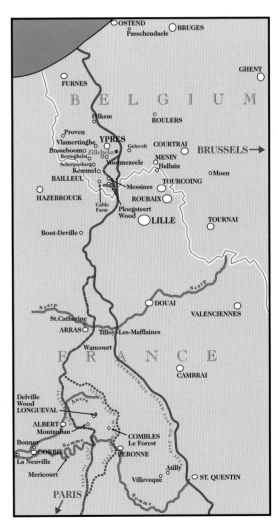

The attack on Passchendaele Ridge took place at 5.40 a.m. on 21st September, 1917. We were engaged all day answering calls from our aeroplanes notifying Boche batteries in action, which we engaged one after another: for our new guns had a range of 13,000 to 14,000 yards, and we were the only battery in the sector able to silence enemy batteries in its back areas. We did some excellent shooting; but as soon as one battery was silenced, we were switched to another by a prearranged system of signals from our planes. Of course we could not expect to get away with this, and the following day saw Boche planes nosing about above the village.

To describe the events of the six weeks that followed would be a monotonous and depressing tale of woes and casualties. In the former category, we had to contend with seas of mud; our new guns heeling over like ships in distress after having fired a few hundred rounds. At the Bellewarde Lake position, the Royal Engineers had erected a special raft platform to combat this, but when fifty rounds had been fired, not only the platform, but the guns themselves were rapidly disappearing in the mud; and eventually we had to abandon the position as untenable, when the two guns were brought down to Zillebeke and put into position near the other four. At the Zillebeke position we pulled the guns out and remounted them in the same place no less than five times – no mean task in the case of 9.2 inch howitzers – and during the process we were subjected to a new feature in the Boche retaliation. Although knowing exactly where our guns were, he no longer attempted a destructive shoot upon them; but as soon as we fired a few rounds, he would drop a salvo into us from several batteries simultaneously. This seldom failed to catch us; not only knocking the guns out of action repeatedly, but also taking a steady toll of the gun detachments. Somehow it was the new men who suffered most: maybe they were not quick enough in getting down flat, or perhaps it was just the fortune of war; but the fact remains that the original members escaped oftener than the reinforcements. Within a month there was no longer any need for Major Hall's threat to reduce the new N.C.O.s; only one of the latter – Bombardier Rosie – was left.

The Boche's penchant for cookhouses has been mentioned before – on 30th September he got an O.K. on our new cookhouse, severely wounding four men, while several others were less seriously hurt. We built a new cookhouse almost on the same spot, and three days later the Boche got an O.K. on it also, when nine men were hit. A few days later, our infantry launched another attack. We were enfiladed all morning by a gun from the south; but had no serious casualties until 9.30 a.m., when a shell dropped behind Number 1 gun, wounding Lieut. Hanson[20] and six of the gun detachment. Lieut. Cruttwell, who was at the rear billets, was immediately 'phoned for, and came up with a gun detachment which had only gone off duty at Zillebeke on the previous day. They came up so speedily that they were in time to assist in getting the wounded safely down the line, when Mr. Cruttwell took Mr. Hanson's place as Section Commander. He had only fired two rounds when a hostile shell dropped right on top of the Section Commander's post. Mr. Cruttwell was killed outright, five gunners seriously wounded, and a signaller buried. The last was dug out alive, but crushed internally and blind.

Every day during this period had its toll of casualties, largely due to the salvo method already referred to; and this sapped the morale of our men – especially the newcomers – more than any destructive shoot ever did. Usually we had to keep in action whether shelled or not; for our infantry in the line could only consolidate their positions under the protection of our gunfire, particularly on enemy batteries in the rear areas.

Certainly we had diversions; but these too seemed to be in keeping with the general atmosphere of the period. One night I groped my way down the pitch black road towards the guns with fresh night-lines. No. 4 gun was firing one round every five minutes; and as I neared the part of the road alongside which I knew the gun ought to be, I realised that a round must be almost due. Just then I heard the sound of a transport wagon ahead of me coming in my direction. It was only yards off when our gun fired. The transport mules stampeded, and without hesitation I threw myself headlong into the ditch alongside the road. It was well that I did so; for the wagon tore past within a yard of where I lay in the slime; and a few minutes later the whole

[20] [Presumably the same officer previously spelt Hansen p. 120]

130

contraption came to grief at the corner of the road. The wagon was over-turned, and the mules, kicking free of the traces, disappeared across country in the direction of Dormy House. The driver, fortunately was uninjured except so far as concerned his feelings; and he certainly did not spare himself in the flow which issued from his lips when he extricated himself from the mud and wreckage of his transport wagon.

Another diversion took place one night before an important attack. We had been warned by Brigade that the barrage would open at 4.a.m., and had special instructions that at no matter what cost, the telephone lines must be kept intact until the attack had been launched. We prepared for eventualities by running reserve lines from the signallers' dug-out to the B.C. Post, to Brigade, to the guns, and to various other points with which we had to maintain contact. The signallers worked hard at this until after midnight, and when the work had been satisfactorily completed (for strangely enough, the night was almost free from hostile shellfire, not even a gas shell coming over), the signallers had run out no less than forty-odd lines from the telephone dug-out. Thus it seemed that unless conditions changed tremendously within the next few hours, maintenance of the lines was assured; for odd shells would not be likely to sever more than one of the communications run out to the various points. Of course, as all lines converged on the telephone dug-out, a direct hit on the latter would undo everything, and this we had just to risk. I sat up all night, phoning brigade every half hour for weather reports (to adjust our lines of fire according to possible changes of wind, etc.). All went well, and at a quarter to four I ascertained from the telephone dug-out that everything was O.K. Then the hum of an approaching Boche plane was heard. I instructed the telephonist on duty to see that no light percolated through the blanket of his doorway. He told me he had already blown out his candle, and I did the same with mine. The plane came nearer, and as it flew overhead I knew from the sound that it must be flying very low. Then there was a whistle, followed by a terrific crackle as a bomb burst very near the dug-out.

Snatching up the phone, I asked the signaller if all was well. No answer. Rushing out (for the plane had continued its course and was now only faintly heard), I found our signallers on duty struggling about in the mud half dressed, shining torches here, there and everywhere. Indeed they had to, for the bomb had fallen just beyond the telephone post and smashed every line we possessed within ten minutes of zero hour. What a babel ensued! Every available signaller was on the job, cursing and working furiously. No one was hurt, and fortunately all lines had been specially tabbed at various points. At five minutes to four we succeeded in getting through to Brigade, where the Adjutant was nearly frantic at our failure to respond to his repeated calls. By four o'clock we had the line through to the guns and to all other points except to the O.P., whose line was 'dissed'. As our trench targets had been previously registered, the last was of no great importance; but had it not been for the precaution taken to tab the lines at different points, we could never have repaired the breaks in time for zero hour. Later in the day the signallers were complimented by Colonel Winter on the manner in which they had re-established communication during those exciting minutes. We wondered if the compliment would have been made had the Brigade heard what the signallers were saying that dark morning; for Brigade came in for as much 'backwash' as the German plane. After all, the plane was gone; but we always had Brigade to fall back on when somebody had to be blamed! It was perhaps bad luck to have an exceptionally peaceful night, and then have a bomb drop on a vital spot; but we were fortunate, for had the bomb fallen three yards further from the roadway, it would have obtained an O.K. on the telephone post; in which case we could not have got through all the lines in time, besides having half of our complement of signallers wiped out.

As the days wore on to November, weather conditions were as bad as ever, and we longed for the rigours of winter to bring a respite from attacks, the result of which we never knew. For one day, walking wounded would tell that not an inch of ground could be held, while on the next, a wounded Australian stated that on going over the top that morning they had been unable to get in touch with the Boche, who they thought had withdrawn. Thus we were in the dark as to what, if any, progress had been made; and our own battery's memories of Passchendaele must always be of the casualties that daily depleted our ranks. Corporal Murray (my fellow B.C.A. at this time) was seriously wounded and later died in Scotland; Idris Williams and Fred. Newsom, the wireless operators, had both gone to Blighty gassed, while Lieut. Leslie had been hit in the head by a shell fragment and sent home also. Thus of all the occupants of the wireless dug-out mentioned in these pages, only myself remained. We still had one of our original sergeants in Quarter-Master Sergeant Thake; the others had either been killed or wounded. We had also lost Lyddite, who was found one morning blistered all over from mustard gas: he got his Blighty at last. Mustard gas took heavy toll of the infantry at this time, and it was a common occurrence to see a string of them being led down the line blind.

One of the saddest features of the battery history of this period was that up to this time we still had two sets of brothers in the battery in the Lambs and the Cartwrights. (It will be remembered that we had a further pair of brothers in Sandy and Tom Macfarlane, the latter having been killed at Montauban in the previous year.) Peter and Billy Lamb were both original gunners of the battery, as was also Corporal Frank Cartwright, whose young brother Louis had joined us as a reinforcement some time before this period. Peter Lamb was killed on 24th September and young Louis Cartwright on the 28th, and in each case the grief of the remaining brother was pitiful to witness. It is a mistake to have two brothers in one unit during a war. "Then shall two be in the field; the one shall be taken and the other one left."

At the beginning of November, Captain Wilson was again in command of the battery, Major Hall having gone to be temporary Colonel of another Brigade. Major Hall had felt the strains of the past weeks; but even the fact that on one occasion (when trying to get wounded bandaged, and the Adjutant of Brigade had phoned to know why we had ceased firing) he had told Brigade that if they wanted the guns to fire within the next twenty minutes they could come and man them, had not prejudiced his prospects of promotion. Our ubiquitous Captain too, was worn out; but early in November the last attack on Passchendaele was made, after which the campaign closed down for the winter. Captain Wilson was ordered home on a Battery Commander's course, while all the batteries in our Brigade were ordered to hand over their guns to an incoming Brigade and prepare for six weeks rest on the coast. We did not believe it, though it was said that the order had been given by Haig personally. But the new Brigade duly arrived; and handing over the guns, we prepared to go with what remained of our battered battery. It was Mr. Fryer who finally confirmed the report that we should go right down to the coast. Slamming the palm of his horny hand into the hollow between my shoulders, he said "No more Zillebeke for you; you've got into a bad habit of considering it your home; but you'll see no more of it, for we're going out for a long rest by the sea."

"Rest by the sea." What a phrase to conjure with – even in November! Yet we could not but think of all those whose voices we had known so well, now silent for ever among the tombs of Zillebeke. And though our hearts were glad, we left the place silently – almost stealthily. It seemed like desertion.

Chapter 26

A journey to the coast – (Ypres to Tardinghen)

I will go back to the great sweet mother,
Mother and lover of men, the sea – Swinburne

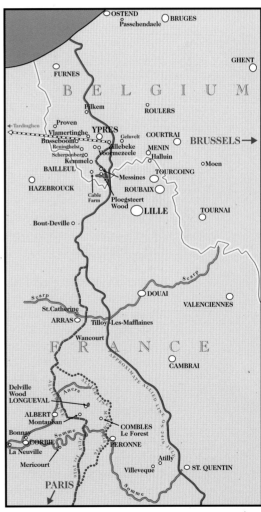

It had been arranged that I should go in the Major's car with Lieut. Clegg (a recent arrival) in advance of the battery, so that billets should be ready for the main body of our men as they arrived at each place where it would be necessary to remain for the night on our way to the coast. Mr. Clegg's job was to drive the car; mine to act as interpreter and arrange the billets.

We departed on Wednesday, 14th November, 1917, and late that day arranged billets at two farms on the road between Steenvoorde and Eecke. All went well during the first stage; and next morning Mr. Clegg and I left in the car at 9 a.m. The morning was beautiful, and after passing through Hazebrouck and St. Omer, the countryside was a feast to the eyes. Green grass, brown trees and hedges – each had an interest of its own after months spent in mud and shellholes. The morning ground mist sometimes gave curious effects, such as a distant monastery appearing to be merely towers suspended in mid-air, the lower parts of the buildings being obscured by filmy mist, while the upper parts were clearly visible.

At St. Omer we picked up two Brigade officers whose car had broken down. The load must have been too much for our vehicle; for after going six miles, we had a bad puncture. While we endeavoured to repair it, the Headquarters car came up; whereupon the two officers, without any hesitation, left us to our fate. It was not long until we were once more bowling along merrily, and in the afternoon reached the village of Wizernes, where we were to stay for the night. Billets were arranged in less than an hour, and the battery arrived in the early evening. After all were comfortably settled, Frank Strachan and I repaired to a small cottage at which I had called earlier in the day, where we had a supper of coffee and brown bread. We spent two happy hours with the three little girls of the family – aged 6, 9, and 11 – pretending to learn a French lesson from a schoolbook. Little [things] amused them, and the mother laughed as much as the children. After the latter had been bedded, she told us that their father had recently been killed; but immediately dismissed the subject with a shrug of the shoulders and that sentence so often heard from these village women, "C'est la guerre."

Next morning the car refused to start, so we travelled in the ration lorry, much to the disgust of Bombardier Mentiplay, then our ration orderly. After passing through some hilly country not unlike parts of Scotland, we made the pretty village of Columbert shortly after midday. It was a very small place, and I had difficulty in securing billets, which were not arranged until darkness had set in. That night was remarkable for one thing: John Smith, the cook, announced that dinner-cum-tea-cum-supper was ready about 7 p.m., when we trouped into a field to get it. We rubbed our eyes when we saw fried steaks. Who in the battery had heard of fried steaks since leaving the civil life? But it was true; and though the steaks were tough enough, never did I enjoy a meal so heartily than on that chilly evening. Fried steaks (chewed au Gladstone), white bread and hot tea – I can remember it now.

That night I slept in a clean little petrol store adjoining the large house in which the officers were billeted. In the morning I was astir early, and laying shaving materials on the window ledge of one of the apartments of the house, went to see if there was any water to be had. Returning after a short, but unsuccessful search, I was debating in my mind whether or not to ask at the house, when the latticed window was opened and a girl handed out a white enamelled pail full of hot water. On thanking her, she told me to knock on the window when I had finished washing. I did so a few minutes later, when the pail was taken in, and almost simultaneously a steaming cup of coffee and some biscuits were handed out. It seemed that I had fallen on my feet figuratively speaking; for later on returning from breakfast in the field where the cookhouse was situated, I again met the damsel of the house, who was loth to believe that I had already breakfasted, and invited me into the house for further supplies. Thinking it might be advisable, with all this kindness, to see that Mr. Clegg was preparing for a start, I went into the kitchen, where *ham and egg* had been served on the table. It was too much to resist; but even after I had finished, Mr. Clegg made it quite clear that he had no intention of going yet awhile. So another recent arrival in Mr. Bottomley took his place on the last stage of our journey. Passing through Marquise, a small market town some six miles from the coast, we reached Tardinghen – our final destination – about 2 p.m. The village was prettily situated, and from the spot on which I stood, the land sloped gently down towards the sand dunes, beyond which white horses capped the grey seas. Then the voice of John Smith, our cook, broke upon my reverie. "What the h--l do they want to stick us in a half-dead hole like this for?" he asked; "I wad raither hae been amun' the mamoselles at St. Omer." His character, I am glad to say however, refuted the sentiment he expressed, which was only his manner of giving vent to his disapproval of this 'half dead hole'.

One strange thing was borne in upon me on our arrival. Though it was broad daylight, the windows of many of the houses were already shuttered, and none of the inhabitants of the village came out to greet us. Indeed, as I arranged the billets, it seemed to me that there was an air which was not quite veiled hostility, but implied resignation to the inevitable rather than welcome to men who had gone through a considerable ordeal during those past months. We learned later that this atmosphere of distrust was not without good reason; and perhaps it was no mean tribute to the battery that within ten days of its arrival these fears and misgivings were entirely removed.

Chapter 27

By the grey sea – Tardinghen (Cape Gris-Nez)

Ships that pass in the night, and speak each other in passing – Longfellow.

Billeting was completed by three o'clock that afternoon (Saturday, 17th November, 1917), when Mr. Bottomley and I decided to go for a walk along the shore towards Cape Gris-Nez. The sky was overcast and a gale blowing; but it was fine to feel the firm sand crunch beneath our feet and to listen to the roar of the great rollers thrashing on the beach. We did not return until nearly five o'clock, by which time our main body of men had arrived and tea was ready.

The battery was billeted in barns excepting "A" sub-section, which occupied a large attic above an old house. The billets were comfortable; and as at one of the farms an unlimited supply of water was to be had – a novel experience to us in France – the whole battery washed in the mornings at this farm. The water came down from the hills and flowed continuously into large water-troughs. It was crystal-clear, and the farmer assured us we could use as much as we liked, as not even in the driest summer did the supply become scarce.

I had, of course, already interviewed some of the villagers when arranging billets; and one old lady expanded sufficiently to tell me that while no troops had been billeted in their village up to that time, the village did not want us. It seemed that at Wisant, some five miles along the coast, billeted troops had created havoc among the farm stock, killing poultry and, on one occasion, a pig. This, however, did not seem adequate cause for keeping the people indoors on our arrival, and it was not until later that I discovered the real reason for their distrust of 'foreign' soldiers.

That evening we held our first concert in the estaminet. It was presided over by Sergeant-Major Clements – a Welshman who had joined the battery when it lost "Old Toobs and Foozes" some time before. The concert was a great success; yet, perhaps with Zillebeke so fresh in our minds, there was no riotous conduct such as there had been in 1916 at Bonnay; and at 11 p.m. all ranks repaired quietly to billets. Our behaviour seemed to have been duly observed by the villagers, whose attitude towards us within the next day or two showed distinct signs of thawing. Doubtless the owners of the barns in which we were billeted had something to do with this; and so also, undoubtedly, had the proprietrix of the estaminet. A buxom, good-natured woman, she never tired of calling us 'bons garçons' after the first few days of our stay, and often refused to take payment for a glass of citron or vin rouge from Si. Arnould and myself, who seemed to have quickly established ourselves in her favour. Her husband was the sleeping partner of the business; for he invariably sat in the estaminet for the greater part of the day, either with a small glass of some strongish wine which we knew as 'Malaga', or with a large plate in front of him, full of what I took to be the remains of several chickens. These remains lay on his plate in such profusion that, as he sat with his enormous paunch threatening to overturn the small round table, he looked the picture of Henry VIII after setting accounts with his capons; and I wondered what number of chickens constituted one of his meals. Later I discovered that he went twice or thrice weekly on a 'shooting expedition', the type and method of which was worthy of its executant.

On the appointed days, he would sally forth to the back garden or 'green', at the end of which stood a low barn with a sloping roof of red tiles. The green had a large patch bereft of grass, and along this bare patch he scattered seed. He then entered the barn, in the roof of which was a ragged hole about a foot in diameter. Beneath this hole, a chair was placed inside the barn in such a way that he could sit – he was too heavy or lazy to stand – and peep through the hole into the garden below. Then taking up a double-barrelled shotgun, he poked the muzzle through the hole in the roof, and waited until thirty or forty sparrows had gathered to peck the seed scattered over the bare patch. Then with a roar that reverberated through the barn, both barrels were discharged in a wholesale massacre of hedge-sparrows. Generally his 'bag' from one shot would amount to about twenty birds, and it was the remains of these I had seen on his plate. I remember one dull afternoon when, on going into the estaminet, the old fellow only gave a grunt in reply to my greeting. Si. Arnould was sitting there, and upon my asking him what had bitten the old man, he informed me that he had that afternoon discharged both barrels of his gun at a congregation of sparrows, and by some miraculous mischance, had killed only two! So all that afternoon he sat by the stove in a gloom within and without. And an ironic fate disposed that twenty yards from his front window, erected for gun drill purposes, stood a 9.2 inch howitzer and a neat stack of shells which may have been percussion shrapnel!

On the evening of Sunday, 25th November, I was sitting in our attic billet writing home, when the battery medical orderly, Bombardier Bodley, came up saying that an excited Frenchman was outside shouting for something – he thought a doctor – would I come and see him? On going down, the man explained that he had come from an inland farm, where a boy had been cleaning a shotgun that day after returning from the dunes. An unspent cartridge had been left inadvertently in the bore, and the gun had gone off while being cleaned; one of the spreading shot wounding an old servant ("bonne") above the eye. Bodley and I drove to the farm in the dogcart brought by the farmer, to find the pellet had flattened out on the old woman's forehead, and then turned downwards toward the eye. Bodley considered it advisable to send to Fromzeele, the village at Cape Gris-Nez, where Brigade Headquarters was situated, for the Brigade doctor. As the farmer decided to stay with Bodley and the old woman (who by this time was in a semi-conscious state), his daughter undertook to drive the dogcart to Cape Gris-Nez. We set off in inky darkness for Fromzeele, arriving at 9 p.m. to find that the Brigade officers were just finishing dinner. On hearing our story, the Colonel not only directed the Brigade doctor to go at once, but insisted on accompanying him. The farm was pointed out on the Brigade map, whereupon Colonel and Doctor set off at full speed in the car, leaving us to follow in the dogcart.

The horse was now tired, and as most of the way back was uphill, we returned at a walking pace. About 10.45 p.m. we were still about a mile from the farm, when we overtook the Colonel and Doctor walking, their car having broken down on the bad road which they had taken as a short cut to the farm. The doctor climbed up into the dogcart, and the girl whipped up the horse to a trot, while the Colonel and I walked the remainder of the way. By the time we arrived, the doctor had settled the old lady for the night; and shortly afterwards he and the Colonel returned on foot to Fromzeele, which lay in a different direction from Tardinghen (the two villages and the farm forming a triangle on the map). As we had eaten nothing since four o'clock – it was now 11.30 – Bodley and I needed no second invitation to sit down to the supper prepared for us. This delayed our arrival at Tardinghen until about 1.30 next morning; on which day the old servant was removed to hospital at Marquise, where she was doing well when last we heard of her. Needless to say, the affair was the talk of the village during that day; and the old lady who had told me about the troops at Wisant, too infirm to stand gossiping out of doors in such cold weather, waylaid me in passing and invited me into her house, doubtless to get the news at first hand. Before I left, her husband escorted me to the yard and showed me the pig they intended to kill at Christmas; making me promise that, should we still be in Tardinghen then, I would join them at their Christmas dinner.

Two days later I received another, and even more intimate invitation, which once more showed to me that if evil strikes deep at the human heart, the inherent goodness of human nature goes deeper still. I had been visiting M. Routtier, the Maire of the village, when to my surprise he asked if I would like to occupy a bedroom in his house during the remainder of our stay. Permission being readily granted, I took up abode in my new quarters that night.

A strange company gathered there each evening, all the combatants on the western front being represented. Two German prisoners who worked on the farm; a wounded French corporal, the prisoners' guard; a Belgian sergeant, M. Routtier's nephew on leave; and myself, were the soldiers; while the civilians were the Maire, his wife, and their daughter Marguerite; their two grandchildren, and a few elderly farm labourers. I had assumed that Marguerite was the mother of the two children and that doubtless their father would be at the front; but in the former supposition I was wrong. The manner of finding this out was curious. One night after supper, I was standing outside the door of the farmhouse with the Belgian sergeant. He was smoking a cigarette before going off to bed; and as we stood for a few minutes looking at the stars, he said "You are fortunate, my friend, to gain the favour of my uncle." Somewhat puzzled by his words, I turned and saw by his expression that some hidden meaning lay behind the remark. So I said "Why should you say that?" He looked at me and smiled, the light from the open door making his countenance quite visible. Throwing away his cigarette, he said as he turned to go, "Demandez au gard champêtre demain: bon soir." And with that remark he left me abruptly.

When next forenoon I saw the French corporal in the field where the German prisoners were working (they had gone from the house long before I arose in the morning), I told him what the Belgian had said. And this is the story related by the French corporal, as nearly as I can remember his words: "It is not a good story. Marguerite is not the mother of the two little ones as you may have supposed. Their mother was Marguerite's sister Lucille, who lived in a large house with her husband and the children in the neighbouring village of Audinghem. The husband was an officer in the army, and after he went away to the war, Lucille and the little ones remained in the house. As the village lies on the main road to Marquise, tramps and beggars passed through it frequently; while at the time of which I speak, coloured French colonial troops were also billeted there. Lucille, somewhat afraid that the cupidity of some of these might be aroused by the general air of prosperity about the house, carefully locked the door of her bedroom each night before retiring. Her worst fears were realised; for one morning it was found that the house had been forcibly entered during the night, money stolen, and worst of all, poor Lucille had been done to death, the murderer having entered the inner room by breaking a panel of the door. A message, simply stating that his wife was seriously ill and not expected to recover, was sent to the husband. Obtaining leave, he arrived at Marquise, whence he set out on foot to complete the journey. On the way he met a man who, not knowing to whom he was speaking, recounted the whole tragedy. So far as we know the murderer has not yet been found, though locally the coloured troops were suspected, since they knew the house well through calling there for water. But the children were too young to be able to give any information. The husband returned in due course to the front, to be later reported missing, and he has now been assumed killed. The children were brought here, and have since been taken care of by their grandparents and Marguerite."

Some time later the proprietrix of the estaminet confirmed the truth of the story, and added "I tell you we were not happy to know that strange soldiers were to be sent to live in *our* village."

Marguerite, the foster-mother, was a fine girl of about twenty-four years of age, and attended the children as though they were her own, as well as looking after the cows in the byre each morning and evening. I had seldom spoken to her up to that time; but had noticed a sadness in her eyes even when she smiled. I no longer wondered why the villagers had remained behind closed doors on our arrival. And it was no less than remarkable that the Routtiers in particular could have such faith in humanity as to invite a foreign soldier to live under their roof after such an experience. Nevertheless I was treated with the very greatest kindness during my stay of over four weeks in that pleasant house among the sand-dunes.

Some of our gunners helped on the farms during the time we spent at Tardinghen; and this, combined with other factors already mentioned, finally won the complete confidence of the villagers. Andrew Garson, an Orcadian, was farmworker in chief; and if not an outstanding personality in the gun team, he was a first-class farm hand whose services, being given freely, were much in demand. He would trot off in the morning to some farm, not to be seen again until evening; when he would crawl into his billet quite happy in the recollection of "a graun' supper washed doon wi' *bocoo* cider."

The battle of Cambrai took place at this time, and of course we completely missed that experience. Not that we mourned our loss; but it was a surprise to us to learn that an attack on such a scale had been made so long after winter had set in. It left an uncomfortable sensation too that we had been 'dodging the column'. However, instead of taking part in the Cambrai attack, our Brigade held sports at Cape Gris-Nez. The field was right on top of the cliffs; and the weather, though fair, was piercingly cold. Our battery did very well, thanks in great measure to the prowess and versatility of Frank Strachan – whose knees, however, had to be massaged before each attempt in the high jump; for his joints froze in the intervals of waiting between each effort. We returned that evening full of spoils, mainly boxes of cigarettes which constituted the majority of the prizes.

Occasionally one of our transport lorries took a party of men for a day's jaunt to Wimereux or Boulogne. The drive along the coast was most enjoyable, the roads winding in and out along the cliffs; and on my first visit to Wimereux, we found that the Army Pay Corps and W.A.A.C.s were staging a splendid show. Unfortunately we had to leave at 9 p.m., when our lorry was under orders to return. Several of our men remained to the end of the performance, thereafter walking back to Tardinghen, where they arrived at 4 o'clock next morning – to parade again with the remainder of the battery at 8 a.m. On another occasion we went to Wimereux for baths. As usual, the place was packed with men, and we could not see each other for steam. I felt someone pawing about my feet, and said "Excuse me, whoever's down there; that's *my* feet you're washing." The voice of Jim Brunton replied "I'm not washing your feet: I've lost my blooming soap."

I remember, too, a splendid evening when I stood on the ramparts of Boulogne at sunset, looking down at the coastline stretching away towards Dunkirk and Ostend – a beautiful sight on that late afternoon. What, I wondered, was happening up there? And it seemed to me that whatever they were doing, they could not be enjoying life better than I was at that moment.

143

But all nights were not so calm and beautiful. One dark night when the wind howled and huge seas were breaking on the shore, I was awakened by the noise of running feet on the cobbles outside my bedroom window. The lights of many lamps flitted here and there; so I rose up, dressed hurriedly, and went out to see what was the matter. People were running past the farm gate for the shore; and following them, I found a number of villagers and several of the battery endeavouring to land the crew of a barque which had been driven ashore. Huge waves were breaking over the little ship as she lay half over on her side; but all the crew were rescued, though one old salt died from exposure before morning.

Christmas Day passed quietly; for despite the Sassenach reinforcements we were now receiving, the Scots element (which favoured Hogmanay) still led the battery in spirit if not in numbers. I had my Christmas dinner of pork and apple sauce with the old couple as promised. I ate too much, I think, for when at last I rose to go, though I had found the dinner excellent and the old couple's 'crack' most interesting, I was, paradoxically speaking, 'boar-ed' stiff!

On 31st December, 1917, we knew that a move was now imminent, and that night held a final concert in the village estaminet. I had explained to M. Routtier and the estaminet proprietrix, as well as to various other villagers, the significance of Hogmanay night for Scotsmen; and had warned them to be in no way alarmed should some of the men arrive in billets very merry. Captain Wilson arranged the detail of the evening's programme, impressing also upon us the importance of keeping as sober as possible in order that on the eve of our departure nothing should mar the reputation we now enjoyed – for indeed, long ere this, we had been completely 'spoiled' by the good folks of Tardinghen.

That night the estaminet was full to overflowing. The large room adjoining the main apartment was also packed; while to make matters worse, as many villagers as could find room squeezed in during the earlier part of the evening. Thus while the concert went famously, liquid refreshment was only to be had at very infrequent intervals owing to the crowd. At midnight the Captain brought our festivities to a close, asking the men to make quietly for their billets, which we did fairly creditably – some indeed, much more soberly than they had intended! But one gunner had evidently secured more than his fair share; and as he went staggering into the night singing lustily, I felt that if any man was entitled to drown his sorrows it was he; for the battery carpenter's time at Zillebeke had been mostly spent in making wooden crosses!

We left Tardinghen on 2nd January, 1918; and when we departed, the entire community turned out to bid us goodbye. Every man of us had his waterbottle filled with cider by some inhabitant of the village, which seemed as reluctant to see us go as it had been to welcome our coming. I said goodbye to the many friends I had made, recklessly promising that if all went well with me I should return to see them after the war. The Routtiers I had left to the last, not only because their home was down at the sand-dunes, but also because I wanted my final farewells to be made there. Even the German prisoners shook hands warmly and wished me good luck: but Marguerite was not to be seen, and as already I had exceeded my time in leave-taking, I went away, though reluctantly, without saying goodbye to her. At the bend of the road that would hide the house from my sight, I turned for a last look at the place which, during those past weeks, had been a second home to me. In the doorway of the byre stood the figure of a girl; as I looked she raised an arm in salutation, and I waved my hand in return. That was the last I ever saw of the Routtiers.

As the battery marched up the hill to the point where our transport lorries awaited us, I saw the old lady with whom I had dined on Christmas Day. She was standing by her garden gate, and I had already bidden her farewell; but on our approach she came out into the roadway, and trotting alongside, wished me 'bon chance' again and again as she grasped my hand, at the same time pressing something into it. Then murmuring some words of which I only caught 'très gentil', she went back to the gate. I opened my hand: in its palm lay a half-franc piece!

The pressure of aged fingers: the wave of an arm. Is it not a symbol of the final triumph of good over evil that the joy of such simple things still lives and brings a glow to the heart when the misery of Passchendaele is gone for ever and its fires turned to ashes – withered, cold and dead?

[21] The names of these places are doubtless of little interest to the general reader; but are given for the benefit of those members of the battery still alive, who did not then know the names of the villages we passed through, and may even now wish to follow our journeyings with the aid of a map.

Chapter 28

February fill-the-dyke — Pilkem (Ypres)

The best-laid schemes o' mice and men
Gang aft a-gley – Burns

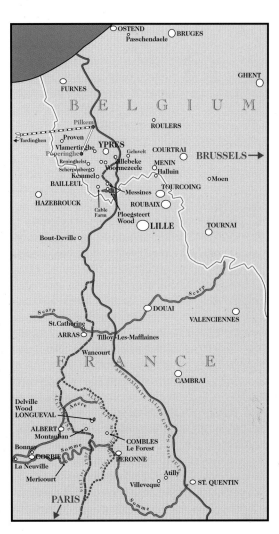

Mr. Clegg and I travelled all day by motor bicycle and side-car on 2nd January, 1918, arriving late that night at a place rejoicing in the name of Lostrat. Here we found an artist lamenting the lack of interest in pictures; but he temporarily forgot his troubles to show us billets in some outbuildings belonging to him. The men arrived at three o'clock next morning, and were not long in finding the 'lost rat'; for Bombr. Bodley (our medical orderly of all people) was badly bitten in the arm overnight, and had slight blood poisoning for some days thereafter.

We left the place at 8 a.m., and travelling via Nordasques and Tournahem[21], reached the village of Moulle shortly before midday. The battery arrived in the afternoon, and we held a concert in the Y.M.C.A. that night. Off again early next morning, we journeyed a long way to Zeggars-Capelle, where we found billets that night in barns half a mile distant from each other. On Saturday, 5th January, we arrived at Esquelbecq, where a very heavy mail awaited us. Within an hour of our arrival, snow was falling; and by

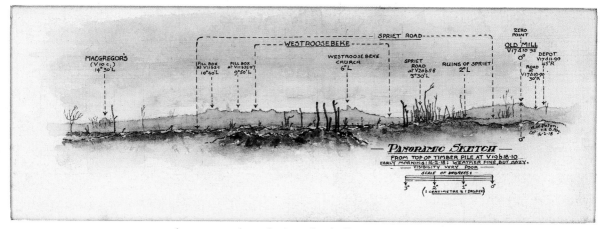

Panoramic Sketch of Westroosebeke Ridge from Poelcapelle (Ypres Sector)

evening it lay six inches deep. The billets were in three barns about a quarter of a mile distant from each other; and that night after tea (which was issued to the whole battery from the most central of the billets), the various sub-sections made their way through the deep snow to their own sleeping quarters. We were to remain a fortnight in Esquelbecq pending the arrival of new guns – it will be remembered that our guns had been handed over at Zillebeke – and during this period the snow melted and rain fell continuously, the whole land being under water, and drill, in consequence, impossible. We had lectures on gas and other military subjects, while I instructed a small gunnery class of B.C.A.s and men who might at some later date be likely to become officers. During this time, Frank Strachan and I were recommended for Officer's Commission for the third time. Third time was not lucky for me; Frank being taken while I was left. Time dragged on wearily in our leaky billets, and exactly one month after leaving Tardinghen, we departed from Esquelbecq to go into position once more in the Ypres sector.

On the night of 3rd February, 1918, we arrived in a deluge of rain at Lancashire Farm (which had been one of our front line O.P.'s when we had been at Vlamertinghe in 1916), and a day or two later pulled the guns into position at Pilkem, some three miles north of Ypres. It was interesting to us to be here, for in 1916 one of our most regular targets had been Pilkem Mill. But now there was little left of Pilkem and no sign whatever of any mill.

We had two observation posts from which we conducted our shoots at Pilkem. One was named "Arbre" O.P. (so called because on the ridge on which the O.P. was situated, there was a tree just outside the little dug-out), and one fine day shortly after our arrival at Pilkem, Major Hall instructed me to escort him up to "Arbre" to conduct a shoot. I had been there three times and knew the way, which led over a duck-board track laid across the open, (the trench system having been abandoned in this part of the sector). The countryside was, of course, shell-swept, and the recent heavy rains made our route almost impassable in places. On this particular morning, however, the rain-filled shellholes were bathed in sunshine; and as we plodded along the duckboards, Major Hall perspired freely, and every now and again gave way to an impatient grunt. The O.P. was one of those small square concrete erections named 'pillboxes' by the troops, and the Major had the greatest difficulty in squeezing himself into it. As a matter of fact, everyone else got out to let him in; and when he had entered, the subalterns who had emerged had to remain outside. But not for long: in a few minutes Major Hall crawled out asking if these "damned engineers can't build a place that will hold a decent man." Then to the consternation of the other officers (belonging to other batteries in the Brigade) he declared his intention of observing the shoot from the ridge itself, outside the O.P. He was warned that it was asking for certain trouble to do so, but retorted that he wasn't going to be cooped up like a sardine in a tin, and prepared for the shoot. Fortunately or unfortunately, the sunshine was so brilliant that afternoon that a shimmering haze made visibility difficult for both sides, and the shoot had to be abandoned, much to Major Hall's disgust – though we were preparing to make ourselves as scarce as possible, foreseeing trouble ahead had he stood there to conduct the shoot.

Our other observation post was "Tim" O.P., situated in the village of Poelcapelle. This O.P. was also a concrete 'pillbox', but of sufficiently large dimensions to hold half a dozen people quite comfortably. But Major Hall never visited it, for he was promoted Colonel and left the battery for a post at the base. He took his servant Bennet with him, and was kind enough to offer me a place on his staff if I cared to go; but though the offer of a safe billet was tempting, I preferred to remain with the old battery at least until the time, if it ever came, to go home for Commission. So once again Captain Wilson was left in command of the battery; and many were wondering why he was not made Major, since despite his youthfulness, he had been so often in command and had recently been through a Major's course. They were unaware, of course, that he had already declined the command of the battery; but I formed the impression that if it were now offered, he would accept.

Meantime, to return to "Tim" O.P.; from the slit in the 'pillbox' – which had been intended for a machine-gun post – it was impossible to see anything but the top of Westroosebeke Ridge, and we used therefore to observe from the top of a large pile of timber within a few yards of the O.P. The timber was heaped up in higgledy-piggledy fashion, and it took some time to get up to the top of the pile of wood and debris. Once there, however, the view of the enemy country was worth all the trouble. The latter consisted not so much in getting up, but in getting down when enemy shelling commenced. The Boche knew it to be used for observation purposes, and never was I on top of the woodpile without his having a go at it sometime during my vigil. I grew quite expert at scrambling down, and our signallers on duty in the 'pillbox' used jocularly to offer me odds when I went up that I wouldn't get down the next three times without a broken limb or a piece of shrapnel. Our tour of duty at "Tim" O.P. was from 6 a.m. on the one day until 6 a.m. on the next; and one night when I was there, we had a word that a raid on a large scale would be carried out by our infantry on the enemy positions in Houthoulst Forest, which lay on our left front. Zero hour was at 10 p.m., and sometime before the hour, I was lying on my stomach on top of the woodpile. Never before and only once since (sometime later among the heights of Bonnay, on the Somme) have I seen such a magnificent display of fireworks. Red, green, and yellow balls, golden-rain rockets, and white star-shells which hung poised in the sky for what seemed an almost indefinite period: and all those in such profusion that, had it not been for the stutter of machine gun fire in intervals between the boom of guns and the crackle of bursting shells, one might have wondered if anyone was left to *fight* over there in the dark. After five minutes of this gorgeous inferno, things began to quieten somewhat; and the display from Houthoulst Forest gradually resumed its normal aspect of soaring star-shells. I was just thinking of coming down, when I heard a whine develop into a shriek as a shell flew over my head and buried itself behind me at the bottom of the timber pile, throwing planks up in the air like a spilt box of Gargantuan matches. Crouching for a moment until the debris fell, I began to scramble down in the dark, shouting "coming down" in response to an anxious enquiry from the 'pillbox'. Over came another shell, this time bursting short of the timber. In my haste to get down in the dark, my leg went down a hole in the pile; and before I could extricate myself another shell flew overhead to burst somewhere behind the O.P. Helter-skelter, heedless now of broken limbs, I scrambled to terra firma and flung myself into the O.P. as the fourth shell scattered broken timber over the roof. The shelling continued for some time after this, but now we sat comfortably in the concrete shelter drinking coffee. We were relieved at 6.30 next morning; and one might have thought that the Boche knew in advance of ourselves that we should not return; for he chased us with 'pip-squeaks' and 4.2's all the way 'home' over the duckboards.

On arrival at the battery position that morning (17th February), I was informed that we had been ordered to pull out as the whole Brigade was moving to another front. We were ready by nightfall, the guns being covered up at the roadside to await the arrival of our tractors. A day or two elapsed, however, before we moved off, as some of the other batteries in the Brigade were not ready. At midday on 19th February, a German plane came over, flying very low, and engaged one of our observation planes just over our heads. We could plainly see the combatants of both planes; and after several long bursts of machine-gun fire, the German made off for his own lines. Meantime our machine went into a dangerous-looking spin, but just as we thought it would crash, it flattened out and proceeded horizontally once more. Tom Matheson (now Bombardier B.C.A. in the battery) said to me "It's all right: I thought it was done for." Then it struck me that there was something queer about it, when I suddenly realised that the wheels were *above* the fuselage. "Look! It's flying upside down," I cried. Almost as I spoke, one of the airmen fell out of the plane, and the machine went into an earthward spin. Just before it crashed, the other airman fell out, and though we were on the spot in a few moments it was all over. The one nearest us (doubtless the pilot) had been shot dead, while the other died immediately from his fall. The plane began to burn the moment it hit the ground; and ten minutes later, all that remained on the scene was a mass of charred material. This was the last incident at Pilkem, though two other items of interest come to mind in recalling that position. The first is mice.

My dug-out, in which I slept alone at night, was also the B.C. Post, and most of the space not occupied by my wired bed was taken up by the table on which the fighting-map was fixed. In previous dug-outs I had experienced rats, beetles, and even wasps; but this one was overrun by little brown field mice, who turned the night-time into an orgy of revelry, and incidentally left tokens of the same in the form of a map-table completely covered over with deposit each morning! To keep my eatables safe, I had stretched a string horizontally across the dug-out about a foot from the roof; and from the middle of this string I tied another piece vertically, at the foot of which hung my bag, containing (among other things) a small Hovis loaf sent from home. Every night witnessed a scene to delight the heart of a Walt Disney – then undreamt of – for the mice used the horizontal string in a tightrope-walking contest with presumably my loaf as the prize; and small squeals of dismay (or was it joyous excitement?) followed each little thud, as one by one they fell from the string on to my bed, and then scampered away to have another go. It was not at all unpleasant to lie awake in the dark during those revelries. As I lay with blanket tucked in over the back of my head with only nose and mouth showing, I often felt that it only wanted a string orchestra to complete the illusion of being an unseen watcher of a fairy ballet. Fairy fantasies were shattered, however on discovering one morning that a mouse had actually succeeded in getting along the horizontal string and down the vertical one into the bag, where it had eaten a nice big hole in my loaf. How he had got out again after such a repast passes my comprehension; but it is certain that he (or *she* – for that mouse possessed all the wiles of the fair sex!) must have climbed out again and up the string. That dug-out could have given overtime to a dozen cats.

Cats. That recalls the second item of interest. One day, an aeroplane flew over our position and dropped some letters, which we found were addressed to someone in Germany. "Open 'em", said Mr. Fryer to whom the matter had been referred. The letters proved to be from German prisoners in England to relations in Germany, and had possibly been dropped on the wrong side of the lines[22]. The letters were sent to Brigade Headquarters; and one of our gunners remarked that trouble might be in store for someone, as only a week previously, "Comic Cuts" (the Official Intelligence Summary) had stated that an airman had been arrested for carrying enemy letters. Another gunner present said, "That was different: the airman was a German – at least he had a German name if I remember rightly." Mr. Fryer contributed the last word to the discussion as he replied to the last speaker. "That don't signify nothing" he said. "Yew cawn't always judge by appearances – if the kitchen cat hed kittens in the oven, yew wouldn't call 'em cakes, would you?"

In the light of later events, those described in these last pages seem like an overture to the gigantic drama which immediately followed. For this chapter began in the atmosphere of a calm and peaceful journey; proceeded to fireworks, and concluded with much scurrying of mice. In the pages that now follow, unaccustomed calm preceded Boche fireworks of unprecedented magnitude, followed by scurrying on our part. But as Mr. Fryer had said, "Yew cawn't always judge by appearances"; and like the mice, we scurried off only to come up again for another attempt. For at 7 p.m. on 25th February, 1918 we left Pilkem bathed in silver moonlight as our caterpillars slowly lumbered down the road through Boesinghe and Elverdinghe to Poperinghe, there to entrain for a destination which was rumoured to be 'down south', and which eventually proved to be the scene of the annihilation of the British Fifth Army – St. Quentin.

[22] *I think letters from German prisoners may at that time have been allowed to be sent in this way as propoganda; for they contained photographs and generally indicated that the writer was better off as a prisoner than the people of Germany.*

151

(See facing page)

[23] *Described in Chapter 11 of this book.*

Chapter 29

'Down south' –
Villeveque (St. Quentin)

The place is silent and aware – Browning

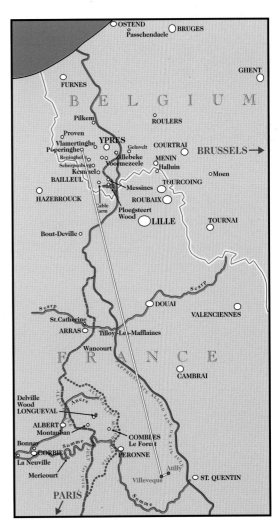

We entrained at Poperinghe at 2 a.m. on 26th February, 1918, and travelled via Wimereux, Boulogne, Etaples and Abbeville to Nesle; and thence to Ham, where we arrived in the late evening of that day. After unloading the guns, we set out on motor lorries for Croix Moligneux, where we pitched tents at midnight, and were then regaled once again with a glorious supper of fried steaks and chips. For such a meal the pangs of hunger we had felt were worth enduring, than which I can give our cooks no higher praise.

Next morning I had a look round the village, which had been burned by the Boche during his retreat in the spring of 1917[23]. The villagers were living mostly in wooden huts, only the charred walls of their former homes now remaining. They would not attempt to rebuild; for as one of them said: "They were burned down in 1914, and rebuilt in 1915: the Germans burned them again in 1917; and who knows but that they may again be in occupation" – an unhappy fear that was to be realised before many more weeks had passed.

153

That night I went forward to a switch road just beyond the hamlet of Villeveque, six miles west of St. Quentin, where we worked all night in the pouring rain preparing our new position. Next day dawned under similar weather conditions; but we had the consolation of knowing that the rain allowed us to pull in the guns without hostile planes spotting the unusual activity in that quiet little by-road. Four of our guns were mounted here, the remaining two being sent forward to a small quarry at Attilly, two miles east of Villeveque. On Saturday, 2nd March, the weather changed from rain to snow; and as we had then no dug-outs made, we felt pretty miserable in our greatcoats, which were like blotting paper and laden with rain. Captain Wilson came to instruct me to accompany him to the forward position at Attilly; and I observed that instead of the three 'pips' on his sleeve, he now wore the crown. He was Major of the battery at last, and his appointment gave great satisfaction to the battery, particularly to those who had been with him since he had been a 2nd. Lieutenant in "B" sub-section.

From 6th March we had a long spell of glorious weather. There was no gun activity, and up the line we learned that the infantry even played football between the lines without a shot being fired. We also heard rumours of a great Boche offensive to be launched very soon, but were told that Headquarters knew all about it, and that we had 'silent batteries' – i.e. batteries in position, but not firing a shot in order that there would be no chance of their existence becoming known to the enemy – cleverly concealed all over the countryside. We had an O.P. near the village of Savy; and as Major Wilson and I trekked across the field to this O.P., we chuckled as we thought how cleverly our batteries were concealed; for in all our visits to Savy (a long way from our gun position) we only saw one battery position, and that we did not observe until one day we chanced to turn round after we had passed, and found ourselves looking down a gun muzzle ten yards distant. It was only later that we realised that the real reason we saw so few battery positions was not that they were so cleverly concealed, but that they were so few and far between. On those sunny mornings, however, we trudged happily across the field, our puttees encased in silver from spiders' webs spun in the long grass, and talked of the surprise awaiting the Boche when he should attack.

Day now followed day of glorious weather; no shelling whatever; games of football every evening in the valley behind our position, and regular, good meals: life was great! Once more my commission papers were completed and sent to Headquarters, though just then I was perfectly happy where I was. One day would be spent at our forward position at Attilly (where Tom Matheson and Balchin were the duty B.C.A.s; Nick Carter and myself being the B.C.A.s in Villeveque); another at the O.P. near Savy; and best of all perhaps, the days spent in a 'crow's nest' build in the topmost branches of a tree in Holnon Wood on the crest of the ridge beyond Attilly. We had a beautiful O.P. there, and when the initial sensation of sickness had been overcome (for the little platform on which one lay swayed about with the branches at the least breath of wind), the view was magnificent. The wood in front sloped steeply down with the village of Francilly-Selency lying directly below, just inside the German lines; while seemingly just beyond it lay the city of St. Quentin. As in the case of Bapaume in 1916, we were not allowed to shell the place, orders being that the city was not to be damaged. So as I lay on my stomach among the tree-tops during those sunny afternoon, I gazed down into the streets of St. Quentin to see Boche decauville trains puffing along, bringing in ammunition galore without the slightest interference from us. The only excitement we had was when the Boche dropped a lone shell into the quarry, to give Tom Matheson and Balchin something by which to remember that there was a war on; and again when our wireless operators, on going one morning to complete a dug-out in progress, found two escaped German prisoners sleeping soundly in it.

On the morning of 20th March, I was instructed by telegram to report next day at Headquarters for an interview with the General in regard to my Commission. We had been informed that the Boche attack would commence on that day, so I hoped he would be obliging enough to postpone it until I had been interviewed. At midday on the 20th we received a few reinforcements just out from England, and in France for the first time. They were very young lads, and all I remember of them now was that the last two in the batch were named respectively Parsley and Raspberry! We had been feeding very well of late; but as one of the officers remarked, we hardly expected the Olympians to send us out fresh vegetables and fruit! That afternoon, I went up to the observation post in Holnon Wood. It was a glorious day of sunshine, and as I made my way across country, I felt in great spirits. Reaching the 'crow's nest' in the trees, I stretched myself out on the wooden platform to see what brother Boche was at. Nothing doing immediately below me – the hamlet of Francilly-Selency was silent as a Scottish Sabbath. Raising my glasses to St. Quentin, however, a different spectacle was presented. German activity seemed greater than ever; trains of stores or ammunition coming in a various points, with men moving hither and thither busily preparing. I was not particularly alarmed; feeling rather that if, as seemed probable, the attack came next day, a warm welcome would await it. So I lay watching interestedly; then from somewhere in rear below me, I heard music. Turning round to look down the other side of the crest – the way in which I had come – I could just discern through the trees far below, a circular group of bandsmen, looking at that distance like toy soldiers. They were playing Gounod's "Marche Romaine"; and as the notes of that stately processional floated upwards to where I lay, I was far from thinking that in a few days' time, we ourselves should be taking part in a march which might be considered processional, but could hardly be deemed stately.

Leaving the O.P. in the early evening, I called at our forward position in Attilly Quarry. While there, the Boche put over some very heavy shells, which, clearing the quarry, fell somewhere about the road by which I should go down to our position at Villeveque. I left Attilly about 8 p.m., and reaching the road, had not gone far when I came across two huge shellholes right on the road and so close together that they practically overlapped. They made one huge cavity roughly fifteen feet deep and thirty feet across, rendering the road impassable for any kind of transport. This boded ill should we require to evacuate our forward position (which we understood was to be done in certain circumstances); for our caterpillars would be unable to get near the quarry to pull the guns out. This I reported on arriving at Villeveque, when the news was passed to Headquarters; but all we could do was to hope that if the Boche attacked on the morrow, we should hold our ground intact. If not, we should certainly lose both our forward guns; for, as previously explained, the 9.2 inch howitzers cannot be wheeled out of position like 6 or even 8 inch hows., but are mounted on fixed platforms and take from six to eight hours to dismantle for a move. Then the gun, carriage and bedplate are mounted separately on wheels and hauled away by the powerful tractors or caterpillars.

Before turning in that night, our guns at Villeveque were 'layed' on our S.O.S. lines. We were in the battle zone of the eighteenth Corps of the Fifth Army, and our guns covered the ground in front of the 30th and 61st Divisions of our infantry. Opposite those two Divisions were no less than five German Divisions in the forward zone and four more immediately in reserve[24]. But our two infantry Divisions hoped to hold all nine of the Boche if necessary.

Late that night, Major Wilson informed me that Headquarters fully expected the attack to be launched at dawn next morning – information from prisoners giving the exact time as 4.45 a.m. – and that I should require to work out the weather corrections for the guns at 3.45 a.m. I rose next morning at 3.40, and made my way to the B.C. Post[25]. It was still pitch dark, and the countryside was silent as the grave. I stood for a moment and listened, but not a sound was to be heard. Major Wilson was awake when I reached the B.C. Post; and about half an hour later, on going out with the corrected lines of fire, I could just make out the forms of the gunners as they flitted about the guns.

The stage was set, and we now only awaited the Boche to bring up the curtain.

[24] *I am no historian, but think it right to give these facts here. Anyone sufficiently interested may see these dispositions clearly marked on Sketch Map 17 of General Gough's "Fifth Army" (facing page 258).*

[25] *[Handwritten note] On returning to my dug-out next morning to get my belongings, I found the place a shambles. The Germans had got a direct hit upon it, and I lost greatcoat and the belongings left there, including the sketches made from the time we left Zillebeke. My diary, however, still rested safely in the large inside pocket of my tunic.*

Chapter 30

The onslaught –
Attilly and Villeveque (St. Quentin)

*The storm is up, and all is on the hazard –
Shakespeare*

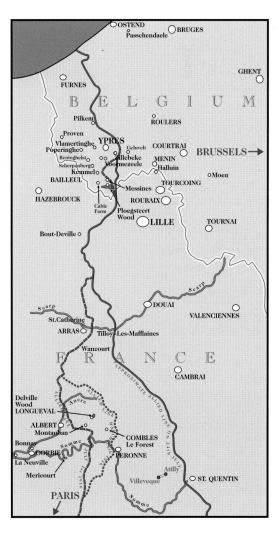

During those minutes before 4.40 on that morning of Thursday, 21st March, 1918, our gunners stood at their posts ready to open fire the moment orders were given. During that pause, we felt instinctively that the attack *was* going to take place. Dead silence reigned; for the guns were loaded and elevated, muzzles pointing skywards; while as many shells as it was safe to fuze were lying ready behind each gun. We waited in quiet expectation.

Nor did we wait in vain; for precisely at a quarter to five the whining of shells commenced simultaneously from all directions. None fell just then in our vicinity; but continuous 'crumps' in the middle and far distance, accompanied by faint though incessant flashes, announced that the great Boche offensive had begun.

A long tongue of flame split the immediate darkness as our own first shell sped screaming towards the German lines; followed in quick succession by another; another; and yet another. Listening to the roar of the bombardment (my own work for the moment was finished), it seemed to me that the 'crumping' of German

157

shells far exceeded the 'boom' of our gunfire; but soon we were too busy to give thought to such matters, message after message coming in from Brigade Headquarters. Strangely enough, one of these was postponing my visit to the General; and it seemed, even to me then, that there was a touch of comedy in the fact that H.Q. had remembered the matter at this juncture – I had forgotten it myself that morning!

The darkness gradually dispelled as day broke; but daylight revealed no visible thing. White mist enveloped the landscape so that we could only see a few yards in front of us. It seemed that nature had added her forces to the already heavy odds against us; for in our forward zone, the defence system no longer consisted of deep trenches manned at every point. Instead, the country lay open except for the barbed wire entanglement – doubtless already cut to pieces by the Boche barrage – and the main defence consisted of 'pillboxes' erected at intervals, the area between each being covered by machine-gun fire. The main condition for such a defence was that our infantry should be able to locate the enemy. The mist made this impossible.

Our telephone line to Savy O.P. was broken, and our signallers there cut off both from Headquarters and the battery. In any case, the thick mist made observation out of the question and we fired all morning on previously registered targets. In the forenoon the sun broke through, and visibility became better. Then low-flying enemy planes came over and circled undisturbed above the battery position. Doubtless our own planes had more urgent business on hand than to engage enemy aircraft; and the Boche leisurely surveyed our activities – we could not, of course, cease fire – and then flew off towards the German lines. We knew that there would be some further excitement for us before long. Ten minutes later, a slow bombardment on the battery position was commenced by a German battery of howitzers firing 11.1 inch armour-piercing shells. The terrifying roar of their approach, the tremor of the ground under our feet as they thudded deep into the earth before exploding, and the spume of tons of soil thrown skywards and falling among us, we must have been appalling to our new young gunners. The more experienced men realised, however, that it would have been much worse had the Boche used instantaneous, rather than delayed, fuzes on those shells. For as it was, it required practically a direct hit on the gun to annihilate both it and its team; and though directed by aeroplane, that direct hit was not obtained. But had instantaneous fuzes been used, pieces of shell would have been scattered far and wide and while the guns would not have been completely destroyed thereby, it is not too much to say that the battery personnel would have been completely wiped out that day.

Later in the afternoon, the hostile shelling was augmented by time-fuzed high explosive, presumably to catch the personnel of the battery; but this burst too high above our heads to do any serious damage. Things quietened down towards evening; but we knew little of how the battle had gone. Nor, apparently, did Brigade; but later in the evening we ceased fire – greatly to our surprise. No one thought of sleep: the men stood round the guns ready to resume at a moment's notice. Every rumour that came through was eagerly debated; but until very late that night, both officers and men were metaphorically as well as literally in the dark. Only one thing seemed generally agreed upon: since we were still in Villeveque, and (so far as we knew) the forward position at Attilly had not been abandoned, the enemy must have fallen far short of his objectives on that first day.

Rumours, of course, were rife. One said that the Boche was completely foiled and had made no headway whatever – that we had been ordered to cease fire lent colour to this report; another said he had walked right through our infantry posts in the mist without being seen, and had reached Marteville. This was a village about a mile and a half from Villeveque; and actually lay between us and our forward position at Attilly, though not in a direct line. If the Germans had advanced to any point in the vicinity of Marteville, then what had happened to our two forward guns? We were not kept much longer in suspense; for before midnight our forward detachment arrived, bringing with them the breechblocks of the guns, which had been 'spiked' and rendered useless (by order of Brigade), when the men had been instructed to evacuate the position. Our gunners stated that the Boche had walked through our forward posts before we knew he was there, and that he had reached Maissemy, almost due north of Villeveque[26]. If this were true, our present position would very soon become untenable, as by a flanking movement, on the enemy's part, he could reach us in a few hours. But we could hardly believe it; for later the night became so quiet that the men eventually lay down and slept round the guns until dawn on the 22nd.

That day (Friday, 22nd March) was a memorable one for the battery. Shortly after dawn – another misty morning with the promise of a fine day: how did the Germans choose the right time for weather while we invariably launched our attacks in rain? – we were informed by Brigade that the Germans were now advancing on Marteville; and as our signallers were still at Savy, the Major realised they must be warned to clear out at once if they had not already done so. No officer could be spared, and Nick Carter and I were the only two who knew the way to the O.P. My offer to go was also turned down, as I was needed at the battery, but Nick had volunteered too; and although we had no idea what point had been reached by the Germans in that direction, off he went after cutting a cudgel to lean on – if, as he whimsically remarked, "I should cop a nice little blighty one."

The next item was a resumption, without aeroplane this time, of the systematic bombardment of our position. We were firing without cessation on Manchester Hill, (where, though we did not then know it, the 16th Manchesters under Colonel Elstob had held out on the previous afternoon until every officer and man had been killed)[27], while at half minute intervals, the Boche dropped an eleven inch shell into us.

Between 9 and 10 a.m. we received our last message from Brigade Headquarters, which was situated on the main Marteville road slightly north of Villeveque. It was to the effect that they were evacuating, and that we were to continue firing as long as we had ammunition, if it were possible to do so without allowing our guns to fall intact into the hands of the enemy. We were then to render the guns useless; endeavour to make for Voyennes, and join the Brigade there. Losing touch with Brigade was a blow; but our job was clear enough. We continued firing for another hour; then our infantry (the 9th Royal Scots) who had been lying out somewhere in front of us) came into sight. A few minutes later, they had passed through behind our guns in orderly retreat; and crossing the valley in rear of our position, hastily

[26] *This was actually the case (see p.271 of General Gough's "Fifth Army"); though it was only one of three breaches made in our battle zone that day.*

[27] *Colonel Elstob was posthumously awarded the V.C. for this gallant stand.*

159

prepared to dig themselves in on the high ridge beyond. One of their officers advised Major Wilson to retire then, as none of our infantry now remained between us and the oncoming Germans. The Major, however, decided to fire off the remaining shells, and placed outposts on each flank of the battery with injunctions to return and warn us immediately the Boche was sighted, lest our retreat be cut off. Meantime we continued firing at about a thousand yards range.

Shortly before midday, Nick Carter reappeared, limping and leaning heavily on his cudgel. He had managed to reach the village of Etreillers (about a half mile from the Savy O.P.), but could get not further by reason of the barrage. Several times as shelling lessened, he had tried to get through, and eventually was hit in the leg by a shell splinter. Then the barrage lengthening, he had found himself no longer on the edge of it, and it had been with the greatest good luck that he had got back at all. (As a matter of fact, while Nick had been trying to reach the O.P., the signallers had got safely away with the exception of Gunner Allen, who was captured).

About 1 p.m. – fully an hour after the Royal Scots had taken up their new position – the Major ordered us to 'spike' the guns. Our last remaining rounds were fired point blank over open sights at the copse six hundred yards in front of us, where we suspected the presence of advance parties of the enemy; and splinters from our own shellbursts were falling round about us, as we were using instantaneous fuzes. The gunners, with the exception of the outposts and a party of twenty-odd men under Sergeant Mentiplay left to render the guns useless, were then sent across the valley to the ridge, there to await our coming, or make their own way to Voyennes if we did not appear.

The Major, of course, was with the rearguard party at the guns. At No.1 gun, several of the gun team were busy destroying the rifling of the breech. One fuzed shell was then jammed tightly into it, while the breech-lock was carried down to the valley and buried by two of the gun detachment. One shell only was left lying fuzed on the ground beside the gun, and only Si. Arnould, Jim Brunton and Bob Baxter were left there. We four lifted the shell and laid it carefully on top of the earth-box in front of the gun muzzle. Then, waiting until the next shell had burst, we climbed up on the earth-box, again raised the shell, and prepared to insert it down the gun – nose first. The slightest touch of that instantaneous fuze on the gun muzzle and the shell would explode. So we handled the thing very gingerly as we began to insert it into the gun. Then we heard another armour-piercing shell coming for us. "Steady", said Arnould quietly, "hold it." The sound of Si.'s calm voice steadied us, and we held the shell until the huge chunks of earth and debris had fallen. Fortunately, none of it touched that fuze, and before the next shell was heard on the way, ours was safely in the bore of the gun. But those seconds in which we held that shell and waited for the other to burst – we knew not where, except that it would be too near for our liking – are the longest I have ever experienced! The spiking of the guns was now almost complete, the last moments being occupied in abstracting bolts and nuts; thus loosening the various pieces, and rendering the guns not only useless but extremely dangerous even to touch, unless by experts.

Then the outpost on our northern flank came running in with the news that advance cyclists of the enemy could be seen on the road below, working round behind us. At the same time, looking straight in front, we could plainly see the sunlight glistening on the Boche helmets as (now that our shellfire had ceased) they emerged from the copse six hundred years away. It was not place for weaponless men! We hurriedly descended into the valley, and climbing up the slope on the other side, passed through the line of Royal Scots who were lying in a shallow trench on the crest, ready once more to delay the advancing horde. Reaching the road behind them, we passed another Company of Royal Scots spread along the edge of the grass. One grimy figure waved to me as we passed, and shouted "Hello." I gave an answering shout and a wave of the hand, though I did not recognise the figure.

Then I observed that some twenty yards off, two of our own small party were carrying between them what looked like a shallow box of gun stores. Overtaking them, I found that they were lugging along a large pan of bully-beef stew which had long since become cold, and now lay, a congealed mess, in the iron tray. "What are you going to do with that?", I asked. "Aw, we rescued it frae the cookhouse as we skidadled," was the reply: "we werna' gaun tae leave *that* tae Jerry."

I had gone down into the valley somewhat despondent, the thought of ultimate defeat working in my mind. But now my spirits rose. For in that moment when things looked black against us, I had a strange feeling that this army of incorrigibles, though presently down in the fight, was not yet out, and would rise even at the count of nine.

Nine. Why, that was our own unit's 'lucky' number, and over it stood – the crown!

161

Chapter 31

In retreat – St. Quentin to Moreuil (Spring, 1918)

The fack can't no longer be disgised that a Krysis is onto us – Artemus Ward

Our little party with the Major at its head now began to make its way to Voyennes, as Brigade had instructed in its last message. We had only gone a few hundred yards, when two German planes came over, flying very low. One circled before reaching us, and seemed to be hovering over a road a quarter of a mile off; the other made straight for the road we were on. Wheeling as he passed, the airman swooped down upon us, loosing a drum of machine-gun bullets as he sped along over our heads.

We scattered and made for the slight shelter afforded by a clump of trees at the roadside, where we were joined by three of the 5th Gordon Highlanders, armed with rifles. As the plane again passed just over the trees firing as it went, the Gordons began potting at it, but as was only to be expected, without any apparent effect. Again with a roar and a hail of bullets, the machine swept past. Then once more it circled – much wider this time, and banking steeply, the airman flattened out his machine and came straight for us, so low now that we began to think he was about to try and fly *under* the trees. As we watched wondering, the solution became evident: the plane was landing. It ran along the ground and came to stop not thirty yards from where we stood. For a moment I though he was about to machine gun us from the ground. The airman, however, stood up in the cockpit of the machine, raised both hands, then began to climb out. We made for him as he came running hatless towards us with his hands up, and took him prisoner. Then I went across to the plane, which our sergeant-major was examining. It was a single-seater Albatross fighter, and contained neither maps nor papers of any kind. Nor at first was the reason for his landing apparent. Further examination, however, revealed that a bullet fired by one of the Gordons had gone clean through the petrol tank of the machine and emptied it. A lucky hit indeed, but rank bad luck for that German.

Resuming our way, our next incident was to be accosted by a mounted red-tabbed Staff officer, who wanted to know who we were, and whither we were going. On being informed by the Major, he said "Well, get going. The Boche is round you on both sides; and if you don't hurry, you'll find yourselves closed in." And with that, he was off at a gallop. We continued our journey as fast as we could, but darkness had fallen long before we reached Voyennes (which would be about nine miles from Villeveque). The sky, however, was luridly lit in many places by our blazing aircraft hangars and army huts, which had doubtless been fired to prevent their use by the enemy.

At Voyennes, we found the remainder of the battery preparing to get some sleep in an old billet. I thought myself fortunate in obtaining a wooden frame over which wire netting had been spread; and though it sagged badly in the middle, Tom Matheson and I shared it. We lay down in our greatcoats about midnight, as there seemed no immediate cause for alarm; but I had forgotten that Tom was a stout lad in more than one sense, and when I awoke some four hours later, I felt that I had been stretched along the wooden bar all night. At five o'clock that morning (Saturday, 23rd March), I was glad to get up for a rest; and shortly afterwards wandered into an abandoned provision shop for something to eat. Already a fair number were inside on the same quest; and as we ambled round, fresh arrivals soon made moving space very limited. Several cases already opened and containing eggs had been propped slantwise against the wall inside the shop; and just as I was making my way to the door with an egg in each hand, I heard a crash. An infantryman, jostled in the crowded shop, had fallen backwards into a case of eggs; and on extricating himself, carried away more egg on the seat of his trousers than he was likely to consume for some time to come. Then Garson, our Orcadian, accosted me with a full tin of something which he thought might be good to carry away for later consumption; could I tell him what was in it? When I informed him it was dried green peas, his language might well have torn the label. By the roadside, the sight was amazing. Everybody seemed to be kindling or searching for wood to kindle – fires and frying eggs in mess-tins; but this came to a sudden end when a stentorian shout of "Hi!" from our sergeant-major was followed by orders to be on the move within five minutes.

We left Voyennes before 7 a.m., and as we crossed the bridge over the river, our engineers were setting the fuzes to blow it up on the German approach. We trekked along for several hours, the heat of the sun becoming oppressive as the forenoon advanced, (for we carried our greatcoats, our only

164

cover at night since we had lost everything we had possessed), and at last we halted by the roadside near Nesle. Everybody was parched with thirst, but no one had water and only a few had any cider. Andrew Garson, however, after discarding his tin of dried peas, had apparently decided to take a bottle of citron; and this he had carried all the way from Voyennes; but this syrupy fluid requires to be diluted with water to thin it down to a drinkable state. Garson, hugging his bottle and perspiring freely, trudged on up the road looking for water while we rested; but his search proving unsuccessful, he returned, and wiping his clammy forehead, said, "Och, tae hell; I'm that thirsty I'll hae a drink o' it 'ithoot watter." He then broke off the neck of the bottle against a fence-post, and holding his head well back to allow the thick fluid to run more freely, he turned the bottle upside down and let the liquid flow into his wide-open mouth. Then spluttering and coughing, he spat out what he had not swallowed, threw the bottle over the fence, and cursed long and fluently. It was castor oil!

We arrived at Nesle about midday and sat down to rest in some billets which were reached through a courtyard off the main street. Ten minutes later there was a terrific commotion outside, and someone came running in to say that a Staff officer had just galloped through the town from the German side, shouting that the Boche cavalry had broken through and was now upon us. We were to save ourselves as we could. I ran out into the courtyard. A motor-lorry was standing, someone in front at the starting-handle. He got the engine running, but never got on the lorry; for the driver nearly ran him down as he drove out of the courtyard like mad. Whether he wanted to save the lorry or his skin will never be known; but a temporary panic ensued, men hanging on and climbing in over the tailboard of the lorry as it went, like bees over a honeycomb. The street was full of running men, and I hurried back to warn our officers, who were in a room of an outbuilding behind the courtyard. All had their boots off for the first time in three days; but at the news (of which they were up to then blissfully unaware) they speedily put them on again. The Major, with some men whom he managed to gather, took a short cut across country; where on the roadside half a mile beyond a little town, he formed up those of the battery with him and any stragglers who came along. I found myself somehow left behind in the courtyard along with Lieut. Gough – a bloodthirsty, but stout-hearted little officer who had joined us at Zillebeke in the previous autumn. "Come on, Paton," he said. "We'll see where the Boche is." I had no particular desire to look for Boches at that moment – we were having trouble enough without looking for it, I thought – but Gough led the way to a ridge beyond the town in the direction from which the Boche would come. We each picked up a rifle en route (any number were lying about just then); and as we lay down under cover of a hedge, Mr. Gough handed me a single clip of cartridges, and said, "We can see them coming from here, and can easily knock out a few of the blighters before we hand in our own checks." I don't know whether or not Gough felt courageous in these moments: I certainly did not. On the other hand, my sensations were not those of fear. Rather were they a mixture of resentment, desperation and obstinacy; and I determined that I would not be shot like a rabbit without first giving a decent account of myself. So we waited, and had I seen a German then, I should have killed him without a qualm – the only time I can remember feeling active enmity to the Boche as an individual. But we could see no Boche to kill, though we lay there for the best part of half an hour. No one was visible in front; but away far in rear, we could see a line of figures drawn up on what looked like a road. We decided to find out who they were; and as we drew nearer, recognised Major Wilson and that party of men already mentioned. Mr. Gough then informed the Major that we had seen no sign of the enemy, and that he and I were going back into Nesle to ascertain whether or not the Germans had arrived. This was news to me, for I had not been asked if I would go – Gough was getting too uppish! Major Wilson, however, would not agree that only two should go, and called for six volunteers. These were obtained without any difficulty; and each securing a loaded rifle, the party set off. It seemed a serious enough matter to us then; but looking back on it now, the whole episode was comedy. Yet Balchin often said later, that the most impressive moment he experienced in Flanders was then, when by the roadside before setting off, I handed him a field postcard with my home address on it. Neither of us spoke – he understood.

The incident which my own memory retains of that episode was very different. Jock Isaacs, who was one of the six volunteers, was sneaking through the woods with rifle ready for emergencies. Gough halted us every few minutes; and during one of those momentary pauses to listen, Isaacs turned round and observed behind him another battery's sergeant-major, the muzzle of whose rifle was within an inch of the small of John's back. In these moments all ranks were equal; for John stretched forward his hand, jammed on the safety-catch of the sergeant-major's rifle, and in Fifeshire accents said angrily, "Here, you; if *Ah'm* gaun tae be shot, it'll be i' the belly, no' the backside." When eventually we crept into the little town, not a soul could be seen. We decided to explore in different directions; Gough going towards the Square, and myself up to the end of the main street. At the far end of the latter, a small party of infantry was lying down behind a barricade of piled up furniture. There we hung on for some time; but still there was no sign of the Boche. The only arrivals were the Major and his party, who having heard nothing and becoming tired of waiting for our return, had come to find out the position for themselves.

So ended the one incident of panic experienced during the entire period of the retreat. Whether or not it was true that a Staff officer (real, or a German spy) had galloped through Nesle, we were never able to ascertain with certainty. But by that evening all was normal, and we lay down and slept all night. Next morning (Sunday, 24th March), it seemed that the situation was more firmly in hand; for once more we came under orders of Brigade, and except for the two days previous, we were never out of touch with Headquarters during the retreat.

We left Nesle at 7 a.m., as the Boche advance had now really reached the vicinity. It was held up until eleven o'clock that forenoon, when the last of our infantry retired and the Germans entered. Meantime we had marched westwards, and at midday reached the hamlet of Rethonvillers, where we loaded up six inch shells for later use by our howitzers in delaying the Boche advance. Then westwards again; and in the late evening we reached a village name Carrepuis, where we lay down to rest in a large Nissen hut. Harris was nearest the entrance; and shortly after we lay down, the door was suddenly opened by a shadowy form armed with a rifle. There was some stamping of horses' hooves and a hum of voices that were certainly not British – and surely that helmet silhouetted against the sky in the doorway was not British either. Then the voice of Harris said resignedly: "It's all up this time, chaps. Here they are." But the intruders proved to be a small detachment of French cavalry going up the line, the first sign of reinforcements we had seen. It had been a day of excursions and false alarms; but at last we slept.

Leaving Carrepuis next morning (Monday, 25th March), we arrived some hours later at a place which looked strangely familiar. It was Rethonvillers, which we had left twenty-four hours previously! We sat down in a large barn, and five minutes later, the sergeant-major put his head round the door and yelled "Hi! come on: you've to clear out at once." We were beginning to feel that our Welsh sergeant-major was too like the shepherd boy in the fable, crying "Wolf, wolf"; but off we went once more, and by early evening were once again in Carrepuis – for what reason we did not know, except that it was in accordance with Brigade orders. We sat down by the roadside; some for a rest, others making themselves comfortable to be ready for another trek. I took off my boots and puttees, and reversed my socks for the second time that day. (This plan resulted in my having no foot trouble whatever; although at this time I wore the same pair of socks for six weeks, during which period we covered nearly a hundred and fifty miles, mostly on foot). The while searching for water, I saw Jim Brunton shaving in a cup of the purest water I had seen for some time. It was surprising enough to see him shaving; but water was scarcer even than cider. "Goodness, Jim", I cried, "water must be plentiful here; where did you get it?" He grinned under the lather as he replied "It isn't water: it's white wine!"

202 Siege Battery were now going into action at Carrepuis with the six inch howitzers for which we had loaded up the ammunition; and some of our gunners manned their guns to give their reduced personnel some help. Orders came to move soon afterwards, however, and shortly before midnight we reached the town of Roye. At six o'clock next morning (Tuesday, 26th March), we were again roused by the sergeant-major's "Hi!", and ordered to clear out at once. The road was already packed with westward-bound traffic, including wagon transport with wounded and nurses being hurriedly removed from the hospital in Roye. We reached some huts at Faverolles (nine miles west of Roye) before noon, and had breakfast at 1 p.m. We remained there until 11 p.m., when we stood by to shift. It was four o'clock next morning (Wednesday, 27th March) before we left, when we travelled west through Montdidier; and then turning northwards, crossed the river Avre. We stopped at Aubvillers (a village some twelve miles from our starting-point that morning); but were ordered on the move again immediately. Then we marched north-east and recrossed the Avre at La Neuville, where it was reported that the Boche had overtaken us. He we were issued with rifles and lay down with a nondescript lot of units of all kinds behind the crest of a hill. It was a relief to feel we were now going to be of some use: but after an hour of lying there without firing a shot, infantry reinforcements of some kind arrived, and we were ordered to hand over our rifles; and once more we became 'nobody's darlings'. Evening found us on the road near Mailly, when we were told to make ourselves as comfortable as we could for the night in a

field. Fortunately for us, the weather still remained good; and more fortunately still, we espied a huge stack of straw, and pulled down enough to make our beds very warm and comfortable that night.

Some French infantry passed along; and finding that we were 'Ecossais', one of them handed over a bundle of photographs which he had found some days previously on the battlefield. To my amazement, the photos. were of the family of one of the Elders of my own church in Edinburgh. I knew that three sons were in France, and could only guess that the photographs had belonged to one of them. It was a strange coincidence that they should be handed to me then[28].

We resumed our way northwards on the morning of Thursday, 28th March, to Moreuil, a small town on the river Avre, which we had been crossing and re-crossing since leaving Montdidier on the previous morning. Entering Moreuil about 4 p.m., we began immediately to explore the possibilities of an old laundry as a billet while we waited in the hope of the cooks producing some tea. Alas! our hopes were shattered by the voice of 'Hi, you' – the men had now bestowed this decoration on our sergeant-major – calling his sheep; and once more we were on the road, a French 75 mm. battery barking defiance at the Boche from the roadside as we went. As at Roye, the road was packed with traffic; but with one difference. Here the congestion was even worse than at Roye, but the situation was better; for the traffic was moving *both ways*. Stray units like ourselves, unarmed, were going down the line to re-form and re-arm; while French civilians – the more fortunate leaving horse-drawn haycarts laden with their belongings, were also going westwards. But on the same road, infantry, ammunition transport, and batteries of field guns were going *up* the line. It was a heartening sight, even if we were taking no part in it; for it indicated not only that the German advance had been slowed up and possible stayed, but that we were preparing to strike back. We began to think that the retreat was perhaps all part of a big plan, whereby the Boche was to be allowed to advance far enough for the Allies to cut off the entire advancing armies by a huge 'pincers' movement.

And here we were, taking no part in it: just wandering, apparently without much object and without means of defence or attack, all over the country. Ah, well: 'San Fairy Ann': our turn would come again soon enough probably. But the sight of those field guns going up had put new heart into us; and as we left the main road to find ourselves no longer accompanied either by other units or civilians, some voices among us were heard in a snatch of song. In a few minutes it had passed down the ranks, and soon all had joined in the chorus, the words of which floated on the sultry evening air with startling appropriateness:-

> We are Fred Karno's army,
> The ragtime battery:
> We cannot fight, we cannot shoot,
> No b----y good are we!
> And when we get to Berlin,
> The Kaiser he will say,
> Hoch, hoch, mein Gott,
> What a ruddy rotten lot
> You've got – in the R.G.A.

[28] *Some weeks after this, when our battery had been re-formed and mails were resumed, I sent these photographs home explaining how they had come into my possession. After discreet enquiries had been made, I received a reply that the youngest serving son had been wounded near St. Quentin, and was in hospital at the time of writing. The photographs were his; and he had already informed his father that half an hour before he was wounded, he had seen and waved to me as his Company of the Royal Scots lay waiting for the Germans. It was he whom I had passed at Villeveque.*

168

Chapter 32

The end of the retreat – Moreuil to Wanel (Spring, 1918)

...smiles that fade in tears,
Like stars half-quenched in the mists of silver dew – Shelley

The long spell of fine weather now showed signs of coming to an end, the evening being very dull and sultry. As darkness gathered, rain began to fall in a steady drizzle, and our song faded away. We plodded on with heads bent; but after three hours we appeared to be no nearer our destination. The narrow road along which we now squelched led on interminably, and at last we realised that we had lost our way. So we sat down at the roadside in the rain to await some passer-by who might be able to direct us to the village of Estrées. There we remained in a continuous downpour for the best part of an hour before there was any sign of a traveller. Then a small light appeared coming in our direction; and soon we were able to guess that a cyclist was approaching. The sergeant-major said cheerfully, "This looks like a bicycle, boys: now we'll soon know where we are." The rider drew rapidly nearer; and as he reached us, the sergeant-major stepped into the road to hail him. "Hi, you", he called out, giving his customary terse salutation; upon hearing which, the cyclist instead of dismounting, hurled the equally terse reply, "Bollocks", and rapidly vanished into the darkness, leaving our sergeant-major standing open-mouthed in the middle of the road. Laughter loud and long, in which the sergeant-major himself joined, reigned for some minutes; but on this occasion the S.M. had the last word, for on returning to the edge of the road, he grinned and remarked to me simply, "Well, that lets us know where *I* am, anyway." That was the last occasion on which we heard him call "Hi, you."

Though now mud-caked and soaked through, it was a good-humoured party that resumed its journey in the direction taken by the cyclist; and this eventually brought us into Estrées shortly after eleven o'clock that night. Major Wilson had gone in advance of us, and had secured billets for the men in a loft full of hay, on which we flung ourselves down, just as we were. We slept soundly all night, the hay being warmer and more comfortable than any feather bed. Perhaps not warmer, if the Major's experience that night is any criterion in the matter; but certainly more pleasant. Major Wilson, writing of that night, said: "A room in the farmhouse was placed at the disposal of the officers. It appeared to be very comfortable; and among other things, contained a fair-sized bed in one corner. As there were five officers, the question arose as to who was to occupy the bed, and my suggestion was to draw lots to decide the momentous problem. The subalterns, however, out of the goodness of their hearts, would not hear of this, and insisted that Captain MacLeod and I should share it. We agreed on condition that the remaining three junior officers tossed and the winner joined us. Clegg won, and wore a grin that wouldn't come off. I did a bit of quick thinking and said I should sleep in the middle. This decision was determined in the belief that if I occupied the outside berth, I should probably be dumped on the floor during the night and as the bed was nearly 5 ft. high and the floor of stone, I did not relish the prospect. On the other hand, if on the inside, I envisaged having my face pushed into the wall and being unable to breathe.

"Ye gods! I remember awakening in pitch darkness, bathed in perspiration and with the certain conviction that my dug-out had fallen in; that a 5.9 had scored a direct hit, and that this was the end. I felt warm bodies on top of me; and self-preservation coming to the front, I heaved desperately. Loud protests and lurid language immediately filled the air; and on regaining full consciousness I discovered that the miserable bed had sunk in the middle, and the Captain and Clegg sometime during the night had gained their objective, lying back to back in a strategical position which met in a line drawn down the middle and on top of mine. I had completely disappeared from view, and was almost smothered – the penalty of occupying the centre of a feather bed. Am I to be blamed for avoiding them now like the plague?"

We left Estrées next day (Good Friday, 29th March), and retraced our steps south-eastwards for five miles to Roevrel, in which we only remained an hour; then west for another eight miles to Oresmaux. As we crossed the river Noye at Jumel, the Boche was strafing the road with 5.9 inch shells – which is recorded as this was the last time we came under enemy shellfire during the retreat.

What the Fifth Army endured and suffered by casualties during those weeks are matters of history. But to many like ourselves who went through it, the tragedy of the retreat did not seem to be ourselves: it lay in the plight of the refugees. At Roye we had seen a genteel, white-haired old lady (doubtless somebody's delicate granny) wandering along the road, her only remaining possession apart from what she wore being a pair of velvet slippers carried in her hand. Outside Moreuil, we had seen such things as a hay-cart furniture-laden, capsized in the ditch and abandoned by its owner; while further on, we passed a stocky little private of the Gordons – one of a stray Company – gradually falling behind and losing touch with his party by reason of trundling a one-wheeled barrow full of bed-clothes, on top of which a child of about three years old was perched; while alongside trudged the Frenchwoman whom he had temporarily relieved of her too heavy burden.

Hamicourt

Now at Oresmaux we had further such experiences. We were again sheltering for the night in a barn, entrance to which was obtained through an archway. The barn had no door; and on waking next morning (Saturday, 30th March), I heard the sound of someone weeping. Si. Arnould heard it too; and going to investigate, found an elderly woman lying half frozen on the rough cobbles in the porch. We spoke to her, but it seemed we could do nothing; she had lost everything and everybody, and only wished she could die. Si. went to the cooks to see if any tea could be had, while I went into the billet and brought out a couple of greatcoats to cover the woman. Soon Si. returned with some bread and a mug of steaming-hot tea; and after some persuasion she took these. Then as though ashamed of her outburst, she rose and went off – goodness knows where. Shortly afterwards, I went up the road to search for firewood for the cooks, who were now preparing breakfast for the men. (By this time we were sufficiently reorganised for the ration lorry to call at a dump for food supplies). Seeing some stacks of faggots in a small field, I knocked at the door of a cottage near-by to ask if we could have them. A woman of about thirty, three children hanging on her skirts, opened the door. She was dry-eyed, but nearly frantic – not for herself but the children, who, she said, had eaten nothing either that day or the one previous. No one wanted her faggots – would we *buy* them? I said we could get wood for nothing, but promised to come back with something to eat. She threw up her hands despairingly and shut the door. I returned to the yard to raise some food. We had little money just then, but no opportunity of spending usefully even what we had. I raised

*Old well at
Hamicourt
(Picardy)*

ten francs in the barn, and two loaves at the cookhouse. "What about some tea?" I asked 'Sniper' Brown, the cook on duty. He would like me to know that he "wasna' a fillinthroapic institution"; but his heart was as big as his words, for he handed me some tea in a packet. When the woman opened the door on my return to the cottage with the food, she simply said "Entrez, monsieur", then sank into a chair and broke down. I was at a loss what to do; so putting the franc notes under the loaves on the table, I laid the packet of tea on the top and left them to it. Then, being of Aberdonian parentage, I scrounged two bundles of her faggots.

We arrived at the village of Taisnil next day, to find the place packed with refugees from Amiens: but banded together, their fate seemed less tragic than that of the aged and solitary ones of the days previous. The villagers at Taisnil invited soldiers and refugees to take potatoes from the pits, and that night we roasted potatoes by the roadside for supper.

Next morning (Monday, 1st April) we travelled via the town of Poix to St. Segree – fourteen miles west of Taisnil. Here we remained for several days, the main incident of our stay being that one of our gunners let chain and

172

bucket fall down the village well, cutting off the entire water supply until we managed, twenty-four hours later, to recover the chain. The local Maire was nearly at his wits' end, and doubtless was glad to see the last of us; for here we had our first real opportunity of washing which we did to the waist. The result was an acute shortage of water in the village even before we dropped the chain, and that despite the weather. We left on the afternoon of Friday, 5 April, for Gauville, a hamlet six miles distant and adjoining the small town of Aumale. The weather was rainy in the extreme; and though in no danger of being caught up in the Boche advance (which had now been stayed), the conditions under which some of the inhabitants of Gauville existed was a heartbreak. I became friendly during our few days' stay with a couple whose miserable hut I had discovered in a wood. It took me back to my schooldays when I saw that hut; for at once I remembered the opening wording in our French book 'Contes et Nouvelles' – "Il y avait une fois un pauvre bûcheron et sa femme, qui demeuraient dans un bois ..."[29]

[29] *"There was once a poor woodcutter and his wife, who lived in a wood ..." (The commencement of the story of 'Tom Thumb').*

It would be about seven o'clock in the evening when I first visited the place to buy wood for the cookhouse. No one was in, and I was just about to depart, when the owner appeared laden with the faggots he had been cutting all day. He was followed immediately by his wife, also carrying faggots; and who, in addition had a baby about a year old strapped on her back. On explaining my errand, they invited me inside. They had been working in the woods since seven o'clock that morning, and all three – baby included -were soaked to the skin. They seemed to think nothing of it; and after lighting a fire and putting the baby to bed, they began to talk. He was a disabled soldier, and the family lived on the proceeds of their faggots which they sold in the district round Aumale. The picture of that couple as I first met them, rain running down their faces; and the woman, laden front and rear, wet through but perfectly cheerful, remains with me now.

From Gauville we went to Hamicourt, sixteen miles north of Aumale; where we spent a few days before leaving (on Saturday, 27th April) for Wanel, six miles north-east of Hamicourt. At Wanel, the Brigade was once more formed into a fighting unit. Reinforcements were arriving almost daily, and here we expected to obtain the remainder of the reinforcements and motor transport column necessary to restore us to full complement; and also

Wanel Church (Picardy)

173

to take over new guns. We had some time yet, however, to wait for the latter; and it was not until Sunday, 19th May, that we eventually left to go into position once more.

On Monday, 20th May, we halted on our way up the line at Longpré near Amiens. Here some of us bathed in the canal, and Gunner Creamer thought fit to lie down in its muddy bed fifteen feet below the surface, until dived for and fished out unconscious. That night we slept in the fields at Longpré. It was a fine night, and above us a line of empty observation balloons swayed to and fro. They were put there in the hope of tempting the Boche to come over and be entrapped; for between each balloon stretched a mesh of wire. Whether or not this ruse was successful, we never learned. The last sound I heard before dropping off to sleep came from Ted Clogg, now battery clerk, who was declaiming to the night air:

> *Ah! fill the cup – what boots it to repeat*
> *How Time is slipping underneath our feet:*
> *Unborn Tomorrow and dead Yesterday*
> *Why fret about them if Today be sweet.*

Next morning we travelled in motor lorries to our gun position at La Neuville, a faubourg of Corbie. We passed through the latter town that forenoon; but what a change from the busy, cheerful little place we had visited in the summer of 1916. Then it had been full of crowded estaminets, and bright shops doing a brisk trade with the troops in silk souvenirs: now it was deserted, and so badly knocked about by German shellfire than on reaching the church, chunks of it had to be removed from the roadway before we could proceed. Nick Carter took advantage of the momentary delay to scrounge a silk bed quilt for his future comfort: this, he said, would compensate for what he had paid when buying a silk souvenir to send home in 1916.

That evening – exactly two months to a day since the commencement of the German attack at St. Quentin – we laid out our new lines of fire and registered our guns. We had been useless too long, of that we were well aware; though it was our misfortune rather than our fault. We were not thinking of our misfortunes, however, now that we were once more in action: indeed it may truly be said that we never thought very much about our fate during the whole retreat. But we often wondered about the fate of the hapless refugees. We had walked – blindly perhaps, but willingly – into this business of war; but they had not chosen to participate in it; they had been caught inexorably in its vortex, tossed hither and thither, and finally thrown out, 'unwept, unhonoured and unsung'

Aged refugees and mules had much in common. They were alike stoic in long-suffering; often so obstinate that they refused to budge until the last possible moment, and sometimes not even then – yet nevertheless the inarticulate heroes of the war. But in one respect at least they differed: the mules generally had a good kick left in them!

Chapter 33

Coming up for more – La Neuville (Corbie : Somme)

But fill me with the old familiar juice,
Methinks I might recover by and by! – Omar Khayyam

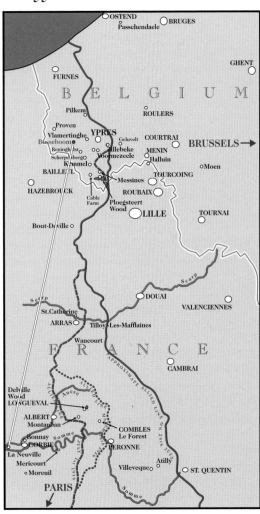

The La Neuville position proved to be a very quiet one; the only causes for occasional anxiety being frequent heavy shelling of the road a couple of hundred yards behind our billets, and the activities of low-flying German planes. Our guns were situated on the edge of a wood near a disused factory, and here the four Battery Commander's Assistants – Tom Matheson, Nick Carter, Balchin and myself – slept in a deserted cottage in which were two iron bedsteads. Each bed had a straw mattress, the interior of which we never examined lest we should find that the beds were already inhabited! But Nick Carter's magenta silk quilt covered a multitude of sins, and when spread on the bed, the place looked almost like being at home! Nick Carter had never left the battery, having had his wound attended at different dressing-stations during the retreat, and in addition, dressed daily by Bombardier Bodly. As a matter of fact we had been nearer to losing Tom Matheson, who was missing for some time, and had only managed to rejoin the battery a week before it had arrived at La Neuville. In the course of his travels, he and a small party of waifs and strays looking for their units had been issued at a dump with a whole leg of mutton, to be cooked and divided between them during their journey back up the line. They put the leg of mutton in a sandbag, intending to cook it at first opportunity. Next forenoon it was very warm, the sun beating down relentlessly upon them. At every step the mutton seemed heavier, while the party grew thirstier; and at midday they came across a wayside estaminet. None of them had any money and all wanted to quench their thirst; so Tom entered the estaminet and drove a bargain with the good lady, who handed each of the party a glass of beer and received the leg of mutton in exchange.

Tom's return to the battery coincided with the arrival of a new officer, whom we immediately dubbed "Little Willie", partly from a faint resemblance to the German Crown Prince, and partly from his extreme youth. He arrived full of beans and curiosity, his attitude plainly indicating "Well, what are you waiting for? I've arrived: what shall we do first?" The first thing we did was to listen to 'one coming over'; that left him thoughtful. The next one – an eight inch – burst near enough to help him to find his true level (horizontally); and by the time he had experienced some more of the same, he became a really useful subaltern. A different type of reinforcement was 'old' Owen. He was a gunner and wasn't old; but anyone with a heavy moustache and apparently about forty was considered old by us then. He was a contradiction in terms, being a Welshman with a soft-toned voice. Not only ignorant of the art of warfare, he hardly seemed to know what the word meant – a veritable sheep in wolf's clothing. He had occupied a post in a bank at some unpronounceable village in Wales, so was installed in the battery office as assistant to Ted Clogg, who as battery clerk was very capable, if somewhat 'hashy'[30]. Old Owen was as efficient in the battery office as he would have been useless on the gun. He plodded industriously and methodically through Army Forms galore, his serenity of demeanour and complete absence of guile disarming any who came to the office to air some grievance about pay or leave. Ted Clogg, on the other hand, was ever speeding up things, his sharp tongue and ready wit more than a match for anyone who might have tried to 'swing the lead' on his mild assistant. Compared one with the other, they were direct opposites; but together they blended like lamb and mint sauce.

One day shortly after Owen's arrival at La Neuville, the Boche was shelling the road behind the billets with eight inch; while every three minutes one shell dropped short (a favourite trick of the Boche) with a terrific crump in the woods just behind our position. After duly waiting for the short one to fall, I went into the battery office for some papers, when Clogg asked me if I had seen Owen, who had gone out but had not returned. I had not seen him; so we decided to go a little way into the wood, lest by any chance he had been caught by one of the 'shorts'. A shell hummed over our heads every half minute, to burst well over the road; so that except for the short one, we were comparatively safe. I was looking ahead without seeing any sign of the missing one, when a voice behind me said quietly, "I think you had better come and lie down, corporal." It was Owen, who had lain down behind a fallen tree-trunk until the shelling ceased. I told him it was he we were seeking; and that there was no need to lie there, as the shells were going well

[30] [SCOT: coarse, rough]

over except for that occasional short one, which we could readily recognise from its sound long before it reached us. He looked at me innocently; and without any sign of 'wind-up', said seriously, "Ah corporal; that is where you have the advantage of me: when I hear a shell, I can't tell its direction – for all I know, it might drop a mile away, or underneath my feet." It was a true statement; for just then I heard that short one coming. I dropped down behind the tree-trunk and left old Owen standing staring down at me. He did eventually collapse in a heap beside me: for I pulled the feet from him just before the shell bust about forty yards away. Then we returned to the office, where Clogg's upbraiding address (if one excluded the oaths with which it was intermingled) was quite maternal. But we did not always have the advantage of old Owen. One day, he came trotting into the billet, such indecent haste on his part indicating that something unusual had occurred. "Hurrah, boys! My bank has declared a bonus to each of the Staff on active service; one to the wife; and half for each child, look you." And even the thought of the sentence which followed did not curb his joy as he added "And I've got five of them!"

At La Neuville, the battery's fire was mostly on enemy batteries and on trenches round Villers-Brettonneux. A great deal of heavy fighting had taken place round the last-named village, on which our guns were registered lest the Boche should attempt to retake it. It had changed hands several times in recent weeks, though at this time was in our possession. It could be seen very clearly through the glasses from our visual observation post, which was situated beside the road on the heights above Bonnay. On my first visit to this O.P., I was astonished to find that it was only a few yards from the spot on which I had stood more than a year previously, when I had so admired the Corot landscape and the silver thread of the Somme.[31] The monument still stood; but though it was now almost the end of May, the trees far down in the valley beneath were blasted and bare; while in place of the silver thread, the recent rains had turned the valley into a series of lakes. Across one of the nearest of these, a khaki-clad Australian, screened from enemy observation by innumerable tree-trunks, was slowly poling a flat-bottomed river punt – a sight strangely reminiscent of a life we had lived once, so long ago it seemed, and now lost for ever.

[31] *See Chapter 12 of this book.*

About the middle of June, we were relieved by a battery which had been on rest behind the lines at the village of Sorel, near Amiens; and here they had been badly hit by influenza, which at that time was raging both at home and in the war zone, often with fatal results. The relieving battery had barely recovered when they were sent to take over our position; and we went straight into the billets they had vacated. Within two days of arriving at Sorel, a goodly number of our men were down with the trouble, which was only kept from spreading by prompt and stringent measures. One of the latter was an early-to-bed order; but our Orkney friend Garson was allowed extra liberty, as he was once more making himself useful to the farmworkers – and in any case, nothing less than a 5.9 would have affected his health. One night he was much later than usual; but shortly after midnight, someone outside was heard fumbling at the iron bar which secured the door of the barn. "That you, Garson?" asked Arnould in a whisper. "Ay," came the reply. "Well, don't make a noise getting into bed, or you'll have the whole barn awake." Garson groped his way across the sleeping forms among the straw; then stumbling over someone, he fell. From the remarks that followed, it was clear that the 'iron' bar was not the only one he had been at that night. Arnould again spoke: "If you make another sound, Garson, I'll run you in first thing in the morning: you should be shot for coming in like that." There was no answer but a grunt, and a few minutes later all sound of movement ceased as Garson stretched himself out to sleep. It was somewhat surprising that no one seemed to have heard the commotion but all was silent. Then the voice of Jim Brunton said loudly enough to have awakened the dead, "Garson!" "What the h--l do you want?" asked the latter, with typical army courtesy. "I only wanted to ask, when you're put against the wall in the morning, which'll you have – a .303 or a Martini-Henry?"[32]

We wondered where Garson had obtained the drink strong enough to put him in such a state: certainly not at the farms, if our previous experience was to be relied upon. In the morning, it proved that in the course of his return to the battery on the previous night, he had gone into an old French billet which was deserted. Looking round to see if there was anything to scrounge, all he could see was a stone bottle of ink on the table. Doubtless many of our troops on the scrounge had looked into that billet already; but all knew enough French to be aware that the word "ENCRE", printed in large letters on the bottle, meant "ink". Garson, however, had been caught before with misleading bottles and thought there would be no harm in smelling it. Extracting the cork, he put his nose to the mouth of the bottle. Funny ink it seemed to be – smelt like rum. 'Makkin' siccar'[33] by tasting, he found that it *was* rum, and at once decided to get his own back for his experience with the castor oil on the Nesle Road a few months before!

We left Sorel on 27th June, 1918[34]; it being rumoured that our Brigade was bound for a new sector of the British front. We reached Longpré, where we were to entrain, at noon that day, and then spent several hours about the railway yard waiting to load our guns. Here in the early afternoon, one of the weirdest figures I have ever seen ran into the yard, stopped short with a jerk on seeing us, and then timidly approached. His face was a mass of wrinkles, and his back so bent that it almost seemed he was compelled to run to keep from falling forward on his forehead. He was no more than five feet high, and as he came running forward, his steps were no longer than six inches. He was more like a chimpanzee than a human being, and his apparel no less curious. Boots of heavy army type; puttees and tight khaki breeches; while above those, glimpses of a dirty army shirt showed beneath a cardigan full of holes and about six sizes too large for him. A large basket, the lid of which was secured by a bootlace, was strapped to his back, valise-fashion. Finally he was crowned with a tassel-less glengarry, and carried a short thick cudgel in his hand. Becoming emboldened by our welcome, he smilingly informed us, in respect to an urgent chorus of enquiry as to where he got the cardigan, that it belonged to "Madame", who was "grande". He greedily devoured some dry bread which we gave him; and for one of his evident age, it was amazing to see how he could eat. I sent him with my tin mug to the cooks who were preparing tea in the yard, and soon he returned rejoicing with the mug full. He said he was seventy-two years of age, and was tramping the country begging his food as he went. He had trotted eight kilos, that day. After

[32] *Different types of ammunition.*

[33] *[SCOT: making sure]*

[34] *[The same date is given for the next day on p. 181]*

finishing his tea, he took the basket from his back and produced from it a filthy sandbag, into which he stuffed the remainder of the bare bread we had given him. After which, he shouldered his burden and prepared to depart. "He would make a good sponge for the gun," remarked 'Sniper' Brown jocularly. The old man looked inquiringly at us; so I said "He wants you to come and help us fight the Germans." "I am too old for that," he replied, shaking his head somewhat mournfully; then looking up, he added with some fire in his voice "But I fought them in 1870." Before more could be said, he wished us 'Bon Chance' about twenty time in quick succession as he tottered out of the yard.

He had fought in 1870. As I lay in an open truck late that night the thought would not leave me. Forty-eight years previously, that old man had been about the age we were now; and I wondered where we might be forty-eight years hence. He had served his country then: how had it served him since? Were his present circumstances his own fault, or simply his misfortunate? And how would our country serve us if this war should ever cease? Time would tell – perhaps: for while I was pondering those questions without finding answers, the train was crawling steadily on through that summer night; every hour bringing us nearer to the scene of an old familiar haunt – the Ypres Salient.

(See facing page)

[35] *[probably 28th
– see previous
note on p. 178]*

THE Book SHOP

We have over 4,000 books in stock including Fiction & Non Fiction, Romance, Detective, Western, Thriller, Science Fiction, Horror, Biographies, etc.

EXCHANGE SERVICE

On any paperback you buy from us you can receive a credit of up to 50% if the book is returned in good condition complete with our price label.

TRADE-IN

Bring us a paperback in good condition and you will receive a credit of up to a third of its UK cover price to be used against another book.

STATIONERY ETC

Writing Pads & Envelopes
Gift Tags & Wrapping Paper

•

Dictionaries, Verb Tables,

•

Phrase Books
& Phrase Books

GREETING CARDS

English & Spanish

We stock a wide range of greeting cards for all occasions:- Birthdays, Anniversaries, Sympathy, Congratulations, plus Mothers Day, Fathers Day, Valentines, Easter, Xmas,

THE BEST RANGE ON TENERIFE

THE Book SHOP

LOS GIGANTES SPORTS SUN CENTRE

Chapter 34

Back to the Salient – (Busseboom – Ypres)

Old soldiers never die ... they fade away – War Song

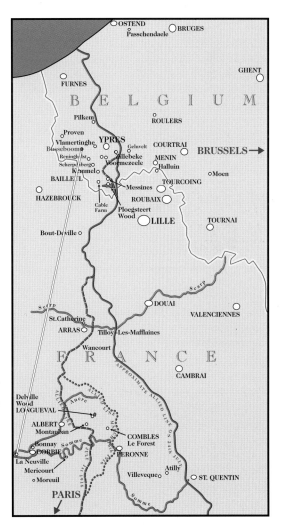

The clanking of the railway wagons over the metals soon lulled me to sleep in the open truck as our train slowly crept northwards through the night; and when next I awoke, it was 7 a.m. (27th June, 1918).[35] We must have been about Lillers; and shortly afterwards we passed several deserted villages which had been heavily shelled, while the railway line itself seemed also to have been subjected to considerable shelling. On reaching a junction (somewhere about Merville, I imagine), we were shunted on to the Hazebrouck line. We had a dry breakfast of bread and bully beef at Blendeques; passed Arques at midday, and at 3 p.m. reached Esquelbecq, where the guns were unloaded. The motor lorries which were to carry us to our new position did not turn up; and eventually we went in parties to billet at Eringhem, seven kilos away. This village was only ten miles from Dunkirk; so that in the three months that had just passed, we had travelled from one extreme of the British line to the other.

The landlady of our billet at Eringhem was blind through cataract. She informed me that she had gone to Dunkirk a year previously to undergo an operation; but while she was waiting there, the Boche had bombed the town, and she was compelled to return to the village without having been operated upon. She was now patiently awaiting the end of the war in the hope that she would then be able to recover both her husband (who was fighting) and her sight.

Next day while waiting for the lorries, Si. Arnould and I entered an estaminet for a cup of coffee. The damsel spoke very little English; and on discovering that she could make herself understood in French, would not continue in English – much to Si.'s annoyance. As we rose to depart, she shook hands with both of us and said to me "Au revoir, Monsieur." Then turning to Si., she said haltingly, "Good after-noon, sare." When we reached the street, Si. growled "Well, perhaps I don't know much French, but I compree 'Au revoir', anyway."

We did not leave Eringhem until 4 p.m. on 29th June, when we journeyed by motor lorry via Wormoudt to our new battery position at Busseboom. From Watou onwards, the road was screened at intervals all the way up, to prevent observation by the Boche from Kemmel Hill. But despite this, we had not gone far when a high velocity shell came whizzing over our heads and dropped thirty yards off. We did not know whether this was a stray shot, or if the lorry had been spotted; but a few yards further on, some high hawthorn bushes hid us from enemy view. Here we stopped the lorry and sat by the roadside to wait until dusk before proceeding further. At the roadside stood a small wooden hut, in which a girl of about twenty-five and her brother (a youth of 18 or 19) ran a coffee shop for the use of the troops. A German shell had buried itself at that point where the wall met the ground, its base protruding from the soil, where it lay neglected. Fortunately it had proved a dud; but I thought if I lived there, I should have had the authorities remove it without delay. But this young pair were not the only young folks in those parts to ignore the war's alarms. One of our observation balloons was up that day not far from where we sat; and we interestedly watched the Boche shelling it with time-fuzed shrapnel. It seemed only a question of time when it would be hit; but the observers showed no sign of coming down voluntarily. As we watched, a family party passed by on the road – two women, two little girls and a boy. The last was propelling a wooden hoop along the road, and betrayed no interest whatever in the balloon or in the shellbursts which flecked the sky round about it.

We arrived at rear position about 9.30 p.m., to find "A" and "B" sub-sections pulling in their guns. I unloaded the mapboards, instruments, etc. forming the Battery Commander's stores, and learning that Major Wilson was at forward position and had been asking for me, I walked up there, finding my way as best I could from the map in the gathering darkness. On the roadside, notices were posted expressly forbidding the use of the road by vehicular traffic except by night. I had about three miles to go before reaching forward position; and when I got there, the Major told me to go back again, when doubtless I should meet the ration lorry coming up, as it was now dark. I was to turn it, pick up the B.C. stores from rear position, and return with them and the lorry to forward position. This had to be done in time to allow the ration lorry to unload at forward position and get back once more before dawn. I met the lorry about a mile from rear position; and after grumbling a bit, the driver turned back. We were loading up the stores at rear position when the Boche opened out on it, and for five or ten minutes we had quite a hectic time from gas shells and time-fuzed shrapnel. We escaped without a casualty, however, except that the canvas roof of the ration lorry was badly perforated by shrapnel bullets – we had taken temporary cover in a dug-out. When the shelling ceased, I got my blessings from cooks and driver for having turned them back to the place. However, we were soon again on our way; but after unloading the stores at forward position, the Transport Officer said that on returning to rear billets, he would send another lorry up to forward position with the wireless operators and their gear. Knowing that this could not be done in time to allow that lorry to return to rear billets before dawn, I mentioned the matter to Major Wilson. He said that on no account must the lorry with the wireless gear be allowed to come up, or the whole battery position might be given away. Already the sky was lightening for dawn; but when the Major went to cancel the order for the lorry, it was to find that the Transport Officer had already gone with the ration lorry to rear billets. As I was the only person who knew the way there – the gun detachments having come up to forward position, in motor lorries, after dark – there was nothing for it but to return on foot to rear billets. I ran most of the way this time, and met the lorry just as it was leaving. The Transport Officer, perhaps naturally, was somewhat annoyed when I told him his orders were countermanded. But having now walked the distance between the positions three times that night and motored once besides – I too was feeling somewhat peeved with the world in general and the Transport Officer in particular; and had it not been that the latter was a very decent type of officer, I might easily have been in trouble that night. Realising this, I added that I was simply delivering the message sent by the Major, who had given the order; whereupon the lorry driver was instructed to remain at rear billets.

I was now anxious to return to forward position without delay; and spying a rusty old bicycle standing against a hedge, I scrounged it, leaving word with the cooks at rear position that its owner could walk up to Busseboom for it if he wanted it before I should again be back, which might not be for some days. (He mustn't have thought it worth the trouble, for it was never claimed). I hope Army Regulations exclude bicycles from the term 'vehicular traffic' for it was certainly daylight when I reached forward position on that creaking old velocipede.

It was now almost five o'clock; and the caterpillars, which had been chugging about the place all through the night pulling the guns into position, had crawled like gigantic beetles into a large, partly ruined barn to wait the coming of the next night before once more emerging to make their way back to the ammunition column behind the lines. The gun detachments – the mounting of the guns completed – had been working furiously to clear away all tell-tale tracks of the caterpillars, lest these should be spotted later that day by any Boche plane which should come over.

On that same morning – 30th June – and at that very hour two years before, our gun detachments under Mr. Phipps had been cutting the corn at Vlamertinghe to cover up the traces of our caterpillars as the guns were pulled into position for the first time after landing on French soil. Many of the gun detachments of that morning, and Mr. Phipps himself, now lay under it;[36]

[36] *Six officers, a sergeant-major, six sergeants, and a hundred and sixty-odd other ranks were at Vlamertinghe in June, 1916. Of these, one officer, one sergeant, and thirty-eight other ranks remained with the battery at this time – June, 1918.*

183

most of them not far away. For it was five miles to Zillebeke and Voormezeele; while Dickebusch and Vlamertinghe lay only two miles distant.

Our first position in the Salient was taken up at the end of June, 1916, at Vlamertinghe: at the end of June, 1917, we returned to the Salient from Messines Ridge to take up position at Voormezeele. Now, at the end of June, 1918, we had celebrated our second anniversary in Flanders by pulling in once more in the Salient at Busseboom. It only required some appropriate memento to mark such an auspicious occasion. Unknown to us, the Boche was even now preparing it for presentation a few days later.

Chapter 35

The toll of the Salient – Busseboom and Heksken (Ypres)

There shall be in that rich earth a richer dust concealed – Brooke

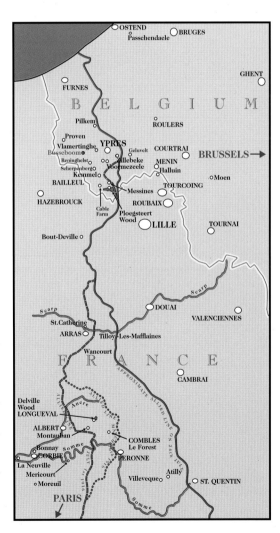

Daylight on 30th June, 1918, revealed our position to be at a farm, from which we could see many of the landmarks upon which we had first set eyes two years previously. But like those on the Somme, they had changed greatly. Kemmel – then a green, tree-clad slope – was now a bare brown mass, on which German observation posts were placed. So much was our forward position in view from Kemmel and from the Wytschaete Ridge, that we had breakfast each day at 6 a.m., dinner at 4 p.m., and tea at 9 p.m.

By orders of Brigade, we lay low for the first two days, during which we did not fire a round. We found time passed quickly enough, and made ourselves snug in dug-outs specially built for us before our arrival by the Royal Engineers. They were very strong, tons of rubble covering the roofs, which were strengthened in addition by heavy iron girders and elephant irons. It was stated – though not by the Engineers who built them – that they were shellproof; but this we doubted. Certainly any one of them would have withstood the impact of a shell with an instantaneous fuze; but opinions varied as to what would happen in the event of a direct hit from a shell with a delayed fuze. We were generally of opinion that no dug-out would withstand the latter except the deep German type we had experienced on the Somme in 1916, and again on the Arras front in the spring of 1917. The dug-outs, however, were excellently built and stronger than anything of ours we had yet seen. "D" sub-section's dug-out seemed best of all; for not only had it girder elephant irons and pillars inside, with tons of rubble on top; but it was actually built right underneath the big barn, whose walls still stood, affording even further protection from enemy shells. At the end farthest from the door, a ventilation pipe had been led in through the roof, in order that there should be plenty of air in the dug-out at both ends.

On 2nd July, we carried out a shoot by aeroplane against a German battery on the Wytschaete Ridge. It was a novel experience for us to be firing by aeroplane observation on the enemy's artillery, and at the same time be able, from the gun position, to see our own shells bursting. We were shelled in return that day to some extent; a German plane apparently registering a Boche battery on us with fair success. A gaping hole was made in the wall which screened "C" gun from Kemmel. "D" gun was knocked out of action, and all its cartridges and fuzes went up in a huge blaze, which would doubtless be noted both by the Boche plane and by visual observers on Kemmel. "E" gun was badly splintered inside the bore and on the buffer – damage which would take some days to repair, if indeed the gun did not require to be sent to the base for re-rifling. At "F" gun, the band flew off the gravity tank of the gun and caught one of the gunners on the head, inflicting a deep wound. Then the tank itself came off, and flying through the air, caught one of our shells which was lying already fuzed. It cut the top clean off the fuze with a glancing blow; and only the fact that it had travelled away from the shell as it sliced the fuze had kept the shell from bursting, the incident being the most remarkable of its kind we had experienced. It seemed no less than a miracle that the shell had not exploded: as it was, the only damage done was to Sergeant Cartwright's foot, which the tank had selected for its last kick.

On 4th and 5th July, we carried out two very successful shoots on German batteries – too successful to be healthy for us. So on the morning of the 5th, on receiving orders for the shoot, we were told to be prepared to pull out immediately after dusk that evening as Headquarters considered the position now dangerous. Incidentally, there was also a message from Headquarters which affected me personally – I was to go there that forenoon to be interviewed by the General in regard to Commission. We completed the shoot (not, however, without some retaliation from the Boche) that forenoon, when I left for Headquarters. The several occasions already on which my papers had been lost, stolen or strayed, made me feel somewhat nervous as I entered the hut where the great man was to interview me. The Brigade Adjutant sat at one end of the table, our own Battery Captain at the other. Between them sat a white-haired figure with head bent over some papers. As I came to a halt before him, he looked up, and I knew my luck was in. For I was looking at old Colonel – now General – Winter, who used to come up to Zillebeke over the duck-boards to visit the little dug-out occupied by Mr. Leslie and me when first we had pulled two guns into Zillebeke.[37]

[37] *See Chapter 21 [p. 112] of this book.*

186

The Captain and Brigade Adjutant – neither of whom had been with the Brigade when we were at Zillebeke – were somewhat taken aback when instead of examination, I was asked what we had been doing in the south since the General had last seen us. Then after a few routine questions, he said "Your O.P. experience and your knowledge of gunnery should take you through without any difficulty. I'll sign those papers and you'll go home for a course – that's all."

On our return to the battery, we found that some more shelling had taken place, Lieut. Gorman and one of the gunners having been wounded. Nothing more happened, however, and at dusk we began to pull out. The wily Boche must have suspected that this would be done, for without warning, he began to pump shells into us; and it was immediately apparent that he had carried out his registration of our battery position very accurately. Well, it was only our turn to receive what we had been giving; and if we were "for it", we couldn't complain. We had celebrated our second anniversary too well, and must now suffer the after-effects. Most of the men cleared away altogether from the precincts of the battery; but half a dozen (including myself) were in a dug-out some thirty yards from the barn while under the latter, the whole of "D" sub-section had taken cover in the strong dug-out previously described. There was little chance to move again, for shells were falling "thick and heavy". We sat smoking in silence, listening to the thud and burst of shell after shell and their accompanying showers of debris, with that attitude of fatalistic apathy born of experience – yet more apparent than real, if my own feelings were any indication in the matter.

There was a momentary lull: then a rush of feet, as old Jack Frost – a man of about fifty – came scrambling into the dug-out., "I think they've got "D" sub's. dug-out, he gasped out; I'm sure I heard someone crying for help, so I ran across here as soon as I got the chance." As the only Corporal in the dug-out, I took it upon myself to forbid more than three to go across under the heavy shellfire, which had resumed, and was as bad as ever. The three dashed across the intervening space, and somehow reached the shelter of the wall near the barn. There two remained, while the third worked his way round to the entrance of "D" sub's. dug-out. It was completely blocked up by tons of debris, and it was very evident that the Boche had obtained an O.K. on the roof of the dug-out, which had caved in. In answer to an enquiry, a faint voice somewhere inside called out they were alive but buried and entreated that no attempt should be made to get at them from the doorway, but to work from the other end. This news was quickly conveyed to the two gunners behind the wall, one of whom – Bombardier Yarnold – went off to inform the Major, whose fighting-post was some five hundred yards from the barn. Meantime the remaining two had secured shovels and were immediately jointed by old Jack Frost, who had disobeyed the injunction to remain in the dug-out until definite news was ascertained. Unfortunately the digging had to be carried out from the end of the barn nearest the Boche lines, no cover whatever being available. It was therefore necessary to drop flat every half minute as another shell fell on the place. In the haste and general excitement of digging under such conditions, there was not very much constructive work accomplished (while Gunner Frazer's eye was cut open by one of the shovels!); but digging went on, and continual calling that we should soon have them out gave encouragement to the unfortunates inside, who were urging haste lest they should be suffocated. In another ten minutes the shelling lessened still further, and at the same time Yarnold returned with Lieuts. Bottomley and "Little Willie". The latter, stout lad, now had a real opportunity of doing something, and quickly brought half a dozen of our gunners on the scene, armed with picks and shovels. As they dug, Mr. Bottomley informed them that the Major was phoning Brigade to neutralise the enemy fire by a concentration of our batteries on that part of the Wytschaete Ridge from which the hostile shelling seemed to be coming; and immediately afterwards, Major Wilson himself came on the scene to direct operations. By this time, the shells had begun to pass over our heads; and in another five minutes they ceased altogether as all the other batteries of our group opened out on the ridge. The men dug for a solid hour before laying bare the top of a corrugated-iron sheet forming the perpendicular wall at the end of the dug-out. Then the end of the iron was bent over sufficiently at the corner to make a six inch hole, from which the hand of Corporal Tom Gordon immediately appeared. The sight of that hand had as cheering effects on those outside as the light from the hole had on those inside, and our energies were redoubled.

It took two hours to make the hole big enough to pull out those inside who were still alive. Sergeants Bell and Cartwright got inside to assist the men up, and sixteen (five of them more or less seriously wounded) were hoisted out. Nearly all of them collapsed on reaching the fresh air; and had it not been for the narrow ventilation pipe sunk through the roof, all must have died from suffocation long before we could have reached them. By this time, Sergeants Bell and Cartwright were feeling the effects of the air inside; so Mr. Bottomley and I went in and hoisted both of them out. We found Gunner Sherlock so badly wounded that we had to obtain further assistance inside before evacuating him. Then we examined what we could of the dug-out. Five of our men were killed – two we recognised: the others were under tons of stuff. We could do no more there that night, and now the paramount necessity was to pull out the guns.

All this happened on the night of Friday, 5th July, 1918, the remainder of which we spent pulling out of the position. The next day was fully occupied working at our rear position; and on the Saturday night we travelled with all our guns three miles further south, to pull into position at Reninghelst – from which our former acquaintances, the Chinese labourers, had long since fled. The work was completed before dawn on the morning of Sunday, 7th July; and by nine o'clock that morning, Si. Arnould and I with a party of six men were on our way back to Busseboom to recover the bodies of our dead. Here we found a party of Argyll and Sutherland Highlanders preparing to commence the work, and cursing us for having, as they thought, abandoned our late comrades without giving them proper burial. I told them drily that our first job was to protect the living, and that it was for their sakes we had been working without sleep for the last forty-eight hours! That brought them round all right; especially when I told them to clear out and leave us to our job. They asked to be allowed to remain; and we were very glad of their help in removing the heavy elephant irons and girders – the latter distorted and bent as though they had been made of lead.

We slaved at the work all day; but despite the additional help of the Argylls, it was 6 p.m. before we were ready to set out with the stretchers for Ouderdom cemetery, when we had to make a long detour to avoid the Boche shellfire on the road we normally should have taken. We reached the cemetery at 8.30 p.m., to find the graves already dug and the Padre waiting. The scene at the graveside in the dusk that evening was impressive and not a little awesome; the words of the burial service being rendered inaudible by continuous rolls of thunder and heavy crumping of German shells in front of us. The sky, too, was a strange colour – dark crimson with great black masses of cloud coming up high over the horizon, their edges trimmed with gold where the setting sun had dipped behind them.

Truly the Boche had presented us with a small memento of our anniversary; but as we lowered the blankets containing those still forms which the Salient was now claiming, to be for ever numbered with its honoured dead, I thought that golden rim over the blackness held the promise of a new and better Dawn.

Chapter 36

The last of the Salient – Reninghelst to Gheluvelt (Ypres)

Farewell! a word that must be, and hath been,
A sound which makes us linger – yet – farewell! – Byron

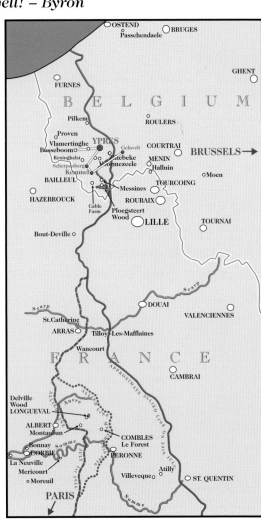

Immediately the service at Ouderdom cemetery was over, Lieut. Gough ran me on the carrier of his motor-cycle to rear position, where a lorry full of gunners was waiting to go up to our new position at Heksken Corner, Reninghelst. We set off in a violent thunderstorm, forked lightning completely eclipsing the gun flashes; while reverberating crashes of thunder drowned what crumping was going on. We arrived at Heksken Corner about midnight (Sunday/Monday), just in time to receive a dozen or more gas shells which dropped right in front of our guns.

I worked out the infantry S.O.S. lines for the guns, and had our mapboards and instruments put under temporary cover; by which time it was nearly 3 a.m. (Monday, 8th July). I was nearly asleep on my feet, not having been in bed since I had risen on the morning of the Friday previous; so Nick Carter and I now began to search for somewhere to sleep. Everything was sodden with the heavy rain, though it was now fair overhead. We found a ramshackle cottage, the roof of which was hanging down into the interior; but it contained an old bed frame with some wet straw on it. We were wetter than the straw, however; and thankful for so comfortable quarters, we lay down. Nick fished out his ubiquitous magenta silk quilt – now mud-caked, damp and slightly lousy. We pulled it over us and slept like logs, in spite of some neighbourly crumps, which threatened to bring the pendulous roof down on our heads. We did not rise until nine o'clock that morning (nobody knew where we had got to), and spent part of the forenoon searching for a permanent dug-out. Eventually we came upon an old French corrugated iron shelter a hundred yards in front of the main road, and by evening we had repaired it, and installed maps, instruments, the wireless station, and ourselves in it.

Next morning (Tuesday, 9th July), seven German 'sausage' balloons were up; and the road behind our dug-out was slowly shelled by a heavy howitzer battery firing a round every half minute. One of its guns, as usual, was consistently shooting short, and each fourth round fell dangerously near to our dug-out. Each time it became due, we sat in suspense, wondering where it would land. And here was I, awaiting orders to proceed home! Was I going to be "pipped at the post", I wondered, as I sat smoking a cigarette and gazing at the roof. If the latter gave any hint, it was one to be ignored, for some French soldier had chalked across it in big letters:

ICI LA MORT NE COÛTE RIEN[38]

[38] *"Here death costs nothing."*

Though cheap at the price, we lived up to our Scots reputation by not having any! That night was quiet, except for a shower of gas shells sent over at 3 a.m., and when we rose on the following morning, all was calm and peaceful. A slight drizzle of rain was falling, and no balloons were up. By reason of the first of these facts, we brought breakfast from the cookhouse to eat in the dug-out. We were in the middle of it, when suddenly the Boche let loose a salvo of 5.9 inch shells, presumably at the road behind. All four shells dropped short, and three of them burst within twenty yards of the dug-out entrance. We abandoned our breakfast and cleared off to a safe distance: not another shell came over.

I was now beginning to feel a sort of permanent wind-up under this cat and mouse existence; for life seemed to have developed into a race between the Boche and Headquarters with myself for the prize – one of very doubtful value, since neither seemed anxious to claim me – and once more I had all the luck. On the afternoon of Friday, 12th July, a message came that my Commission papers were through, and I was to proceed next morning to Esquelbecq, and entrain for Poperinghe and home.

Home! What visions it brought to me. Yet next morning, when the time came to say good-bye to those who had so long been my companions, the wrench of parting was so great that I almost felt like staying. The wistful look on the face of such men as Si. Arnould, Tom Matheson and Jimmy Edwards as they wished me the best of luck, seemed to be saying (though they were too generous-hearted to let the thought have more than momentary lodgement) "You've always been lucky here, and your luck has held out to the end." I felt a guilty conscience at leaving them all like this; it seemed like abandoning them to their fate. But I have to confess that even that thought did not prevent my leaving them 'while the going was good'. Major Wilson, last to bid me goodbye, was good enough to say that if I would let him know when I was 'through', he would make an application for me to be posted back to the battery.

I journeyed to Esquelbecq in the Major's car; and arriving in Boulogne that evening, spent the night under canvas at St. Martin's camp. Shortly after midnight we had a call from a party to whom I had forgotten to say goodbye – the Boche; whose planes bombed the camp for twenty minutes. The occupants of my tent cleared off to the 'slip' trenches provided for such an emergency: but I had so strong a feeling that nothing could happen to me now that I elected to remain alone in the tent.

Sunday, 14th July, saw me on the boat for Folkestone once more. Was ever such a welcome sight as the white cliffs of Dover then? Only one – when shortly after dawn on the following morning the train sped across the border into Bonnie Scotland and from my carriage window I looked down on the cliffs of Berwickshire.

Going back over the years it seems to me that only step by step did it become clear that war held for us youths on the one hand, romance, comradeship and unselfishness to the point of sacrifice, on the other hand – monotony, degradation and often apparently futile suffering. In my experience it embraced almost all human emotions except, strangely enough, personal hate of the enemy. I found too that while in my early teens I had been appalled at the thought that some day I must die, in moments when it seemed that the end was imminent, the fear of death passed away. Then I felt I was going over (and not alone) to some new experience; and though my time had not yet come, I think I then learned that whatever may be over there – life goes on.

So in that respect, the war to me was something of a spiritual experience.

My diary up to this point has, I hope, told the story of the Battery more than my own. This it was meant to do, and it is fitting that its completion should deal with what happened to the battery rather than with any account of my own doings elsewhere. But for any who are interested, it may be added that though eventually obtaining my Commission, I was still in England at the time of the Armistice; and demobilisation shortly afterwards put an end to any hopes of again joining the battery as an officer.

The pages which now follow tell the final chapters of this history of the battery as recounted to me by Major Wilson; Corporals Si. Arnould and Tom Gordon; Bombardiers Tom Matheson and Jim Edwards; and Gunners 'Sniper' Brown and 'Auld Dougal' Brebner.

The gun position at Heksken Corner in Reninghelst proved much quieter than at first had been anticipated. Our infantry seemed content to remain comparatively inactive, while the Boche on Kemmel did likewise. Our artillery, nevertheless, gave the observers on the hill no peace of mind or body; for one battery or another was always 'strafing' it. So much was this the case, that it was said later by the Germans themselves that the average life of an observer on Kemmel at this time was estimated at six tours of duty.[39] It was now generally realised that the supreme German effort had finally failed; and that our own comparative inaction at the moment was attributable to the

[39] Quoted on p. 224 of "Outline History of the Great War" (Carey & Scott).

193

Allied plan of co-ordinating every front before once more launching an attack of our own on a scale never before attempted. Meantime the initiative was passing swiftly into our hands with every day that passed.

On 8th August, 1918, the first of our attacks was launched further south with immediate success, and not without effect on our position; for it began the process of straightening out the Salient. Towards the end of that months, Major Wilson was summoned to Headquarters, where he had a meeting with the Brigadier-General in charge of the infantry. The battery was to be entrusted with a very important and dangerous shoot on the front line of German trenches on Kemmel. Observations would be carried out by aeroplane, and the airman had been given strict injunctions to report each round with absolute accuracy, as the Boche front line was only twenty-five yards from ours.

On the evening previous to the shoot, the airman came along to the battery, when final details were arranged. Next day, as the shoot was about to commence, our own infantry quietly evacuated their front lines. Immediately word was received that they were clear, we began the shoot, and fired in all 300 rounds, laying the Boche front line of trenches practically flat. This was fully confirmed by our infantry, by the many official photographs which were taken from the air, and later by our own gunners going over the ground. That night the aeroplane observer came up to the battery, and seemed only with difficulty to restrain himself from throwing his arms round the Major's neck! This was one of the most successful shoots ever undertaken by the battery; and if it was wholesale murder it was our duty. We had returned in those days to the Law of the Jungle – eat or be eaten – and from our point of view, we were preserving our infantry in the sector from the latter fate. This particular shoot also contributed to an event of far-reaching importance; for about the end of the first week in September, the Germans abandoned Kemmel altogether, leaving it finally in our hands.

Then we moved to the Scherpenberg, preparatory to driving the Boche from the Wytschaete Ridge. Here one morning early, a Staff car drew up at the battery position, several "brass-hats" of high rank alighting. They accompanied a heavily-built old man, who walked some little distance up the hill examining the remnants of the trenches, now only a foot to eighteen inches deep. He was the French Premier, Monsieur Clemenceau – *The Tiger!* I do not know whether or not that morning he took away a souvenir of the occasion; but a field gunner further up the hill could possibly have given him one: he was searching the pockets of a dead German with a pick.

There was now no peace for the harassed Boche: and following his abandonment of Kemmel, we took four of our guns forward to the foot of that hill, the remaining two being pulled into position at Belgian Battery Corner, near Vlamertinghe. While at Kemmel, our gunners had opportunity of seeing the fearful damage done by our artillery during the weeks which had passed. The trenches were nowhere more than a foot or so deep, while here and there the remains of wrecked machine gun emplacements might be descried almost buried in the earth.

Towards the end of September, 1918, the battery pulled out once more, and following a fortnight's rest at Busseboom, passed some of its old haunts on the way to its new position. Back through La Clytte, Reninghelst and

Vlamertinghe; past our 1916 billets at Shrapnel Corner, and up to Ypres; round by the Cloth Hall and down the Menin Road. The Menin Road! What a name: not only to us, but to every man who served in Flanders! In 1916 we had crept along it to our observation posts; in 1917 we had traversed it on foot down to Bellewarde Lake, and by Hellfire Corner into Zillebeke: now in 1918, we came with our guns down the road for the last time, and pulled into position at Inverness Copse, near Gheluvelt. It too, held memories; it had been the scene of many a sanguinary struggle, and the grave of many a brave man on either side. It had been one of our first targets during the bombardment which preceded the battles for Passchendaele in 1917; and now our guns were mounted on the spot where then our shells had fallen.

The copse was roughly a thousand yards long by five hundred deep and its whole area was a mass of sticky mud of varying depth, blasted stumps and rusty barbed wire. A place of decay and desolation, it seldom showed sign of human life even when we lived in it. For, as had been the case in our position at Bellwarde Lake more than a year earlier, the mud made a sustained shoot impossible, and the men spent most of their time in the part-demolished German dug-outs which remained to form the only available cover. At this time, Bombardier Jimmy Edwards was in charge of the ration lorry, which came up nightly shortly after 7 o'clock. On reaching the position, his only thought was to get away again from such a ghastly place with all possible speed. But usually he had to call several times to produce any signs of life; when a few heads would emerge from the bowels of the earth, take in the rations, and vanish like outcast lepers back to their colony. It was such a God-forsaken place, that the gunners went to bed at five o'clock at night to shut out the sight of it! Yet here, though we did not then know it, was fired the last shot from our guns during the war. For it was nearing the middle of October, and the Boche was in full retreat.

During the four years preceding, the struggle in the Salient had been intense. Its front areas, such as Polygon Wood, Glencorse Wood and Inverness Copse, had now been in our hands, now in the hands of the enemy. Neither side had been able to claim them permanently – it seemed they belonged only to the domain of Death. The flower of Britain and of Germany had withered and perished there: *now the Salient itself was gone.* No more now would the grisly spectre of death ride iron-shot and triumphant across that ground over which he had so long held sway. Here Death might deal not again for ever – Swinbourne's words recurred to the mind; and the lines which followed rang no less true:

> *Here now in his triumph where all things falter,*
> *Stretched out on the spoils that his own hand spread,*
> *As a god self-slain on his own strange altar,*
> *Death lies dead.*

Chapter 37

How the end came – Gheluvelt to Moen (Courtrai)

But such a tide as moving seems asleep,
Too full for sound and foam – Tennyson

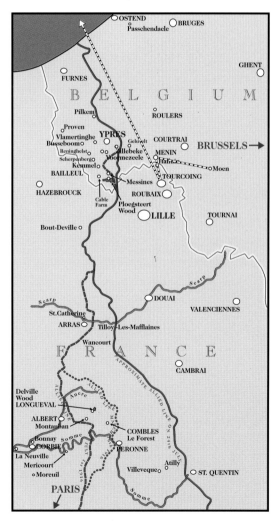

About the middle of October, 1918, the battery began to pull out from the Gheluvelt position to follow up the retreating Boche. But even now we were unaware that we were moving silently, but rapidly, in the flow of a tide that in little more than a fortnight would sweep irresistibly over the enemy and overwhelm him.

Yet Tom Matheson might have had some inkling that the end was near. For one day just before we left Inverness Copse, he was standing looking down at Nick Carter as the latter sat cross-legged on the ground with his everlasting silk quilt across his knees. At first it seemed he was about to mend it; but instead of using a needle, he produced the stump of a candle which he lit and stick upright in the earth. Then taking up the quilt, he began to run its multitudinous seams over the flame, to the accompaniment of a merry crackling like hundreds of fairy fireworks. Tom might have guessed that here was one member of the battery preparing for civilisation once more; for he was burning the lice eggs out of the seams of the quilt!

197

Leaving Gheluvelt behind, we went down that part of the Menin Road which had hitherto been in German hands; through Menin itself, and into the town of Halluin, where we remained for a week without mounting our guns; for the Boche had retreated further than could be reached even from here. One day, Jim Edwards was standing beside the ration lorry just outside Halluin, when a French farm cart came along. It was full of furniture; while, as usual, baskets were hanging from every available corner. On top of the cart, a girl of about twenty was sitting; apparently one of a family returning to their home now that the Germans had gone. As the cart passed our motor lorry, the girl gave a cry; and rising to her feet, she called out excitedly in English, "Good old Scotty: good old Crown-Nine Battery." It was Marie, who two and a half years before in Vlamertinghe, had served us with eggs and chips, and upon whom Sandy Henderson had first tried his French.[40]

[40] See Chapter 1 of this book.

From Halluin, we moved eastward into Courtrai, where billets were found in an old German hospital that had once been a training college of some kind. We were still out of touch with the Boche on the ground, but were visited nightly by his bombing aeroplanes. One night as they came over, a light was observed to be emanating from a cellar across the way, and in which the civilian inmates of the house above had taken shelter on the approach of the planes. Knowing that they would be bombed if the light was seen by the planes, one of our signallers ran across to warn the people of their danger. He knocked at the door of the house; but as the inmates were in the cellar below, and would not come up until the danger was past, the message could not be delivered. But the bomb was dropped as one of the planes passed; and when, some minutes later, the door was opened, it was an inanimate form that lay across the threshold. This was the battery's last casualty during the war, and perhaps it was not out of place that it should have been incurred in such a manner.

Courtrai was now rapidly becoming repopulated by families returning after long absences; and the place offered several unaccustomed attractions in the evenings at this time. Here, one evening, a certain young member of the battery was temporarily smitten by the charms of a pretty French damsel. He had accompanied her home that night; and next day he announced to his friends in the battery that he intended to call upon her that evening. He had been wiser to remain silent on the subject; for two or three other members of the battery insisted on accompanying him to see that, as one of them put it, the damsel's intentions were honourable! He was too young to be without a chaperone or two, they said. The party duly arrived at the house, and stood a few yards off while the smitten one went up to the door and knocked. "Who is it?" asked a voice from the interior. "Me," was the ungrammatical reply, uttered in a somewhat plaintive tone. A long period of silence followed without sign of anyone coming out; then some faintheart among the chaperones suggested that all should get back to billets, as it was bitterly cold. "Try her in French", someone else suggested. Nothing loth, our hero called out, "Il – est – tres – froid – pour – *nous* – ici." Whether or not it was the word 'nous' that caused the silence, it is impossible to say; but the weather was not more chilly than that silence; which still reigned; and at last, the disappointed swain, accompanied by his chaperones returned disconsolately to billets. Ah! Willie; to think that your courage failed at the end after what you had done in these past months! Or was it that you had bought your liberty too dearly to throw it away so lightly?

At Courtrai the officers had some entertainment in the shape of boxing, as our Transport officer had been a middle-weight champion of the Army (a fact which I had not known when I had that argument with him at Busseboom!) After several essays by the junior officers, however, no one would take him on with the gloves. One day, Major Wilson, who so far had taken no active part in these proceedings, offered to have a spar with him, on condition that there would be no slogging. Unfortunately, after some moments of quiet boxing, the Major 'socked' the other on the jaw. Dropping his hands to apologise, he received an upper-cut which nearly lifted him off his feet. Then the bout stopped – we were not there to knock each other out, but the Boche; and at the end of October, we pulled into position at Moen, some ten miles east of Courtrai, and thirty miles north-west of Mons.

Here we were close enough to the enemy; for he now occupied the line of the Scheldt, and at Moen was sitting on the ridge above us. He made so little movement however, that the battery played football with the Boche as spectator. One day the game was brought to a premature conclusion, when several rifle bullets came whistling across the pitch but generally we ignored each other. He seemed content to await our next move, while we waited for orders either to fire or to move on. Still we had little idea that the end was imminent; and when on the evening of 8th November, rumour became rife that Germany had thrown up the sponge, nobody would believe it. Though we knew that the enemy was stated to be at the end of his resources, we could not imagine him yielding in an ignominious fashion. After all we had gone through, we felt a great respect for the Boche as a fighter, and our idea was that if he was done up, he would go out in a blaze of some kind.

So the end came upon us very suddenly, quite quietly and without any display of fireworks. Early on the morning of 11th November, 1918 one of the signallers, flushed with the news but trying to give the appearance of calm, looked into the pig-styes in which our gunners were sleeping, and woke them up to say that hostilities were to cease at 11 a.m. that day. He was told to go away. The officers, doubtless, knew to some extent what was coming; but they too were showing an outward calm. For when the same signaller entered the B.C. Post and said, "A telegram sir, to say that hostilities will cease at 11 a.m.", the officer on duty simply said "All right; lay it on the table." The signaller went sadly back to his post – his bombshell had proved a dud.

Some minutes before eleven o'clock, the battery was paraded under Lieut. Fryer. The occasion was too great for an ex-sergeant major of the regular army not to make it the subject of a lecture. So he occupied the minutes of waiting by informing the battery that, although the war would end within the next few minutes, they were not to think they would be allowed to slack off. There would be 'spit and polish', infantry drill and... What else might there have been was spared to the battery by the Boche; for at that moment, Mr. Fryer's homely words were interrupted by two terrific crumps right above us. The Boche, like ourselves, had tired of sergeant-majors; and as no casualties resulted from those two last shrapnel shells – fired just on the stoke of eleven – the Boche had done us one good turn in bidding us adieu.

Still the battery stood lined up by sub-sections waiting for the arrival of Major Wilson. It had been a disappointing morning so far: it was all very well to take matters coolly; but we could not get over the astounding fact that *the war was over*, and we had only a fragment of an army lecture to show for it up to now. Not a word of congratulation that we had, after many vicissitudes, at last seen it through. But all that would be put right, we knew, when our O.C came on the scene. That was it – he had reserved to himself the right to make the speech that would fit the great occasion, and make us all pleased with ourselves. Had he not gone with us all the way, the only survivor of our original officers? For he's a jolly good fellow, and so were all of us! Even now, he would be thinking what he was going to say to us: he knew all about what we had done – and where we had failed – during those years of struggle; now, please God, gone for good. And here he was, coming over the stubble towards us.

The Major walked across to the spot where Corporal Si. Arnould now stood at the head of "A" sub-section. "Good morning, Arnould," he said in his usual cheerful manner, "Is everything in order?" "Yes sir," Si. replied, wiping his great hand down the seam of his trousers in anticipation of the warm handshake which he was about to receive.

"That's all right," said our Commander quietly. "I think you had better have the guns all cleaned up."

THE END

A.W. Paton
23 Silverknowes Terrace,
Davidsons Mains
Edinburgh, 4.

January, 1939

Appendix 1

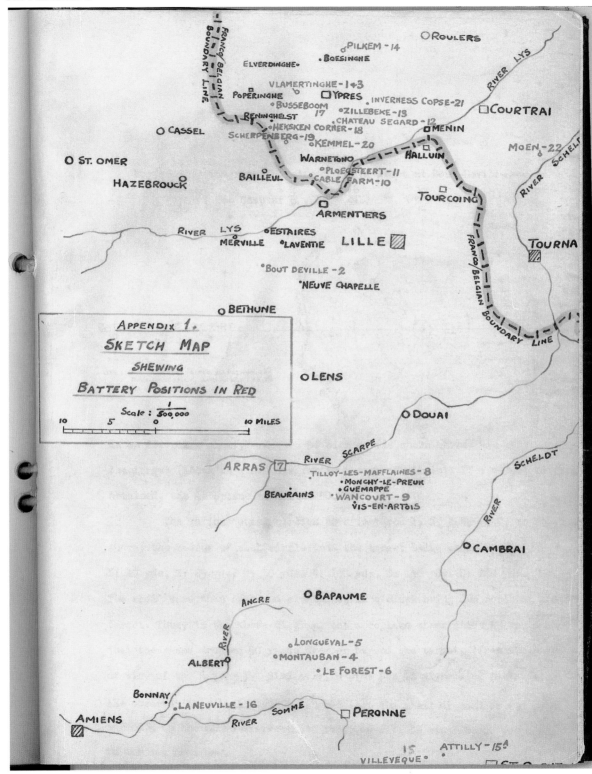

Sketch Map shewing Battery positions in red: scale 1/500,000

APPENDIX 2

Explanatory diagram of Incident
during Shoot at Bout-Deville
(See Chapter 2: Page 9)

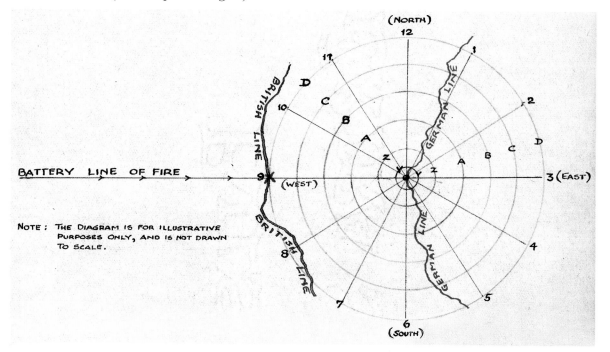

In an Aeroplane shoot, a series of circles (as shown above) was made round the target (shown on the above diagram in centre of circle). If a direct hit was obtained, the aeroplane signalled "O.K."

The various outer circles were lettered Y, Z, A, B, C, D, as shown above; the radius of each circle being as follows Y: 10 yds; Z: 25 yds; A: 50 yds; B: 100 yds; C: 150 yds; D: 200 yds.

The radii were then numbered clockwise, 12 o'clock being due north of the target. Thus, in the above diagram, the aeroplane observation A3 would show that the round dropped 50 yards over or beyond the target, (from the point of view of the battery). Similarly, D- (or Don in signalling parlance) 9, the observation actually given, showed that the shell dropped at the point marked X on the above diagram; and this as will be seen above, was actually in our own trenches.

APPENDIX 3

118 SIEGE BATTERY POSITIONS

From	To	Position	Notes	Chapter(s)
1916				
27 Jun (?)	13 Jul	1 Vlamertinghe (Ypres)		1
16 Jul	21 Jul	2 Bout-Deville (Armentiers)	Wick Salient 19 Jul	2
22 Jul	10 Sep	3 Vlamertinghe (Ypres)		3
13 Sep	end Sep	4 Montauban (Somme)	personnel attached to other batteries	4
1 Oct	1 Dec	5 Longueval (Somme)		5, 6
		Bonnay (Somme)	rest for 2 days	7
1917				
8 Dec	15 Mar	6 Le Forest (Somme)		8, (9), 10, 11
22 Mar	13 Apr	7 St. Catherines (Arras)		12, 13
15 Apr	6 May	8 Tilloy-les-Mafflaines (Arras)		14, 15
8 May	25 May	9 Wancourt (Arras)	1/2 waiting 1/2 in reserve	16
28 May	17 Jun	10 Cable Farm (Ploegsteert Wood)	(Messines Ridge battle 7 Jun)	17
18 Jun	early Jul	11 Ploegsteert Wood (Messines Ridge)		17, 18
mid Jul	28 Aug	12 Chateau Segard, Voormezeele (Ypres)		19, 20
28 Aug	14 Sep	13 Zillebeke (Ypres)	old Mk I guns destroyed	21, 22, 23, (44)
end Sep	early Nov	13 Zillebeke (Ypres)	Mk II guns (4 here, 2 at Westhoek Ridge)	25
1918				
14 Nov	2 Jan	Brigade relieved for 6 weeks rest at Tardinghen (Cape Gris-Nez)		26, 27
5 Jan	2 Feb	Battery personnel at Esquelbecq awaiting new guns		28
5 Feb	25 Feb	14 Pilkem (Ypres)		28
28 Feb	22 Mar	15 Villeveque (St Quentin) (15a Attilly)	18th Corps 5th Army battle zone	29, 30
23 Mar	19 May		Guns spiked: army in retreat	30, 31, 32
21 May	mid Jun	16 La Neuville (Corbie)		33
29 Jun	5 Jul	17 Busseboom (Ypres)	first shoot 2 Jul	34, 35
8 Jul		18 Heksken Corner, Reninghelst (Ypres)		36
		19 Scherpenberg (Ypres)		36
	end Sep	20 Kemmel (Ypres)	with 4 of 6 guns (2 at Belgian Battery Corner)	36
end Sep	early Oct	Busseboom	fortnight's rest	36
early Oct	mid Oct	21 Inverness Copse, near Ghelevelt		36
mid Oct		22 Moen (Courtrai)	guns not mounted: enemy out of reach	37

APPENDIX 4

Officers and men of 118th Siege Battery, Royal Garrison Artillery
June 1916 – November 1918

The names are as given in Occasional Gunfire, with their latest rank where known. Where a surname is shown with two different ranks, this may be one individual whose promotion is not specifically mentioned in the book. If stated in the book, the man's job in the army or in civilian life is shown to aid identification.

Men indicated with an asterisk went for Officer's Commission, but since none of them returned to the battery as an officer they are not included in that category.

Officers

(S) indicates known Scottish origin

Bottomley, Lieut
Clegg, Lieut
Cruttwell, Lieut
Fownes, Captain
Fryer, Lieut
Gibbs, Lieut
Gorman, Lieut

Gough, Lieut
Hall, Major
Hansen/Hanson, Lieut
Leslie, Lieut Hubert
'Little Willie', Lieut
Lovell, Major E H
MacLeod, Captain

Phipps, Lieut
Rees, 2nd Lieut
Reid, Lieut(S)
Walker, Mr
Wilson, Major Robert(S)
Winter, General

Men

Allen, Gunner (signaller)
Arnould, Corporal Si(S)
Baga (Lt Crutwell's servant)
Baird, Frank (servant)
Balchin (BCA)
Bale, Sergeant
Baxter, Bob
Bell, Corporal
Bell, Sergeant
Bennet (Major Hall's servant)
Betts, Albert (BCA)* [Notts
Betts, Claude (BCA)* cousins]
Bird, Bombardier
Bodley, Bdr (medical orderly)
Brebner, Gunner Dougal(S)
Brown, Gunner 'Sniper'(cook)
Brunton, Jim
Carter, Nick (BCA)
Cartwright, Corporal Frank
Cartwright, Louis
Cartwright, Sergeant
Clements, Sergeant-Major
Clogg, Ted (clerk)
Cox, Gunner
Craig, Gunner
Creamer, Gunner
Duncan
Dunkley, Sam (telephonist)
Edwards, Bombardier Jimmy
Fakes, (Section) Corporal
Frazer, Gunner
Frost, Jack
Galliford, Dick

Garson, Andrew (Orcadian)(S)
Goldie, Gunner
Gordon, Corporal Tom
Gregory, Alf (aircraft scout)*
Grubb, Chris (Fife miner)(S)
Harris, Gunner (cook)(S)
Henderson, Sandy(S)
Hill, 'Ginger'
Hope, Sid(S)
Hutchison, Jimmy
Innes
Isaacs, John (Jock) (Fife miner)
    (Capt Wilson's servant)
Jack, Sergeant
Lamb, Billy
Lamb, Peter
Lewis, Sandy
Loveland (telephonist)
'Lyddite'
'Lyddite' the second
McAllister, (Section) Corporal
Macfarlane, Sandy (teleph'ist)(S)
Macfarlane, Tom(S)
McGill
MacPheat(S)
Marchant, 'Tiny'
Mason (sanitary orderly)
Matheson, Bdr Tom (BCA)
Mentiplay, Bombardier
Mentiplay, Sergeant
Millman, Gunner
Murray, Corporal (BCA)
Murray, Gunner

Newcombe, Cpl (gun capt)
Newsom, Fred (wireless op)
Nowell, Sammy (Fife miner)(S)
Owen, Gunner (asst clerk)
Parsley
Paton, Corporal Alec (BCA)*(S)
Payne, Gunner
Price, Gunner
Raspberry
Reid, Harry (servant)
Reid, Jim
Rosie, Bombardier
Ross, Bombardier Tommy
Sherlock, Gunner
Sidebottom
Sinclair, Gunner
Smith, David
Smith, John (cook)(S)
Spencer, Sergeant
Stanway
Stevenson, Gunner
Strachan, Frank (clerk)*
Thake, Quarter-Master Sgt
'Toobs & Foozes', Sgt-Major
White, Arthur (signaller)
Williams, Idris
    (Welsh wireless op)
Williamson, Andrew
    (Glasgow police)(S)
Wood, 'Sticky'
Woods, Corporal (clerk)
Yarnold, Bombardier

GLOSSARY

(The definitions given here are not in any way authoritative, but are given simply as a guide to the reader of the Diary. I am indebted to "Soldiers' Song and Slang" (Eric Partridge Ltd) by John Brophy and Eric Partridge, for many of the definitions given in this Glossary.)

AE	One
ALLEMAND[E]	German (used generally to denote an enemy airman)
AULD REEKIE	Edinburgh (literally "Old Smoky")
AUSSIES	Australians
BARRAGE	A curtain of artillery fire put down in front of advancing infantry to afford them protection.
B.C.A.	Battery Commander's Assistant.
B.C. POST	Battery Commander's post – where fighting maps, etc. were kept, and whence shoots were conducted if not from the visual Observation Post.
BLIGHTY ONE	Non-fatal wound sufficiently severe to take one to Blighty (i.e. to England).
BOCHE	German. (Generally the term used by Officers, the ranks mostly using the word "Jerry")
BOMBARDIER	The artillery equivalent of Lance-Corporal.
BREECH-BLOCK	The circular steel block which closed the breech (or rear end) of the gun – in simple language, the "door" of the gun.
BUITS	Boots.
BUSES	Royal Air Force slang (facetious) for aeroplane.
CAMOUFLAGE	Screens usually composed of green or brown rags stuck into wire mesh.
CATERPILLARS	The tractors used to pull the guns; so-called because their wheels were fitted with a caterpillar tread to enable them to pull the heavy parts of the gun over rough ground.
CHIT	A note; generally to or from Headquarters.
COOTY	Lousy.
CORDITE	One of the two types of explosive used in artillery cartridges (the other was N.C.T.). Cordite, when taken from its muslin cover, was in sticks about 3 inches long, and if put in the fire in small quantities, crackled and jumped about. N.C.T., on the other hand, was made up in pieces about half an inch long, and if put in the fire, simply flared up. Consequently, when a full charge of N.C.T. had not been used, the odd quantities were sometimes (against orders) used to assist in boiling water – particularly when the Gunners were boiling their underclothing in empty cartridge tins in the open air.
CRUMPS	Enemy shell-bursts. High explosive shells burst with a crackle or crump, and emitted black fumes; shrapnel (in the air) burst with a musical 'pring', and emitted white fumes.
CUSHY	Comfortable (from the French 'Coucher', to lie down)

DECAUVILLE	The narrow gauge railway line used for bringing ammunition and stores up to the forward areas.
DELAYED FUZE or FUSE	Fuze (No. 101) used on shells which buried themselves in the ground BEFORE bursting; used to shell dug-outs or shelters, and sometimes enemy batteries. (See also INSTANTANEOUS FUZE)
DISHED or DISSED	Disconnected: Signallers' term when the telephone line had been severed by shell-fire or from any other cause.
DOUBLE SHUFFLE	A term popularly used when a double share of anything had been obtained by trickery.
DUCKBOARD	Roadway composed of two narrow planks across which were nailed horizontal wooden slats 18 inches wide. Used for flooring trenches or making footpaths across marshy ground.
DUD	A projectile which failed to explode – generally by reason of a defective fuze.
DUG-OUT	Shelter: so-called because it was generally dug out of the side of a trench or bank at the roadside.
DURATION	The duration of war.
ECOSSAIS	Scottish.
ELEPHANT IRONS	Heavy semi-circular or channel iron sheets used by the Royal Engineers in roofing strong dug-outs. They were too heavy for carrying about by mobile units, which generally used corrugated iron sheets and sandbags.
ELEVATION	The angle at which the gun muzzle was pointed when ready to fire the shell.
EMPLACEMENT	The area occupied by the gun when in position (i.e. the gun pit)
ENFILADE	Looking down the line end-on, as opposed to from the front.
ESTAMINET	The type of restaurant where light wine, coffee, eggs and 'chips' were obtainable.
FAUBOURG	Suburb.
FUZES or FUSES	The fuzes for the shells were packed in wooden boxes, and were screwed on to the nose of the shell before the latter was put into the gun breech. Responsibility for the safety of fuzes lay nominally with the Battery Sergeant-Major. (See also DELAYED FUZE and INSTANTANEOUS FUZE)
GALLISES	Trouser braces
GUNLAYER	No. 4 on the gun detachment. His duties were to 'lay' (or aim) the gun when in action.
INSTANTANEOUS FUZE	Fuze (No. 106) used when the shell was required to burst at the precise moment of impact. With this fuze, the shell burst into fragments which flew in all directions. It was used for cutting or destroying enemy barbed-wire entanglements, scattering troops, etc., but not against dug-outs or concrete shelters. (See also DELAYED FUZE)
JERRY	The term generally used by the rank and file for the Germans.

K.R.R.	King's Royal Rifles.
LAYED	Aimed (See GUNLAYER).
LUM	Chimney.
M.P.	Military Police.
MAIRE	The Mayor.
MAIRIE	The Mayor's House.
NAPOO or NAPU	Finished; Gone (literally "Il n'y en a plus")
NISSEN HUT	A removable hut built in sections.
N.C.T.	See under CORDITE.
NO MAN'S LAND	The 'dead' area between our own and the enemy front line trenches.
O.C.	Officer Commanding.
O.P.	Observation Post.
PANORAMIC SKETCHING	Drawing (with the aid of field glasses) enemy trenches and prominent features as seen from the O.P. These sketches were sometimes useful in helping young or new officers to locate points in the enemy lines visible from the O.P.
PAVÉ	The part of the street (usually in the middle of the road) covered with cobbles or stones.
PILL-BOX	Concrete fortifications built as machine-gun or observation posts; first built by the Germans, and later copied by us.
PIP-SQUEAKS	Small shells (77 m.m. dia. or about 3 inches), known also as "whiz-bangs". They were of such high velocity that the 'whiz' of their coming, and the 'bang' of their burst were heard practically simultaneously.
R.A.M.C.	Royal Army Medical Corps.
REEKIN'	Smoking.
REGISTERING	Recording for future use the normal elevation, etc. required to hit a given target. This was done by an experimental shoot which ceased when the correct range was obtained. This was then recorded so that the same target could be engaged on any future occasion without observation, but with the certainty of doing damage.
R.O.D.	A popular army phrase indicating the desire for home and peacetime (roll on, duration)
SALVO	A group of four or more shells fired simultaneously at one target.
SAN FAIRY ANN	(Literally Ça ne fait rien – It matters nothing). Used popularly by all troops, and meant "It doesn't matter" "Why worry")
SARK	Shirt.
SCROUNGING	Stealing from a department or store or dump – not personal belongings. The losers usually replaced their loss by "scrounging" from someone else!
SHOUTING THE ODDS	Drawing attention noisily (Doubtless derived from Bookmakers' cries)

SPIKED	Rendered useless by destroying the vital parts.
SPONGE (GUN)	The mop used to cool and clean the interior of the gun muzzle after firing the shell.
STAR SHELLS	See under VERY LIGHTS
STRAFED	Shelled; Bombarded. Also used in the sense of receiving punishment.
SWINGING THE LEAD	Malingering or evading duty. A 'lead-swinger' was one who let others do his work.
TIME FUZED	Fuzed so that the shell will explode after a set number of seconds (generally in the air), and not when making contact with anything.
TOUT DE SUITE	(Toot Sweet) At once.
TRACTORS	See under CATERPILLARS.
TRANSOMS	Heavy beams of hard wood reinforced with iron used to form a bed or platform for the heavy guns.
TRENCH FEET	A loathsome disease caused by standing for long periods in waterlogged trenches.
TUBES	T-shaped piece of metal inserted in a small hole in the breech-block of the gun, and giving access to the cartridge. The gunner firing the gun attached his lanyard to the Tube, which ignited the cartridge when the lanyard was pulled. The pressure of accumulated gases from the cartridge fired the shell. The safety of the Tubes (along with the Fuzes) lay nominally with the Sergeant-Major.
UP WE GO, AND THE BEST OF LUCK	A popular phrase used by the infantry as they climbed up out of their trenches to go 'over the top' for an attack.
VERY [or VEREY] LIGHTS	Rockets fired from a brass pistol. Used in the front line to illuminate No Man's Land at night, so that sentries could 'spot' wiring or raiding parties of the enemy.
WHIZ-BANG	See under PIP-SQUEAK.
WIND UP	Fear. To have 'wind up' implied no disgrace and could be casually mentioned in conversation, though usually referring to an incident in the past.
WINDY	Apprehensive of personal danger. Derived from 'wind up' but unlike that term, was used in a derogatory sense. To say 'I had the wind up' was a mere statement regarding an isolated incident; but to say 'I was windy at that place' meant the speaker had been in a state of CONTINUOUS 'wind up', and was disparaging himself in consequence.
ZERO HOUR	The precise moment of launching an attack.

INDEX